HATERS

HATERS
Harassment, Abuse, and Violence Online

Bailey Poland

Potomac Books
An imprint of the University of Nebraska Press

Library of Congress Cataloging-in-Publication Data
Names: Poland, Bailey, author.
Title: Haters: harassment, abuse,
and violence online / Bailey Poland.
Description: Lincoln: Potomac Books, [2016] |
Includes bibliographical references and index.
Identifiers: LCCN 2016017213
ISBN 9781612347660 (pbk.: alk. paper)
ISBN 9781612348704 (epub)
ISBN 9781612348711 (mobi)
ISBN 9781612348728 (pdf)
Subjects: LCSH: Internet and women. | Sexism. | Misogyny.
Classification: LCC HQ1178 .P65 2016 | DDC 305.3—dc23
LC record available at https://lccn.loc.gov/2016017213

Designed and set in Minion Pro by L. Auten.

For my mom, who has always been my first and best reader

Contents

HATERS

1 THE MANY FACES OF CYBERSEXISM
Why Misogyny Flourishes Online

Online spaces are fraught with the abuse of women. The past few years have produced one high-profile case of harassment after another, suffusing news headlines with the lurid details of women forced from their homes, their online and offline lives shattered by a torrent of sexist, racist, and transphobic abuse. Hate mobs like those associated with Gamergate and individual abusers and stalkers have proliferated online in recent years, causing women to fear going online at all. Whether it's organized campaigns of unrelenting harassment, "doxxing," and violent threats loosely coordinated on various message boards and social media sites or abusive spouses taking their violence into cyberspace (once ending up in front of the Supreme Court), hardly a month goes by when the news isn't following yet another extreme example of the price women pay for being visible online.[1] What is it about online spaces that makes abuse so common? And what can we do to make the Internet safer?

Before we can begin to explore the answers to those questions, it's important to understand the core terminology used to describe the online abuse that characterizes so much of women's experience with the Internet. A grasp of how this book talks about sexism and cybersexism is essential. While other definitions of sexism and cybersexism may exist and the definitions themselves are fluid, for the purposes of this book the two terms have specific definitions that are used as frames for the concepts discussed.

In this chapter I discuss the basic terminology used throughout the book in discussing sexism and cybersexism. I also explore the prevalence of offline sexism that informs women's day-to-day lives and how such attitudes moved online, and then I examine the mindset that leads to cybersexist harassment.

Sexism is a combination of prejudice against persons based on their gender, combined with the privilege and power required to cause harm. In other words, because men as a group hold the majority of social privileges, such as political and financial power representation, their prejudices against women as a group are more likely to hurt women, limit their opportunities, and cause other difficulties for women trying to go about their daily lives. Further, as women do not hold the majority of the privileges or power that exist, their prejudices against men (frequently a reaction to already-existing injustices and unequal levels of power and opportunity) do not rise to the level of sexism.

"Privilege" in this context is often misunderstood as primarily class or financial power; however, the definition of privilege used here takes a more nuanced approach. Privilege is, for the purposes of this book, the set of social advantages associated with particular axes of identity that are considered to be dominant. These social advantages are often unnoticed by those who have them, but they nevertheless carry a great deal of weight. Privilege is often associated with those forms of identity (and the associated benefits) that are considered default by virtue of overrepresentation. While having privilege will not correlate to success or power in all cases or situations, it simply increases the likelihood that it will. The term "privilege," therefore, is used to describe the broad social attitudes that impact power, access, safety, and representation along the axes of gender, race, sexuality, and more.

Male privilege, for example, is associated with greater representation in media, business, politics, and journalism, as well as easier access to positions of power, employment, capital, and so on. The same attitudes that produce sexism in the form of negative stereotypes about women often find footing as positive stereotypes about men—where women are seen as irrational or overly emotional, men are painted as levelheaded and logical.

The Many Faces of Cybersexism

As a result, while sexism is often understood solely as prejudice against someone on the basis of their sex—and, under that definition, it is often said that women who push back against sexism are themselves engaging in sexism against men—the ability to cause harm to a group (women) while conferring benefits on another group (men) is a core part of the definition of sexism used throughout this book. Sexism as it affects online life is the major focus of this work, with the key caveat that online harassment and abuse are rarely—if ever—linked to gender alone.

Although this book addresses women as a group and uses sexism as the guiding framework, racism is another key element of online harassment and one that, as a white person, I discuss but cannot ever fully speak to. Online harassment of women of color, and specifically misogynoir, requires far more in-depth analysis.[2] A call to action for addressing that issue is a central part of my goal here; while this book is intended to start a discussion, it is only the first part of a much broader and deeper conversation that must take place in order to improve the well-being of online communities.

With that said, cybersexism is the expression of prejudice, privilege, and power in online spaces and through technology as a medium. While this book focuses on the verbal and graphic expression of sexism in the form of online harassment and abuse aimed at women, it's important to note that cybersexism can also occur in less overt forms not directly as a result of ill intent. For example, the design of technology to suit an ideal user (presumed to be male) or to make it more difficult for women to access and use is also cybersexism. Some examples include making smartphones too large for the average woman's hand, health and fitness tracking apps that exclude menstruation (or regard the tracking of menstruation as only for cisgender women and aimed only at pregnancy), or designing a "revolutionary" heart implant that works for 86 percent of men and only 20 percent of women.[3]

This book examines the use of harassment and abuse aimed at women in online spaces, with an understanding that cybersexism often has a goal of creating, enforcing, and normalizing male dominance in online spaces—

norms preferred by straight, cisgender white men, primarily located in the United States. While online harassment is a global problem, the norms established in the early years of the Internet tend to reflect Western-centric patterns of use and abuse. The types of cybersexism examined here include everything from casual sexist harassment to overt abuse, illegal threats, doxxing, and other behaviors that make online spaces uncomfortable, unpleasant, and unsafe for women's participation, along with a discussion of the justifications used for such behavior and women's ability to respond. While sexism itself is the overarching focus here, issues of race, sexuality, disability, and others also play a role in determining which women get targeted for certain kinds of abuse and how that abuse functions.

This book also looks at the ways in which this cyberabuse affects women in their online and offline lives—and the increasingly blurred boundaries between the two. Chapters address the ways women cope with abuse, the solutions currently in place, and why so many of them fail. This book also attempts to outline possibilities for long-term changes to the way we live, work, and play online.

Sexist attitudes color the majority of women's interactions with the world, from expectations about how—and if—women should talk (online and off), to the skewed media representation of women, to male dominance, to violence against women, and more. Stereotyping and gendered abuse are a common fact of life for women. The continued and rapid erasure of the lines between online and offline activities makes it impossible to fully separate online and offline harassment. Online harassment is rooted in offline beliefs, and those offline beliefs are supported and reinforced by the prevalence of sexist behaviors online. Domination of specific spaces deemed important is, as ever, a central goal for those who engage in sexist activities. With the Internet the quest for male domination is disguised by a mythology of level playing fields and equal opportunity, and it is backed by the vicious and constant harassment of women.

Understanding how cybersexism works requires an understanding of how sexism itself functions in offline spaces. Attitudes displayed online—whether in the form of YouTube videos, Facebook comments, Twitter replies, Reddit threads, or blog posts—do not occur in a vacuum nor do they exist only in online spaces. While people may be more comfortable expressing extreme views online than they would in person, such expressions often reflect the true beliefs they hold. Those views, extreme or not, are also not confined to or created solely in online spaces.

The United States in particular has a strong set of expectations regarding appropriate gender roles for men and women, and sexist, demeaning beliefs about women's roles are still common. Power, money, violence, and control continue to exist along highly gendered and raced lines, and taking a serious look at the ways sexism operates in offline spaces is key to understanding how it became so prevalent online.

DOMINANCE AND VIOLENCE OFFLINE

The decision to target women with abusive, gender-based harassment online is rarely random or spontaneous. While individual actions may not be impelled by a goal other than disagreeing with a woman and wanting to put her in her place, as it were, the decision to engage in obviously sexist harassment to achieve such ends indicates how cybersexists think the Internet should work. In many ways activities aimed at building and reinforcing male dominance online are conducted in order to re-create the patterns of male domination that exist offline. In offline spaces sexism occurs in a variety of ways, from the obvious examples of financial and political control to violence, including almost invisible factors, such as policing the ways in which women talk.

Political and Financial Power

Offline, men remain in powerful positions throughout the world. From a political standpoint every U.S. president through 2016 has been male and, with the exception of President Barack Obama, white and male. The 114th U.S. Congress consisted of roughly 80 percent men and more than 80 percent white people, regardless of gender.[4] Among countries around the globe, however, the United States is not even in the top seventy countries in terms of representation of women in political bodies. The top five countries are Rwanda, Bolivia, Cuba, Seychelles, and Sweden; the United States stands at an abysmal seventy-first place, and the United Kingdom is thirty-sixth.[5] Of the top five countries only Rwanda and Bolivia have equal or greater numbers of women in a lower or single legislative chamber; no country in the top five has parity in an upper chamber.

Around the world women are often grossly underrepresented within the legal bodies that govern the everyday lives of citizens. As a result, decisions are made that affect women without women's input. Men's ability to control the legal environment in which women live and work is a source of much conflict and power. However, this overrepresentation of men is not unique to the political arena.

From the highest ranks of business, where women occupy fewer than 5 percent of Fortune 500 CEO positions, to the individual level, where working single mothers are disproportionately likely to be women of color who are living in poverty, men have significantly more control over the economic fate of the world and, as a result, most of the women in it.[6] Financial control is an issue from the most senior positions within a business to the most entry-level role, with men consistently making more money than women, controlling more resources, and having easier access to higher levels of power.

The wage gap remains a gender issue within the United States and around the world, with men still making more than women at every level of employment. Further, it is important to remember that women's wages vary widely by race, with white women having the greatest advantage.[7] Although all women are at a disadvantage where financial impact is concerned, race plays a major role, as do sexuality, disability, and gender identity. In the United States companies in twenty-nine states can legally fire gay employees for their sexuality; in thirty-four states companies can legally fire transgender people solely for being transgender.[8] In addition, the Fair Labor Standards Act permits organizations to pay disabled workers less than minimum wage—often far less than minimum wage.[9] The ability to find and retain work, and to be fairly compensated for that work, without being discriminated against based on race, gender, ability, or sexuality continues to be an immense challenge across the globe.

Media Stereotypes

Beyond the world of finance and politics, even something as seemingly simple as entertainment remains a male-dominated field—on the screen, at the writer's desk, and behind the camera. The Geena Davis Institute on Gender in Media found that men still make up 93 percent of directors and 83 percent of writers. The Geena Davis Institute also found that there is a 5 to 10 percent increase in women on-screen when women are writing and directing media rather than men, who consistently write more male characters and cast more male actors.[10] Movies and TV shows still feature significantly more men than women, and even when women are present they are often relegated to supporting roles or are characters whose existence only matters in relation to a main male character. Women are more likely to be sexualized than men in entertainment, and degrading comments about women's bodies and intelligence are common across all types of media.

Sexism in media and entertainment is linked to numerous problems for women and girls. Media and advertisements often reflect unattainable and deeply manipulated imagery of women's bodies, and a company such as Unilever (owner of the Dove brand) sells a version of empowerment with one hand while selling skin lightening creams that contribute to racist stereotypes with the other.[11] Multiple research reports across decades have shown that exposure to sexist, racist stereotypes in media—such as consistently portraying women as irrational and hyperemotional or only casting people of color as a variety of stereotypes (the nerdy Asian, the strong black woman, the hotheaded Latina)—can have serious real-life consequences.[12] Eating disorders, feelings of inferiority, reduced personal and educational goals, feelings of invisibility, and more all result from people's limited opportunities to see their lives accurately and intelligently portrayed on TV, in books and comic books, through music, and even in the news.[13]

Although media stereotypes might at first glance seem harmless, as easy tropes needed to quickly convey information, research has also shown time and again that the images we see on the screen both reflect and reinforce our preexisting social beliefs. While the media do not bear full responsibility for the creation of sexist attitudes and other negative problems, the representations of casual sexism and racism in media become part of the way viewers see the world around them. Cybersexists and sexists who operate offline both try to argue that something like a book, movie, or video game is "just entertainment" and that seeing social patterns reflected within entertainment is the work of people who are looking too hard.

The refusal to critically examine media or acknowledge its effects is often known as the "third-person effect": people who assume that they are not affected by stereotypes in media are often the ones who are most likely to absorb harmful messages and beliefs from it, because they do not interrogate the messages presented by the shows and movies they watch and the video games they play.[14] A failure to examine something like sexist messages leads to passive acceptance of them as reflecting something true about the world, often leading to a reinforcing and strengthening of sexist attitudes about women.

This pattern of behavior contributes to a cycle of reification and reenactment of negative social beliefs. People who do not examine the attitudes implicit in media are less likely to examine their own beliefs and more likely to absorb those messages from the media they consume—whether or not the messages are deliberately included. People who go on to create their own media then unthinkingly perpetuate the same stereotypes, further reinforcing the validity of sexist portrayals of women for new audiences.

Violence

Economic power and the erasure and sexist portrayals of women through entertainment and media are not the only ways that gender comes into play. How people interact with one another at the personal level is keenly shaped by gender, expectations of proper gender roles and behaviors, and the power structures that uphold men and degrade women. Too often these interactions include violence. Violence remains closely linked to gender, and its intersections with race, sexuality, gender identity, and other factors increase the likelihood that certain groups of women will experience violence.

Even violence against the self is gendered, for while men commit suicide more frequently, women attempt it significantly more often than men do.[15] And while the number of young men with eating disorders has been rapidly climbing in recent years, women still make up the bulk of people who develop anorexia and bulimia.[16] Eating disorders are deeply linked to mental health, and their catalyst is often an attempt to deal with the constraints society places on women's bodies. Thinness is an ideal, and girls and women starve themselves trying to reach it. Eating disorders remain the form of mental illness with the highest mortality rate, and for those who survive it, recovery is an ongoing, lifelong process.

Violence committed by the state is another aspect of offline violence. Although men of color make up the largest segment of the prison population, the incarceration of women of color—especially black women—is rapidly increasing, reflecting the racist policies enacted across the country.[17] Racism remains all too common offline, as it does online. The American legal system disproportionately affects people of color, especially black and Latino men. People of color have significantly higher rates of policing, incarceration, and death sentences than white people, who are more likely to receive lighter sentencing for similar crimes.[18] Despite the preponderance of men already in the prison system, women are now incarcerated at nearly double the rate men are, and since 1985 the rate of women's imprisonment has increased by 800 percent and has disproportionately affected women of color. Black women are three times as likely as white women to be imprisoned, and Latina women are nearly 70 percent more likely than white women to be sentenced to prison.[19]

Legal and social biases around race remain thoroughly ingrained in American society, leaving white men firmly in the most advantaged position. In addition to systemic racism, racist hate crimes remain a fact of life for many individuals, especially within the United States. In late 2013 the FBI released the collected 2012 hate crime statistics, which showed that 48.3 percent of nearly six thousand recorded hate crimes were racially motivated and that a further 11 percent were due to bias against the victim's ethnicity or national origin.[20] Around the world, xenophobia, racism, and gender-based violence intersect with government surveillance, control, and violence.

Intimate partner violence, domestic violence, and rape all occur with astonishing frequency across the world. While the most readily available statistics are for the United States, similar statistics can be found for nearly every country. Within the United States 20 percent of women experience nonfatal partner violence, compared to only 3 percent of men.[21] Additionally, 33 percent of female murder victims were killed by an intimate partner, versus only 4 percent of male murder victims. Overall, 84 percent of spousal abuse victims are women. One in twelve women is likely to be stalked in her lifetime, versus one in forty-five men, and 87 percent of all stalkers are male, regardless of the gender of the victim. Furthermore, most people who are stalked know their stalker, who is frequently a former spouse or boyfriend. While all domestic violence is serious, the majority of interpersonal relationship violence between adults is directed at women, and when men experience such violence it's most often at the hands of other men.

Rape also occurs along gendered lines—78 percent of rape and sexual assault survivors are women. Sexual violence is inextricably linked with domination of women and is frequently committed as an assertion of masculine power, which is also why most of the people who commit rape and sexual assault are men. For example, one Department of Justice study found that nearly 100 percent of acts of sexual violence committed against women over the age of eighteen were perpetrated by men, as were 92 percent of physical assaults and 97 percent of stalking incidents.[22] When men are attacked, other men commit 70 percent of rapes, 86 percent of physical assaults, and 65 percent of stalking incidents.

However, gender is not the only factor leading to domestic violence and rape. Violence against women offline, like online violence, also has a highly racial component. For example, 17 percent of American Indian women within the United States are stalked, compared to only 8.2 percent of white women, 6.5 percent of black women, and fewer than 5 percent of Asian and Pacific Islander women.[23] Nearly half of all black girls have been sexually assaulted before they turn eighteen.[24] Rapes of American

Indian women are frequently committed by white men and take place on reservations, a situation in which men abuse women knowing that they are unlikely to have to deal with the legal consequences of doing so; in 1978 the Supreme Court of the United States handed down a decision prohibiting tribes from arresting and prosecuting non–American Indian individuals who commit crimes on tribal land.[25] Race and gender both provide opportunity and motive for violence, and women of color are far more likely to be on the receiving end of it.

Violence extends along multiple axes of individual identity, especially when that identity is seen as deviating from an expected norm. Acts of violence against LGBT (lesbian, gay, bisexual, transgender) people are common, and anti-LGBT violence often begins in childhood. A study of nearly forty European countries found that more than half of LGBT students reported dealing with bullying in school that related to their sexual orientation or gender.[26] Violence against adult members of the LGBT community is also common, with verbal and physical attacks being a regular occurrence for many individuals.

The highest tracked anti-LGBT homicide rate that GLAAD (an organization originally founded as the Gay & Lesbian Alliance against Defamation) has reported was in 2011; even though 2012 saw a 16 percent decrease, that year still saw twenty-five homicides directly tied to anti-LGBT attitudes.[27] As with all types of violence, violence against LGBT people often occurs along intersections of race and other factors, with LGBT people of color at a significantly higher risk for hate crimes, suicide, and homelessness. In 2012, of all anti-LGBT homicide victims in the United States, 73 percent were people of color.

Transgender women, and particularly black transgender women, face even higher rates of homelessness and suicide, as well as violent attacks and murder due to hate crimes aimed at them for their gender and often their race; 53 percent of homicide victims of anti-LGBT violence in 2012 were transgender women, and the high percentage of attacks on people of color makes it likely that many of the murders of trans people were also attacks on women of color. In another testament to the inequalities of the legal system in the United States, few of the people who attack transgender women of color ever face legal or even social consequences for doing so; many of the attackers, who tend to be white cisgender men, face no jail time.

The "trans panic" defense, so called because it allows cisgender men to claim that they found out that a woman was transgender, "panicked," and killed her, allows many men to walk free after committing violence and murder.[28] In summer 2015 a U.S. Marine, Joseph Scott Pemberton, was being investigated for murdering a transgender woman named Jennifer Laude after he discovered that she was transgender. In his defense testimony Pemberton said that he "felt violated and angry," which was what led him to strangle Laude and leave her to die.[29]

In 2002 a transgender teenager named Gwen Araujo died after being brutally beaten for several hours by a group of cisgender men, who used a similar defense.[30] The assailants received sentences for second-degree murder and voluntary manslaughter, but the charges likely would have been much more severe had Araujo not been transgender. While Araujo's murder was a turning point that led the State of California to ban the trans panic defense, such a "defense" remains a viable option for many attackers. At the same time, trans women of color, such as CeCe McDonald of Minnesota, are frequently imprisoned for defending themselves from such attacks and often incarcerated in men's prisons, exposing them to further attacks and abuse.[31]

Violence is a fact of life for women, and women who experience multiple axes of oppression, including racism, homophobia, transphobia, classism, discrimination due to disability, and bigotry due to being a religious minority, are more likely to be attacked. Additionally, women with fewer social privileges are less likely to receive assistance or find justice following an attack and are often unable to report violence due to fear of further violence or even criminalization at the hands of the state. The attitudes that result in violence toward women are an extension of the social, financial, and political privileges already held by men—beliefs about what roles women should play in society, what can be done to keep them there, and what kinds of behaviors are permissible in enforcing those roles. Violence that affects women's physical bodies is all too common, yet it is not the only kind of violence that occurs.

Male Control of Conversation

As with economic domination and media control, there are subtler forms of violence against women. Policing the ways in which women interact with men—the very ways that women talk—is a form of verbal violence that maintains systems of control favoring men and masculinity. Although not as overt as physical violence, socially permissible male domination is no less dangerous for progress toward equality and justice.

Men tend to be the primary speakers in any mixed-gender group. The deliberate, although often subconscious, silencing and erasure of women's voices contributes to systems of male control, and deviations from the expected norm are met with harsh retaliation. This pattern is perhaps most visible in the business world, where the more highly placed a man is, the more he talks. The opposite is true for women, however; the more highly placed a woman is within a company, the less likely she is to be talkative.[32] Women who are seen as assertive in the workplace are more likely to be the target of negative gender stereotypes that paint them as "ball-busters," "abrasive," bad managers, and overly emotional, which can impede career advancement.

Outside the realm of business women are frequently characterized as chatterboxes; although the stereotype includes seemingly positive aspects about women's facilitative role in conversations, it has negative effects on women's ability to be seen as authoritative or worthy of respect. This type of benign sexism has insidious undertones, painting women as "emotional" and men as "logical," or women as "caring" and men as "harsh"—characterizations that are then used as excuses to restrict women's access to equal power—in addition to limiting the acceptable emotions men can exhibit. There is a commonly used saying based on this type of benign sexism, which is that women talk three times as much as men.[33] The statistic has been repeatedly shown to be false but nonetheless persists, as it is allows for men to insist that women are talking too much and supports other stereotypes about women's appropriate place in a conversation.

The stereotype that women talk too much is, in fact, an offshoot of the fact that men have a tendency to dominate all casual and professional discussions. The prominence of men's voices in conversation even extends to how much they interrupt women; in one study of mixed-group conversations, men were found to have interrupted more than forty times on average, while women interrupted only twice.[34] Interruptions are a common tactic for establishing a hierarchy of power within a conversation and are used to keep women from taking up too much verbal space. Men tend to be socialized to assert themselves in conversation, including interrupting other speakers—especially women—to position themselves as the most authoritative individual in the discussion. Most studies on linguistic patterns and gender find that men use interruption to take control of a conversation.

The dominance of men's voices in conversation doesn't end with simple interruption, however. Men also talk significantly more than women in group situations, despite the chatty stereotype applied to women's conversational styles; while men and women use a roughly equal number of words each day, men begin to talk more and women begin to talk less in mixed-group discussions. As a result, men are so used to being the primary voices heard that any violation of what they perceive as the norm becomes an oddity and is often seen as an injustice.

In situations in which women do talk as much or nearly as much as men, the men begin to perceive women as having taken up more than their fair share of conversational space. One example from a study cites a male teacher who created space for his students to spend equal time speaking in class sessions, yet he felt that he was devoting 90 percent of speaking time to the girls in his classroom. On top of that the boys agreed with him, and many complained to the teacher about how much time the girls spent talking. In a similar vein, public speaking events at which men and women are given equal time to speak also result in men feeling as though women have spoken too much.[35]

One researcher describes the attitude toward women's speech as being a comparison between women and silence, rather than a comparison between women and men.[36] That is, the amount of time women speak is judged based on a comparison to silent women, not the amount of time that men speak. Any woman who speaks at all is seen as violating the acceptable social role for women, and the closer to equality of speaking time groups get, the more unequal men believe the speaking time to be. As a result, many men resort to domination tactics such as interrupting women and attempting to return control of the conversation to men, leaving women silenced. In chapter 2, I discuss how these behaviors play out in nearly identical ways in online spaces.

Women's Vocal Patterns

Silencing women in casual conversation is not the only tactic for establishing male control. Even the ways in which women vocalize are subjected to deep scrutiny and sexist stereotypes. Conversational patterns that eventually reach the entire population typically begin with young women, but in their early stages such patterns are discredited and examined as a sign of women's weakness, largely because of their origin. Column after column in popular news outlets decries the latest vocal fad among teen girls and announces yet again that the way women talk is unacceptable, yet everyone begins using those vocal patterns. For example, the common use of "like" or "you know" as conversational filler, despite now being present throughout all demographic groups, is still presented as the trait of a certain type of "Valley Girl" who should not be taken seriously. The stereotype persists in contrast to research that shows people who use such fillers tend to be more thoughtful and conscientious in conversation.[37]

Another speech trait closely associated with women—and denigrated as a result—is vocal fry (also known as creaky voice). The lowering of the voice at certain points, as at the end of a sentence, is in many ways the opposite of another trait stereotypically and negatively associated with women: uptalk. Uptalk is the habit of ending sentences on the same note as one would a question; it's often seen as a mark of insecurity or immaturity. And yet, at the same time, vocal fry's lowered tones or the rasping sounds used at the end of sentences have been stereotyped in the same way. Vocal fry and uptalk are portrayed as a problem for women in the workplace, an indicator of girls' low self-esteem, and more, even as both speech patterns have moved outward to all demographics and as research has shown that neither truly reflects problems with women's self-esteem, intelligence, or maturity.

The stereotypes used to decry women's voices are deeply linked to sexist ideas about the proper ways for women to speak, if they are expected to speak at all. Nonetheless, linguistic researchers consistently cite young women as being progressive forces that generate popular vocal trends, many of which spread throughout the entire population and every demographic, including the men who tend to lead the charge in initially deriding their use. A great deal of commonly used slang, along with linguistic patterns, originates with women, while the women who created and use those traits are mocked and taken less seriously than the men who eventually pick up on those trends anyway.[38]

Sexism and male dominance offline range from overt, gender-based violence and murder to policing the very ways women are expected and permitted to speak. The offline world remains one in which violence against those who are seen as lacking social power or worth is built into the very systems in which we live and work. Violence against women is incredibly common and occurs along intersecting axes, leaving the women who are already most vulnerable to social and economic disadvantage even more vulnerable to physical violence. Casual verbal violence exists in the gender stereotypes that impact even how—and how much—women speak and in attempts to keep them from doing so.

The types of attitudes bolstering high rates of violence offline do not disappear when someone turns on the Internet, as discussed in detail in chapter 2. Cybersexism, along with the racism, homophobia, and transphobia that often accompany online harassment of women, is a manifestation of offline beliefs and behaviors, enacted in online locations. As with offline violence, online harassment and abuse are intended to reinforce existing patterns of power and dominance over people who have historically been disenfranchised or oppressed.

MALE DOMINANCE ONLINE

Despite the oft-repeated narrative characterizing the Internet as a free-wheeling "Wild West" space in which everyone is seen as equal, there is significant evidence that points to racist, sexist biases appearing online almost as soon as the Internet became available to the general public. The Internet, despite the optimism, was not designed as a level playing field, and it certainly has not become one. In her book *Cyber Racism* Jessie Daniels points out that racist and white supremacist websites were among the first websites to appear and be consistently maintained.[39] Online spaces have always been, and remain, areas where dominance and control remain deeply important, and the same types of domination tactics that are used offline appear online.

"Trolling" is the most common term for online domination tactics. While trolling originated as an attempt to disrupt chat room or message board conversations (often by making deliberately inflammatory racist, sexist, or otherwise derogatory remarks or by simply filling chat rooms with spam), and while it is still characterized as someone casually or jokingly engaging in antisocial behaviors, the act of trolling has taken on new meanings. Online harassment and abuse are often called nothing more than trolling and portrayed as an aimless activity—pointless, juvenile, and ultimately the result of harmless pranks.

Yet the presence of trolling and the frequency with which trolling is cybersexist in nature provide extensive evidence that online harassment, even when called trolling, is far from being either pointless or harmless. Cybersexist harassment is in fact intended to restore and reinforce the power and control of men—particularly straight, cisgender white men—given the amount and types of abuse and harassment that are aimed at women of color and LGBT women. Cybersexists utilize the same types of stereotypes, violence, and silencing tactics online that appear offline in order to achieve their goals and drive women away, especially from positions of prominence and power.

The perception of cybersexism as an ultimately meaningless activity that shouldn't be taken seriously helps disguise its effects on women and throw up a smokescreen around its causes. The deliberate nature of the decision to specifically target women with abusive online communications is intended to establish men as dominant and keep women's participation in online spaces low, invisible, or nonexistent. Tactics used by cybersexists—such as derailing (an attempt to disrupt a conversation and refocus it in a way more comfortable to a male participant or a man who has interrupted the conversation for that purpose), mansplaining (a tongue-in-cheek term for a man condescendingly explaining something to a woman that she understands better than he does), gendered harassment, abuse, and threats, which will be discussed in depth in chapter 2—are all aimed at re-creating aspects of the offline world in online spaces. The goal of cybersexism is to build places in which women must either be silent or invisible, reinforce the sexist attitudes that see women's proper role as silent and objectified, and develop an Internet where men are not challenged on their use of stereotypes or violence against women.

Male Control of Conversation

Online, as offline, men tend to dominate mixed-group conversations. Men write the majority of articles for news outlets (more than 60 percent of bylines and on-camera appearances for news organizations are men's), and they are more likely to take precedence in casual conversations on forums and social media.[40] Susan Herring's work on the topic of online communication reveals that women "tend to enjoy less success than [men] in mixed-sex computer-mediated interaction."[41] Overall, women not only speak or write less than men when communicating online, but they also receive fewer positive responses to the topics they do raise.[42] Men, it seems, are unlikely to respond well to women's presence online, even in a limited capacity, and frequently resort to harassment and abuse as a result.

As in offline situations, "'equal' behavior" from women is seen as inherently unequal by the men involved.[43] Men are accustomed to dominating online spaces, often because they are equally accustomed to dominating offline spaces. Since the Internet was largely (although certainly not

The Many Faces of Cybersexism

entirely) developed and accessed by a male user base in its earliest years, many of the norms established reflect both unconscious and deliberate patterns of male dominance and control. The Internet was not designed to be a level playing field, and its earliest users ensured that the ingrained expectations of incoming Internet users reflected the attitudes they most often held. As a result, the ideals espoused, especially around the libertarian interpretation of free speech, reflect the beliefs and values of the initial users of the Internet. Although many still insist on describing the Internet as an open range where everyone has an equal shot at success, systems of prejudice and power have always been in place online.

The distinct lack of neutrality in Internet spaces, which is the lingering result of the Internet's creation and history, allows men to frame women as interlopers in what are perceived as male-only online spaces and to justify men's abusive reactions to women's presence, even though men have not been the primary users of the Internet for more than two decades. When women do participate on anything close to equal footing with men, it "threatens the asymmetrical, dominant position that some men apparently assume is theirs" and that they assume is the mythical level playing field.[44] Women who expect to be able to take up as much space online as their male counterparts quickly find that men do not agree with that expectation. Through cybersexist harassment, men attempt to re-create offline conversational patterns that privilege male voices, opinions, and ways of speaking. Sexist harassment and abuse in these situations are intended to silence women entirely or force them to conform to men's chosen norms for a specific space.

While social media and casual forums might seem like the most common space for harassment due to the ease of immediate interaction, abusive tactics are common throughout all spaces online. Researchers have found that even academic spaces are not free from such tactics of silencing and control. On news sites, during personal conversations, across social media, within online classrooms, and more, women are consistently subjected to conversational and rhetorical strategies that attempt to position men as powerful actors and women as subordinate participants, if not silent or invisible watchers.

In her book *The Internet of Garbage* Sarah Jeong describes online abuse through two frameworks: through harassing content and harassing behavior. "When looking at harassment as content . . . the debate ends up revolving around civil rights versus free speech," she writes. She does not regard this characterization as a helpful frame, as it sets up a spectrum on either end of which might be violent threats or simply annoying comments. It reduces the conversation to "where is the line between mean comments and imminent danger?" Instead, she writes, "behavior is a better, more useful lens through which to look at harassment. On one end of the behavioral spectrum of online harassment, we see the fact that a drive-by vitriolic message has been thrown out in the night; on the other end, we see the leaking of Social Security numbers, the publication of private photographs, the sending of SWAT teams to physical addresses, and physical assault."[45]

This framework allows us to position the online behavior on a spectrum and determine a response that is in proportion to the behavior, not whether the First Amendment protects the content. Jeong's framework provides an invaluable guideline for the remainder of this book. While both content and behavior are discussed in depth here, approaching the research and anecdotes as analysis of activities rather than specific things that have been said helps paint a more accurate picture of the environment and how we must respond. The content of a single message is important to consider not only in terms of its direct impact on another individual but also in the way it reflects larger patterns about online behavior and harassment.

Active and Passive Harassment

Researchers such as Barbara Ritter have also identified two primary forms of cybersexist harassment that offer another framework for understanding how online harassment functions. Using the standards often set for sexual harassment in an offline workplace or business, Ritter identifies gendered harassment as "misogynist behaviors that are hostile or degrading towards women."[46] She then identifies two forms of online harassment stemming from offline beliefs and behaviors, classifying the types of harassment as active and passive verbal and graphic gender harassment.

"Active verbal gender harassment, for example, includes unwelcome, offensive messages purposely sent. . . . Active graphic gender harassment also fits this description, but includes pictures. Passive verbal gender harassment . . . includes intentional messages posted to many potential receivers," which can include creating a username that incorporates an offensive slur, or passive graphic gender harassment, such as a user photograph or avatar with graphic content.[47] Active verbal harassment is one of the most common forms of online abuse, although using images and usernames to harass women also occurs regularly. Passive harassment has the effect of being visible to many potential targets at once, while active harassment requires a specific target.

Active verbal harassment is especially common on forms of social media like Facebook and Twitter, where participants have a defined name and identity used to send comments; those comments typically contain the bulk of the harassment and are the most noticeable. However, sites like Twitter and YouTube, along with comment sections, are particularly suited for passive verbal and graphic harassment; abusers can create a handle or name aimed at their target or targets (for example, a woman might receive a written threat from someone with a username that incorporates a gendered or racial slur) and use an avatar or other picture designed to harass, frighten, or disgust.

Ritter's discussion of these forms of harassment helps illuminate some of the new ways in which technology enables sexist harassment to thrive in the course of otherwise casual-seeming conversation—a common tactic for making women feel unsafe or unwelcome. Additionally, new aspects of technology allow for the transmission of sexist content and harassment in ways not possible before the advent of the Internet. In their analysis of online gender-based humor Limor Shifman and Dafna Lemish found that a good deal of Internet humor relies on conservative gender stereotypes and sexism, and it is transmitted in new ways, creating new kinds of harassment and reifying already existing harmful stereotypes. "New visual humor genres, such as funny photos or PowerPoint™ presentations, were either rare or non-existent prior to the internet," they write, while the advent of widely available Internet access allows for the creation and distribution of content to a much larger audience.[48] Offline, harassers have to target one individual or a handful at a time; online, images, comments, and memes can be spread in next to no time across dozens of accounts and websites, where they are more likely to be seen by large numbers of women.

The use of memes as a messaging strategy online often incorporates both sexist and feminist aspects of communication; cybersexists frequently create and share image files with stereotypes, sexist jokes, or other commentary over a chosen image. Feminists also use memes in order to respond to sexist harassment or to promote their own messages in easily transmitted and re-created formats—think LOLcats, the Shiba Inu "doge," and the ubiquitous Success Kid. The complex ecosystem of commentary through memes alone, on the many subjects that end up as memes, is well worth further study.

Anonymity

Cybersexists also rely heavily on anonymity—or perceived anonymity—to conduct their activities online. Derailing, mansplaining, gendered abuse, and threats are somewhat easier to combat when the people engaging in those activities do so under their real names. Often, online activities conducted while connected to an offline identity can backfire spectacularly. One woman, Justine Sacco, was fired from her public relations position after she sent a racist tweet in which she joked about not being able to contract AIDS on a trip to Africa because she's white. While she was on the flight her tweet was picked up, publicized across multiple social media sites, and eventually reported by various news sources, resulting in the loss of her job.[49] People regularly post jokes similar to Sacco's and worse, including abuse and threats, without any serious legal or professional repercussions, because they work under an assumption of anonymity. Anonymity makes it easier for cybersexists to act and much harder for women to respond effectively.

One report demonstrated the ways perceived anonymity online "may encourage individuals who would not engage in such conduct offline to do so," since the impression of being both anonymous and physically

The Many Faces of Cybersexism

separate from a target makes it easier to justify and engage in abusive speech.[50] Cybersexist harassers often use anonymity to say they didn't "really" mean the harassment, abuse, or stereotypes they posted, because the account was anonymous—it wasn't truly them, and therefore they weren't truly expressing their own opinions.

Claiming that opinions anonymously expressed don't reflect actual beliefs is a common strategy for avoiding criticism when those views and behaviors are noticed and criticized: it simply becomes labeled as trolling and thus not worth discussion. research demonstrates, however, that many online harassers are simply more comfortable expressing harmful beliefs or engaging in abuse when they're anonymous, because they assume they will not be able to be held accountable for whatever they said or did.

The sensation of anonymity is regarded as a sort of "get out of jail free" card to express opinions or engage in activities the harassers know to be wrong in a social or legal sense, without dealing with any of the repercussions of having those opinions connected to their offline identity. Instead of using anonymity to say things they don't mean, anonymity is used as a shield between an individual's real beliefs and their real identity: cybersexists feel free to engage in the types of harassment that they cannot commit under their real names but wish they could.

Many cybersexists add to the sense of security provided by anonymity, using multiple "burner" or "sockpuppet" accounts to harass women and engage in intimidation and abuse, then quickly shutting them down. This practice allows them to engage in harassment without having to deal with the effects of engaging in those behaviors offline or under their real name. Although anonymity is more difficult on websites that require identification, such as Facebook, it's still possible for people to set up multiple fake accounts for their own use. As Jeong writes, however, "*anonymity is not the problem*. It's quite apparent that anonymity can be a shield against" online abuses like doxxing, by protecting an individual who might otherwise be targeted.[51] Anonymity is a tool used by abusers, but it is also one that has many other valid uses that must be considered.

Justifications for Abuse

Most cybersexists appear to feel a sense of impunity regarding the harassment and abuse they commit. It can be observed in the ways they talk about their own behavior, both to each other and to their targets. As Whitney Phillips has pointed out in an interview about online harassment, cybersexist abusers often use the concept of trolling "as a way of repudiating responsibilities for their own actions" by framing violent misogyny and other behaviors as nonserious or conducted in jest.[52] There are a number of beliefs cybersexists display when they justify their own behavior, reject responsibility for it, or place blame on the targets of their behavior.

The first such justification is the argument that they are entitled to engage in abusive activities by virtue of being a man online, again relying on the concept of women as invaders or interlopers in male space. The sexist beliefs they hold offline are also a strong motivation for engaging in more extreme forms of abuse online, where female targets are more easily found. Online harassers also assume that the Internet is an inherently sexist place, and therefore they see accepting abuse as the cost of entry for women; the prevalence of this attitude and its roots in the Wild West idealization of the Internet give online sexism the appearance of being an incontrovertible norm.[53]

As a result of these pervasive attitudes, bystanders are also less likely to step in when harassment occurs, or they may accept the visible online abuse of women as part of the atmosphere of the Internet. The passive acceptance of abuse and sexism as an Internet norm contributes to the sense of impunity for those actively engaging in cybersexist harassment. After all, if only their targets notice or say anything about it, they must not be doing anything truly wrong.

In addition to the perceived lack of penalties for cybersexism, the ability to rapidly recruit additional harassers creates the conditions for more and more extreme examples of online abuse, such as mobbing activities and coordinated harassment campaigns aimed at individuals or small groups of targeted women. The feeling of anonymity helps lower inhibitions to acting on those sexist beliefs: cybersexists feel that they can act on their

The Many Faces of Cybersexism

opinions about women online, while simultaneously feeling secure that they will not be caught and that their public identity will remain safe and untarnished.

As a result of all of these factors, cybersexists are comfortable derailing women's conversations, positioning themselves as the authority on subjects they don't understand—often confronting women who study the topic, harassing women who disagree with them, and even sending violent threats to women. The culture of online cybersexism is pervasive.

A PORTRAIT OF THE CYBERSEXIST
AS A NOT-SO-YOUNG MAN

While I most frequently refer to cybersexist abusers as such throughout the book, it is important to explore the idea of "trolling" as it relates to cybersexism and online abuse. The persistent image of a troll is that of a bored, angry teenage boy, hiding in his parents' basement, typing insults with Cheetos-stained fingers and chugging Mountain Dew. Trolling, under this use of the term, is the act of a child, someone who clearly doesn't mean the things posted online, no matter what those things might be: it is no more than adolescent angst spread across the Internet. While incorrect, this image is pervasive. Despite the fact that most trolling activities (and particularly the most violent and illegal forms of cybersexism) are committed by adult men, many people refuse to acknowledge cybersexism as a serious issue, often because they think such activities are carried out by children and teens and therefore are not serious or dangerous.[54]

As discussed earlier, however, this old definition of a troll no longer fits the current online environment. Trolling, if defined as irritating but ultimately harmless distractions and disruptions, does not describe the pervasive culture of online abuse and harassment experienced by women. However, such cybersexist abuse and harassment are frequently defined as trolling. This misdefinition leads to a deep disconnect in the way we discuss online abuse.

Too often, we are prone to labeling any disruptive behavior as trolling—no matter how harmful it is—and to simply encourage women not to feed the trolls, as though ignoring a problem will make it go away. The concept of trolling is no longer useful for describing an online environment that includes actively damaging, frightening, and illegal behaviors unless we dramatically change our understanding of the term. Trolling is not simply the mild interruptions to online activities that can easily be ignored or that have no impact beyond being annoying. Trolls and cybersexists may be one and the same, engaging in different behaviors at different times. At the least, they are engaging in behaviors on a spectrum not nearly as wide as is often assumed.

Meet "weev." He is a consummate troll under both the old understanding of the word and the new. Offline he goes by Andrew Auernheimer and is a white man in his thirties from Arkansas. Offline he spent several years deeply entangled in the legal system because of his hacking, which included exposing an AT&T security breach to the website publisher Gawker and thus releasing the data of more than 114,000 iPad users.[55] Auernheimer nearly spent a forty-one-month sentence behind bars, but he was able to avoid the full sentence when the Third Circuit reversed the conviction on a legal technicality about the location of the criminal case.[56] He's frequently referred to as a hacktivist for his exposure of security flaws, a champion for free speech, and one of the closest things the Internet has to a folk hero—a David who triumphed over AT&T's Goliath. Libertarians love him. So do other trolls and cybersexists.

In addition to his hacking activities, as weev, Auernheimer was—and remains—a prolific cybersexist troll. One of his greatest successes, such as it is, came in 2007 when he instigated the harassment of the programmer and game developer Kathy Sierra, which escalated to the point that she canceled all of her speaking events and put her career on hold, vanishing from the Internet for six years while dealing with the fallout and still keeping her online presence minimal.[57] Her Social Security number and personal information were made publicly available, along with a fake account of her career that depicted her as a former sex worker, with the sole intention of damaging her future opportunities in the tech field.

She began receiving death and rape threats, as well as manipulated images of her with a noose by her face or being strangled. The threats just kept coming—so many and so violent that she had to leave her job and public online spaces for her own safety. Although weev has since distanced himself from the events that took place, he still receives the dubious credit for having obtained her information and encouraging the harassment and abuse that ended her career.

Before he started having serious legal troubles, weev also spoke publicly on his motivations for harassing people online. He has been profiled in multiple publications, including in a lengthy *New York Times* piece.[58] In preparing to write that piece its author listened to Auernheimer pontificate about his attempts and successes at creating online destruction and chaos, which he likened to eugenics (in addition to the actual anti-Semitism the author noted, Auernheimer now sports a large swastika tattoo on his chest).[59] The writer of the piece also met with weev and a number of other trolls in person, and in that encounter weev at one point expressed ideas focused on trying to "kill four of the world's six billion people in the most just way possible."[60] When spoken, weev's beliefs are deeply misanthropic but wrapped in a polished zeal that gives him the appearance of being an expert in his own convictions.

He also appeared on a segment of a show called *Insight*, speaking remotely to a room full of people.[61] On-screen before the audience the bearded, articulate Auernheimer is quiet, calm, and good-humored, listening patiently to the host's questions. He looks like your average thirty-something white guy. With his curly hair and sweatshirt he could be any young man sitting in a college classroom or start-up office. The content of his responses, however, is where the surprises are.

"Do you not take any kind of responsibility for initiating those kind of comments?" the host asks, referring to weev's online insults, one of which was displayed on the screen as she spoke.[62] "You don't have to respond that way, why choose to respond that way?"

"You know, I think the problem with our society is that everybody is so politically correct, because they've grown up in a bubble of Fisher-Price rounded corners and bright colors where costumed animals will tell nobody anything that might hurt their feelings," he responds, watching closely to see how the audience takes his statement.

As the people in the room begin to react to weev's pronouncements, smiling slightly or laughing, he increases the violence of his rhetoric in response: "Kids these days, they should be out welding, they should work with caustic chemicals, you know, controlled demolitions, throw spears. . . . How are we supposed to stand up to countries where people want to hate us?"

Then, greeted by the audience's visibly growing disagreement with his statements, especially the coded racism of imagined foreign people at whom we might, apparently, need children to throw spears, he wraps up his reply with some suggestions that will be familiar to many women who have dealt with online abuse and harassment.

"Get over it," weev says. "Grow up. Grow up and learn to deal with people on the Internet not liking you, and if you don't like it, shut down your Facebook page, make your Twitter private, don't engage in a public discussion, and you'll never run into a conversation where I can say something that can hurt your feelings."

While weev does not target only women for his trolling, the immensity of the damage done to women at his behest, as well as the highly gendered nature of his attacks on them, qualifies his harassment as often being cybersexist in nature. To weev and his fans and copycats, many of whom use his photograph as their avatars, as well as to other trolls (and those who offer well-meaning but ineffective advice), cybersexism is seen as something that must be endured as part of spending any amount of time on the Internet. Deliberate, targeted, sexist harassment is presented as the cost of entry into public discussions online and something that women need to just "get over."

Auernheimer is far from the only troll to suggest that people who receive harassment are responsible for it by virtue of existing where the trolls can see them. Online journalist Patrick Klepek reported in his blog about an extensive back-and-forth email conversation with a troll regarding the motivation for trolling and what the troll sees as the appropriate response.[63] Klepek protected the anonymity of the troll when writing about the discussion—an interesting decision, given that the troll's targets do not have the same choice when interacting with him, but one that was likely necessary to secure the conversation.

Throughout the emails exchanged with Klepek the troll offered extensive and contradictory philosophical ruminations on his own trolling, including the insistence that he would not be responsible if his targets chose to kill themselves as a result of his harassment. Despite that, the troll fully acknowledged that his behavior—which he described as a pattern repeated across many years—is inappropriate. At the same time, the troll insisted that online harassment isn't serious and that people who think it is are foolish.

"Imagine the 'older street tough' of lore taking your lunch money every day, or to be a woman and have a male coworker slap your ass or make other unwelcome advances. These are serious issues that have a real impact on a person's life and psyche." Here the troll acknowledges that offline sexist harassment and other forms of abuse exist and are serious issues, while discounting the fact that online harassment could also be serious to those who experience it. "It is entirely another matter to be on the receiving end of a completely anonymous voice, with no physical presence whatsoever, spilling words into a medium that one has complete control over. At any time, I can block anyone on Twitter, I can tell them to go away in whatever terms I choose, or I can even delete my account or make it private at no cost to myself. I simply don't see the connection."[64] Echoing weev's words, this troll insists that shutting down or locking an account is a feasible solution to online abuse and that the person on the receiving end is ultimately responsible for the situation.

Oddly, neither this troll nor weev seems to consider that threats anonymously made can be more frightening than threats from a known source, since threats from a named source can be tracked and dealt with, while threats coming from someone who is anonymous often cannot. This troll also, when suggesting that blocking trolls or telling them to go away is a solution, ignores the fact that cybersexist harassers frequently make multiple accounts from which they send a barrage of harassment or threats. Women can block harassers, true, but those harassers have a tendency to just regroup and come right back. The fact that blocking is a possibility is also not an excuse for an individual choosing to engage in the initial cybersexist harassment.

Additionally, both weev and the troll Klepek talked to seem to believe that turning off the computer is a viable solution for avoiding cybersexist harassment. While turning off the computer may seem like a good way to deal with trolls and abuse at face value, it is at best a temporary solution for briefly avoiding seeing further comments: it stops no one from making them in the first place. Women's choices should not be a decision between avoiding online life (a laughably improbable suggestion) and dealing with unrelenting harassment. As Laurie Penny states in her book *Cybersexism: Sex, Gender and Power on the Internet*, men "declared early on that there were 'no girls on the Internet.' That idea sounded like sweet freedom for a lot of us, but it turned out to be a threat."[65] Women's presence online is already seen as an anomaly and harassment of women, as a given; if women raise an objection, men's solution is to tell them to shut up or get lost.

To add to that, as Danielle Citron points out, "even if women go offline (or never availed themselves of online activities in the first place), online rape threats, sexually demeaning comments, and damaging statements remain online, accessible to anyone searching targeted women's names."[66] Even if the woman herself goes offline the harassment remains—visible to employers, friends, family, and strangers, some of whom may elect to continue the abuse or, lacking a response or rebuttal, believe that whatever has been posted about a woman is true. Unlike a harassing comment shouted from a car or made by a coworker, abusive statements made in online spaces have a near-permanent existence. And, as most people would readily acknowledge, deciding to permanently leave the Internet is in most cases just not an option anymore; even a temporary absence can result in personal and professional losses.

To counteract their own contradictory arguments, cybersexists often change tactics, further reframing their behavior to remove focus from their culpability in it. Like many trolls, the particular individual with whom Klepek spoke uses both "I don't mean what I say" and "It's anonymous trolling, so why take it seriously?" as thin excuses to justify his harassing

The Many Faces of Cybersexism

and abusive activities online. There are a few problems with this troll's defense of his own actions, which stem directly from the combination of those excuses.

Individuals who rely on these pretexts to explain their behavior insist that their own subjectivity and intentions should trump the subjectivity and reactions of their targets, while they simultaneously take great pains to prevent the targets of their abuse from being able to discern those intentions. That is, trolls assume that they should get to dictate not only the content of their statements but also the emotional reaction those statements elicit, as well as the content of any responses, and that any negative reaction is entirely the fault of their target.

Regarding threats, whether or not cybersexists believe they're joking when threatening to rape or otherwise harm women tends to be irrelevant to the women on the receiving end of what often appear to be serious threats and abuse from men they don't know. Even when humorously phrased these "jokes" also reveal the underlying beliefs and attitudes of those who tell them.

One report on the sexism of online humor notes that "sexist humor has been an integral part of many patriarchal cultures for centuries. Underlying such humor are sexist beliefs about the inferiority of women. It portrays them as stupid, illogical, ignorant, or irresponsible, and it tends to build on sexual objectification."[67] Whether a joke is a statement made at the expense of women generally or used as a way to backtrack from an offensive or threatening comment to a specific woman, its content is not neutral. Sexist humor is frequently used as a way to reinforce attitudes about appropriate gender roles and remind people of their appropriate place in a certain environment.

Cybersexists may insist that their intent was to use the threat to tell a crass joke or elicit an angry reaction, but what they say their intent was has little effect on the actual outcome of such statements. Acting as if harassing women online or issuing violent threats is a prank or a joke that can be waved away by insisting that the goal was to be funny in no way makes such actions acceptable, which even cybersexists themselves will sometimes acknowledge. The existence of threats from people who later say they were joking puts women in the position of attempting to discern whether or not a threat is serious.

Given the knowledge that online threats do sometimes correlate to offline attacks, women must assume the burden of further analyzing communications that are already upsetting or frightening. As some threats are serious, all threats must therefore be taken seriously—whether or not the person sending them thinks they were funny or if they think their belief that something was funny justifies sending it in the first place. One must also wonder about the offline behaviors of a person who considers harassing strangers or sending violent threats an amusing online pastime.

The suggestion that the relative anonymity of the Internet is a reason not to take trolling or abuse seriously also fails to hold water. As noted earlier, many individuals find threatening comments or abuse coming from anonymous sources to be significantly more frightening than the same types of comments coming from a known source or individual. It is more difficult to protect oneself from an anonymous threat, whereas a threat from a named person, or someone known to the target, can usually be more readily dealt with. That a threat or harassing comment comes from an anonymous account does not, as Klepek's troll suggests, make it less serious.

Furthermore, most cybersexists are perfectly aware that their threats will be taken seriously and that their anonymity is useful as an additional intimidation factor. That is in fact often the point: the ability to engage in deliberately sexist harassment of women is seen as amusing—it is a demonstration of power over their chosen target. By insisting on being allowed to both issue the threat or harassment and attempt to control how it is received, cybersexist abusers make it plain that they want to be able to dominate the entirety of their interactions with women while never fully acknowledging their role in the situation or the consequences of their actions for the people they target.

Although they claim to be joking and suggest that the Internet is not a space for serious discussion, this defense is a disingenuous tactic that cybersexists use to, again, divest themselves of responsibility for an abused target's fear or suffering. "Since I say I didn't mean it," they seem to insist,

The Many Faces of Cybersexism

"it shouldn't be taken seriously and it's your own fault if you do." The individual who is on the receiving end of abuse is not required to agree with the abuser simply because the abuser finds engaging in harassment to be entertaining. The deflection of responsibility for dealing with harassment onto the harassed is a tactic consistently used by cybersexists to avoid truly examining their own behavior and the effects it has, regardless of their stated intent.

Cybersexists often adopt an air of being equally offended that their harassment has been noticed at all. In terms of offline abuse such a switch is referred to as DARVO—deny, attack, reverse victim and offender. This strategy is especially common in situations of interpersonal or domestic violence, where abuse is first denied and then blamed on the person who was in actuality abused. DARVO is a useful strategy for cybersexists, as it allows them to deny that their behavior was actually abuse, to attack the people criticizing them, and then to claim that being criticized for being abusive is itself a form of abuse.

For example, the troll with whom Klepek spoke refers to the early years of the Internet in familiar terms, fondly using the Wild West trope, with the implication that back when the Internet was seen as lawless (or, phrased more honestly, seen as a space only for white men), no one would have been upset at racist, sexist, or otherwise abusive trolling. If the targets of such abuse are invisible or silent, the reasoning goes, the abuse must not be that serious. "I'm an embittered, resentful, and defeated vestige of the old Internet," as he puts it, apparently upset at the changes that have brought attention to his hobby of encouraging people to kill themselves—making him, he seems to believe, the real victim.

Another of the common themes throughout cybersexists' self-defense, when they offer it, is that people shouldn't be so sensitive to having their feelings hurt; we shouldn't be so "politically correct" as to get upset when women are threatened with abuse or rape. It's "just the Internet," as the saying goes—an attitude addressed in depth in a later chapter. This defense is a useful tactic for further redirecting focus from the cybersexist's actions to the victims' reactions to the abuse they receive. By forcing the conversation to analyze women's responses to abuse rather than the abuse itself, cybersexists reinforce the idea that abuse is as inevitable as bad weather and, as a result, make it seem like our only option is to choose how we react to it.

This misdirection also disguises the fact that cybersexist harassment and trolling are not components of a neutral or harmless activity that merely results in hurt feelings. In fact, the harassment and abuse that women experience online have an immense effect on their lives and well-being; cybersexism itself is also rarely an unfocused lashing out, instead tending to be deliberately conducted and purposeful. Although trolls occasionally acknowledge their behavior as being inappropriate or deliberately harmful, many men still engage in cybersexist activities.

Even men who insist that they are not trolling will engage in activities that are associated with cybersexism, such as mansplaining, acting dominant in some way, and resorting to sexist stereotypes to position themselves as the authority within the conversation. However, these conversational strategies are not the only tactics used by cybersexists to attempt to retake control of the Internet and drive women away. Threats, doxxing, hacking, and mob harassment are all strategies used by cybersexists to reinforce the unequal nature of the Internet, damage women personally and professionally, and attempt to intimidate women and minimize their presence online.

So what is the motivation for cybersexism? Why do men decide to seek out and harass women, sometimes for hours, days, weeks, or months without stopping? What is the relationship between seemingly less serious actions, like mansplaining, and illegal threats of violence? And why do so many people defend those activities?

The Many Faces of Cybersexism

2 TYPES OF CYBERSEXISM
What Online Harassment Really Looks Like

There are many reasons that cybersexism occurs, from mere boredom to much more dangerous and deeply held convictions about the appropriate gender roles for men and women and the best ways to enforce those roles. Although there are as many individual reasons for trolling as there are individuals who decide to troll, there are a number of patterns that link cybersexist behaviors, revealing attitudes that are similar to the sexist beliefs many men hold offline as well.

Men don't seek out women to harass simply because women are natural targets and men are natural aggressors. The motivation for cybersexist activities is deeply linked to believing that's true, however; cybersexism is used to create, support, and enforce norms of male dominance in online spaces. Even as individual men engaging in cybersexism may claim they are not sexist—and this chapter explores many of the types of cybersexism— the patterns of online abuse and the particular targets of that abuse suggest that the same sexist, racist, and other damaging attitudes that influence offline behaviors are behind online abuse as well.

Cybersexism is often seen as nonserious: comments that most closely align with an older definition of trolling can often be shrugged off, or so the reasoning goes. A deliberately inflammatory comment can generally be ignored, but its relationship to the more serious, frightening, and violent forms of cybersexism cannot. As women who have been harassed on the street know, what starts off as a simple comment can quickly escalate into violence. Toward the end of 2014 a number of women—most of them women of color—were physically attacked and even murdered for doing nothing more than rebuffing a street harasser.[1] Similarly, in online spaces, ignoring, rebuffing, or simply responding to a harasser can quickly escalate the conversation from irritating to frightening. No response (or even a lack of response) guarantees that the situation won't escalate, which is one of the reasons cybersexist abuse is so frustrating, and so frightening.

TYPES OF CYBERSEXISM

Understanding the varying types of cybersexism, from basic conversational strategies focusing on male dominance to vicious and illegal threats of violence, is key to understanding the relationships between them.

Derailing and Mansplaining

Much like interrupting and critiquing women's use of slang offline, male-driven derailing and mansplaining, both prevalent online, don't seem that serious at first glance.[2] However, these two acts have in essence become the online versions of interrupting and critiquing women's speech patterns, as discussed in the previous chapter, and they happen with equal or greater frequency than their offline counterparts. Derailing is a form of interrupting, in which a cybersexist will attempt to redirect women's conversations to focus on something he is more comfortable with or to reassert his preferred norms. Derailing often occurs when an individual begins asking questions only tangentially related to the topic at hand, such as asking questions that could easily be answered by using a search engine when women are discussing complex ideas. Derailing effectively demands free education and labor from those women, repeatedly enters a conversation to challenge the participants' understanding of their own conversation, and tries to refocus women's attention on another topic or even on the derailer himself.

The "not all men" claim is a particularly common and pernicious form of derailing, one in which a man (or, more often, men) respond to women's discussions of sexism by reminding the participants that "not all men" engage in whatever form of sexism is under discussion. While it's true that not every man engages in every type of sexist activity, this form of

Types of Cybersexism

derailing has the immediate effect of re-centering the conversation on men who want some kind of credit for not doing what's being discussed. It also reduces focus on the problem at hand (the men who do act in sexist ways) and often takes the form of forcing women to defend their language choices, never mind that "all men" weren't under discussion in the first place.

In a turn that demonstrates the power of the Internet to respond to cybersexism, "not all men" has become a meme—its popularity as a mocking response to this derailing tactic is attributed to writer Shafiqah Hudson; she made a joke in early 2013 on her Twitter account (@sassycrass) about how common this response is.[3] While the concept has existed for years, the tweet and subsequent meme helped make it a way for women to regain control of their own conversations by undercutting the derailing attempt with humor.[4]

However, point-blank interruption is not the only way for men to disrupt women's conversations online. In one example of online interruptions, an academic listserv chat described by Susan Herring included a particularly dedicated method used to disrupt women's online speech. Although the listserv used an asynchronous communication style similar to email, leaving gaps and periods of time between each addition being posted, "interruptions" are performed by men who quote at length from another participant in the conversation and break up the quote with their own extensive commentary.[5]

This strategy deliberately mimics offline and real-time online conversational tactics of interruption, in which a man's average number of interruptions is significantly higher than a woman's. In the particular listserv conversation referenced by Herring, 90 percent of men's messages used this interruption tactic, compared to only 8 percent of women's comments.[6] By re-creating the appearance of interrupting, even asynchronously, men attempt to develop the same level of control over the conversation as they have offline, disrupting women's speech and giving themselves the ability to shape how women's statements are perceived and read.

These behaviors are enacted in other ways in online spaces, through activities such as taking screenshots of a woman's tweets, blog posts, or commentary and framing comments around them. The strategy also relies heavily on taking women's words out of context and reinterpreting them to suit the cybersexist's point of view. As discussed throughout this book, a common tactic is to paint women who resist sexism as attempting to censor free speech; decontextualizing a woman's statements makes it easy to twist a statement and give it the appearance of censoriousness when such an attitude does not exist.

Mansplaining is another form of derailing, one in which men will interrupt a conversation between women to explain something to them about the subject, whether or not the men know anything about it and regardless of the men's level of expertise in the topic.[7] Often mansplaining is done to let the women know men think the women's opinions are factually wrong and that men's opinions should be more carefully considered, even if the men's ideas have already been addressed during the course of the discussion.

Mansplaining is often regarded as a condescending and unnecessary addition to a conversation. Whether it's a comment on a blog post, a response to a tweet that merely repeats the woman's point in different words, or a YouTube response video used to explain a point a woman already made, mansplaining is incredibly common. Women with any following on any social media or online platform come to expect that a certain number of men will attempt to explain their own points back to them and that reminding those men that those points have already been made will be regarded as insulting.

Often a mansplainer has little to no expertise in the area on which he is attempting to appear authoritative. In Rebecca Solnit's article in which the term originated, she describes an offline encounter with a man who tried to tell her about the importance of her own book, which had been published that year, under the assumption that it had been written by a man. "Being women," Solnit writes, "we were politely out of earshot before we started laughing, and we've never really stopped."[8] While common in conversations about women's issues specifically, mansplaining occurs on any subject when women are perceived as taking up too much space or appearing too authoritative.[9]

Types of Cybersexism

A counterpart term, whitesplaining, has been coined to address the issue of white people explaining racism to people of color. These two types of derailing tactics are meant to assert that individuals who have privilege in a conversational setting (e.g., white people, especially white men) should be taken seriously, whether or not they have any expertise in the topic at hand.

Gendered Abuse and Harassment

Although scant research exists on cybersexism and intersecting forms of online abuse compared to other forms of violence and abuse, one area where some research has been conducted is gendered harassment and how that harassment tends to play out in online conversations. The available research tends to predate today's social media heavyweights, Facebook and Twitter, where a great deal of abuse occurs, but the patterns are largely consistent. Herring and other theorists have identified common themes that occur during gendered abuse and harassment. While Herring's research uses two specific case studies, drawn from a live chat and a listserv, multiple independent studies have reported similarly abusive language choices and harassing actions.

Additionally, the same types of harassment can be observed simply by visiting most comment sections of blogs and news websites or popular social media sites. Gendered abuse and harassment typically take the form of overt sexual harassment, gender stereotypes, and sexually explicit insults intended to demean, objectify, or assert dominance over women. The use of gender as a tool to silence women is a dominance tactic that aims to restore control of online conversations to men either by painting women as inferior and objectified or by reducing them to silence.

In the first example Herring cites in her article, three women were conversing on a public chat forum when two men interrupted and attempted to refocus the discussion on themselves. The initial derailing involved immediate sexual objectification of the women conversing, with the instigator referring to them as a "babe inventory" for the other male participant to examine.[10] The expectation that women online should be present only to serve as fodder for heterosexual male fantasies is common, and a great deal of cybersexist harassment begins with sexual objectification as a method of asserting dominance over women encountered in online spaces.

All three women in the conversation resisted the attempt at derailing, at which point the men immediately escalated the sexist harassment they had begun to deploy. Escalating from what's seen as standard or acceptable levels of sexual harassment is a common tactic in the face of women's resistance. The harassers called one target a bitch and told her to "quite [sic] the stupid Valley Girl talk" before using a "kick" command to forcibly remove her from the conversation multiple times.[11] The gendered nature of the insults and the reference to stereotyped women's speech patterns directly mirror the ways in which men attempt to assert control over women in offline conversations.

The immediate escalation of the violence of the rhetoric used to assert dominance over the women matches the way such conversations can escalate offline—much like a street harasser insulting a woman who hasn't responded favorably to his initial overture. The act of "kicking" a woman out of the chat space not just once but repeatedly emphasizes the rhetorical and, in some senses, physical control the men felt they had or deserved over three women's ability to speak to one another in a public chat space. The sense of entitlement to women's time, attention, and bodies is a hallmark of sexism—cybersexism and otherwise.

These demonstrations of power achieve the harassers' goal. All three initial women participants were kicked off of the forum at least once (one of the harassers, as a moderator, could remove women from the conversation; the women, as chatters, could not do the same to either harasser), and the harassers continued to escalate the nature of their sexist harassment, adding racist elements after each woman rejoined the conversation. Upon recognizing the force of the overt power displays and the futility of continuing to resist, the women began to alter their topics of discussion, refocusing on their harassers and redirecting all of their discussions toward them and other men.[12]

The accommodation of male demands even extends to one of the original harassers using an action command in which he "mounted" one of his targets, which "supports the feminist adage that sexual harassment

Types of Cybersexism

is not fundamentally about sex, but about exercise of power."[13] Repeated interruptions of the women's conversation, followed by escalating sexist and racist harassment, along with power displays in the form of kicking women off of the channel and "mounting" those that remained, succeeded in allowing the men to take complete control of the women's conversation, scattering the women throughout the forum, and ending the discussion that had initially been solely among the three women.

The behaviors these harassers displayed reflect the most common patterns of cybersexist abuse across the Internet. An initial interaction with a cybersexist is likely to involve an assessment of women's physical appeal according to narrow standards (objectification), displays of power and dominance in traditionally patriarchal ways in the face of resistance, and an escalation of aggression until the women acquiesce. Such interactions often culminate in threats of sexual and physical violence or death.

These acts are not random or thoughtless, either; sexist abuse is a deliberate choice, and it is used to establish men as superior while at the same time reinforcing gender stereotypes. Harassers might be hard-pressed to frame their behaviors so succinctly (or to reflect on them honestly at all), but these behaviors align with what cybersexists feel should be the "natural" roles for men and women in cyberspace.

Cybersexist harassers use "sexual objectification and gender stereotyping to make women feel unwelcome, subordinated, or altogether excluded" in an attempt to limit or end women's participation in online conversations.[14] The tactics chosen by cybersexists are common in offline spaces as well, but the lowered inhibitions of online interaction—along with the ability for harassers to quickly recruit others to their cause, as was demonstrated in Herring's example—mean that sexual harassment becomes a powerful tool for reinforcing male-dominated norms online.

Free Speech and Gender Essentialism

While the use of power displays such as demeaning language, objectification, and sexual harassment are common in instances of cybersexism, Herring identifies another aspect of cybersexism. When overt attempts at asserting dominance fail, cybersexist harassers frequently change tactics and begin "[depriving] the women of any legitimate grounds from which to voice their concerns. . . . Worse, women in general are essentialized as inferior to men."[15] The delegitimizing of women's voices occurs as harassers use less sex-based but no less sexist gender stereotypes, such as referring to women as hysterical or distorting women's writing to make it appear morally or intellectually inferior, often by referring to women's resistance to sexist behavior as a form of censorship.[16] From there the imagined deficiencies of the targeted woman are applied to all women generally, positioning men as inherently superior to women.

Herring's second example of cybersexist harassment includes instances of all of the above strategies. The example chosen is a conversation from an academic listserv, where professors, graduate students, and undergraduate students could meet to discuss issues of the group's choice (thus also demonstrating that academia itself is not free from sexist or cybersexist problems). The discussion group Herring examined was "Paglia-L," devoted to examining the works of Camille Paglia and other, tangentially related topics.[17] The specific thread Herring chose to examine began as a discussion of a professor who had been forced into early retirement after writing an article in a student newspaper that blamed women for date rape.

The harassment of a female user of the listserv started when she described the professor's article and comments as offensive to women; this descriptive effort kicked off a discussion that included attempting to undermine her positions based on spurious claims made about her points, to essentialize her (and through her, women generally) as inferior to men, and to create a double standard that permitted criticism of all of her conversational tactics, while ignoring or promoting the ways men spoke—even when those methods were similar to hers. By analyzing the conversation in depth Herring identifies the strategies used to put the woman in her place as core components of cybersexism.

Throughout the discussion on the "Paglia-L" group, as the conversation continues Herring notes a marked decrease in the number of contributions from women and an increase from men. As in offline conversations mixed-group online discussions frequently allow for more speech from men while attempting to silence women who are seen as talking too much. Herring

Types of Cybersexism

points out that, "in asynchronous [computer mediated communications], women's messages rarely exceed two screens in length, and longer messages are frequently accompanied by apologies, whereas men write messages as long as 20 screens and rarely if ever apologize for message length."[18] That is, men tend to take—and accept as inherently theirs—ten times the space of women in online conversations, while women are accustomed to trying to validate their presence through the use of apologies, self-effacement, and strict limits on how much they speak. While it can be argued that such limits are self-imposed, it is important to remember that women who take up more space tend to become targets for more serious and sustained forms of harassment.

In "Paglia-L" the participant named Mary introduces her opinions as an additional aspect of the discussion around the professor's forced retirement, mentioning that she disagreed with his suspension but found his views distasteful.[19] Although her statement conformed to the pro–free speech interpretation line of argument in the thread, her dislike of the professor's commentary itself drew the ire of male participants because it was seen as feminist in nature and therefore threatening to the male-dominated space of the discussion thread. From there the harassment began and continued to escalate throughout the entire listserv. This pattern reflects the underlying drive of cybersexism to reject any attempt at gender equality; even when women agree with one aspect of the male-dominated position, any feminist critique is seen as a threat and must therefore be wrong.

One of the tactics used by the men in the group—one common to many online discussions that result in cybersexist attacks—was to reformulate Mary's arguments against a specific man as being against all men (similar to the "not all men" argument referenced previously), converting it into a perceived threat to their free expression.[20] In reconstructing Mary's argument this way they deprived her of a reasonable point on which to base her opinions; she must then respond by restating her original arguments in a way that conforms to the expectations of the men in the group or by defending herself from charges of censorship, despite having explicitly supported free speech in her initial comment.

Reshaping a woman's argument to make it seem as though she said or implied something damaging to freedom of speech is one of the fastest ways to gain support for harassing her, as cybersexists frequently use their own interpretation of free speech as a way to demand that women refrain from criticizing their sexist statements. That is, sexists assume that free speech also includes the ability to be free from criticism or social repercussions. This line of reasoning ignores the reality that, in the United States, the First Amendment is related to government censorship and has nothing to do with whether women approve or disapprove of sexist statements.

Additionally, the tactic of reframing criticism of sexism as an attempt to impose limits on free speech falls in line with the cybersexist strategy of intentionally redirecting focus from the damaging speech itself and onto the reaction to that speech, acting as though the reaction is the real problem. In this case mischaracterizing the reaction (dislike of a piece of writing that blames women for rape) is used to discredit an argument that was never made (the imagined threat to free speech), leading to the hyperbolic response: that criticism and dislike of sexism are clear pathways to censorship. Women who resist sexist statements are likely to be told that they're impeding someone else's freedom of speech. While this argument is clearly absurd, it is incredibly common and frequently applied to feminist critique of media such as video games, movies, and TV shows.

Another common cybersexist tactic is to put women on the defensive by deliberately misinterpreting their statements as an attack, rather than an analytical perspective. By framing Mary's comments as a restriction on free speech, the men in the group were freed from addressing the substance of her arguments, as well as able to position themselves as the victim of feminists, while going on the offensive. Mary herself had to contend with a purposeful distortion of her writing, while the group's participants largely ignored what she had said.

As in the other chat Herring analyzed, Mary attempts to defend herself against the attacks and is joined by another woman, Gail, who points out that the men in the group are not responding to arguments Mary actually put forth. And, as in the other chat, this resistance is met with an immediate escalation of harassment from the men. Men in the group

Types of Cybersexism

chat begin introducing sexist stereotypes to accompany the earlier ad hominem attacks, suggesting that feminists "bitch" about oppression and that Mary is "verging on the stereotypically hysterical," that her posts are not "reasonable."[21] Referring to women as hysterical and unreasonable relies on old sexist stereotypes about hysteria (the idea that an issue with women's wombs prevented women from being logical) and the assumption that women are incapable of engaging in serious, logical discussions with men, or at all.

Positioning women as hysterical has the effect of creating a positive contrast for men—positioning them as calm, reasonable, and authoritative. The implication is that women cannot participate in conversations without becoming overly emotional, while men can. Men's opinions, according to this line of reasoning, should be taken seriously, while women can be dismissed out of hand on the assumption that their opinions are illogical by virtue of being expressed by a woman. The deeply ingrained gender stereotypes used by men are a rhetorical tactic intended to undercut women's authority on the topic of discussion and reinforce the existing power hierarchy by placing women in opposition—and subordination—to men.

Gender essentialist arguments are a useful strategy for cybersexists to avoid addressing the content of a woman's argument, as seen with the response to Mary. In open forums such as social media, essentialist comments are also likely to draw the attention of those who will engage in overt sexist harassment on the assumption that the stereotype being applied to a woman is true. This situation enables the original individual to recruit other people to harass the woman while still putting himself in the position of being logical and rational. In instances when gender essentialism occurs, it's common to see a cybersexist man speak to a woman with condescension or outright hostility, while seriously and respectfully considering the same argument the woman made if it's presented to him by another man.

Creating Double Standards

In Herring's example the men in the "Paglia-L" discussion finally resort to developing double standards for the ways in which women are permitted to communicate and to using that double standard as a way to discredit everything said by the women in the group. Following the escalation of harassment, both Mary and Gail begin to engage in more directly adversarial tactics, similar to those the men had consistently used toward them throughout the entire conversation.[22] While this change also represents an accommodation to the expected male norms—a norm in which disputes involve aggressive discussion on the listserv—the women's use of these tactics is met with immediate disapproval from the men. Eventually both Gail and Mary fall silent, leaving the conversation to be totally dominated by men.

As a result, whether the women in the group responded to arguments using the conversational strategies they preferred or by accommodating the men's conversational patterns, they were censured by the men—who presumed they had the inherent right to do so. This tactic allowed the men to take control of the conversation and thus position themselves as the authority figures on what strategies for dispute were acceptable. In changing their tactics to criticizing how the women spoke instead of addressing what the women said, the men created an environment in which the outcome of the dispute was not decided on the merits of an argument but on whether the men chose to engage with the arguments in good faith. Meanwhile the men could participate in the dispute by engaging respectfully or by utilizing cybersexist harassment and aggressive tactics, and both strategies were regarded as valid—or, at least, none of the men received criticism for how they spoke, regardless of the tactics they used.

These types of behaviors appear everywhere on the Internet; anywhere people congregate and talk, such tactics are likely to make an appearance. Women in many conversations online are placed in a no-win situation in which their speech becomes grounds for disagreement and harassment regardless of topic or conversational strategies, and their points are ignored or discarded. Meanwhile, men assume the role of arbiter and engage in whatever conversational tactics they please, expecting their choices to be regarded as valid.

The strategy of creating these double standards is sometimes referred to as tone trolling or tone policing.[23] While anyone can engage in tone policing, it is frequently aimed at women as a way to prevent a woman from making a point in the discussion. When an online disagreement changes in focus from what women said to how their male interlocutor feels about how they said it, there is no longer a debate but an attempt to establish dominance within the conversation. Many men suggest that women appear to be too angry or emotional to be taken seriously, as determined by those men, and therefore they exempt themselves from actual engagement with the argument made by the woman.

Tone policing is a form of derailing that creates a double standard that allows men to act as the judges of what counts as acceptable speech for women online, while also ignoring the substance of what women are saying. In both examples of harassment cited by Herring, men denounce women's chosen forms of expression from the start and disapprove of the women for subsequently adopting the same rhetorical strategies the men had been using, meaning that no matter how women spoke, men reacted negatively.[24]

Herring also pays attention to women's reactions to online harassment. The conversations recorded by Herring demonstrate that two of the most common responses to cybersexism are to conform to the conversational norms demanded by men or to fall silent entirely.[25] These methods of dealing with online abuse have the effect of restoring conversation to male control, achieved either by using harassment as a punishment for deviating from accepted subjects and methods of discussion or by removing women from the equation, thus reproducing the hierarchical power structures often found in offline discussions.

As noted earlier, it's easy to blame women for acquiescing to the strategies that are designed and used to produce exactly that effect. However, positive change cannot come from women choosing to remain in hostile spaces and enduring harsher and more violent forms of harassment solely to make a point of not leaving; as discussed later, the effects of exposure to such cybersexist harassment can have serious online and offline consequences. We should not expect women to shoulder the burden of intense harassment; instead, we should expect men to treat women as equals in the conversation and refrain from engaging in sexist abuse in the first place.

When discussing cybersexism, it's easy to act as if harassment is impossible to overcome and that it's women's responsibility to grow a thicker skin (an argument discussed later); however, harassment is a chosen activity that is deliberately engaged in—we can demand and expect better behavior from the men with whom we interact. While the examples used in Herring's research are specific incidents of online harassment and sexism, they reflect the larger patterns of online discourse and the tactics used by men to reassert male dominance over women's discussions. One aspect not included in either example cited by Herring (with the possible exception of the "mounting" discussed earlier) is the use of threats of violence and abuse to control discussions and silence women.

Online Threats

At the time of this writing I had recently reported to Twitter a threat of violence I received. It's not the first time that I've had to file such a report, and I don't imagine it will be the last. As with the above forms of derailing and attempts at establishing conversational control, most women online have had to learn how to deal with men overtly threatening our safety and well-being. While many of these threats are not "serious" in the sense that the person sending them probably will not show up in person to actually carry out the threat, threats have other functions and purposes. As in offline spaces, threats are often intended to intimidate and silence women.

The particular threat I received is a good example of this principle. With apologies for the crudeness and a trigger warning that this threat is about rape, Twitter user Jimmydeanskills (@drkillerkills) said, "How about I shove my dick in your mouth and you shut the fuck up?"[26] Although the comment made in that tweet is direct enough to constitute an illegal threat that could be reported to the police, the hashtag this user included at the end of the threat, #twitterlovesrape, also indicates that the individual has a good understanding of how to make his threat more effective: that is, he knows that Twitter has a very poor track record where protecting its users from such threats is concerned.

This cybersexist, given the throwaway account (which has no followers, isn't following anyone, uses no profile picture, and has tweeted only threats

Types of Cybersexism

and abuse), also likely knows that the anonymity of the account will probably serve to protect him from any legal consequences, since tracking him down is beyond the capacity or interest of most police departments. My awareness of those factors is also what prevents me from filing a police report: the time-consuming and emotionally draining labor of filing a report that is unlikely to produce results, dealing with explaining how and why such a report would occur, and potentially being harassed in turn by the police (a more common reaction than you might think) just isn't worth it. Instead, as many women do on a daily basis, I submitted a complaint with Twitter and will wait days, weeks, or months for the account and the threat to be taken down, if it is at all. Twitter has, in the past, declined to suspend users for sending much more graphic and specific threats than the one quoted above.

The text of the threat, however, is what's truly revealing about the mindset behind it. The overt threat of violence is not enough for the cybersexist—it is explicitly stated here that the intent is to silence me. Silencing me on a specific topic is irrelevant, apparently, as the threat was not issued in response to anything I said but just sent directly to me. It is enough that I should be silenced in a violent and sexually degrading way. While the content of the threat is vile and dangerous, it is also common. My experience with violent threats is, compared to women with bigger platforms than mine, quite limited; although I keep a file of them in case I should ever need to pursue legal action (and please think for a moment about the burden of doing so: in addition to receiving the threat, I must also keep a permanent record of it to prove that I experienced it at all; I am far from the only woman who does this, and my file is comparatively small), the privileges associated with being a white, thin, cisgender, heterosexual, able-bodied, educated, middle-class woman have the tendency to shield me from a multitude of threats aimed at women who have fewer or none of those privileges.

Even threats are not exempt from the Internet mythology of the Wild West. In 2015 the Supreme Court of the United States handed down its decision in *Elonis v. United States*. In this case a man was arrested for issuing violent threats to his ex-wife, coworkers, and even the female FBI agent who met with him once as part of the investigation. Despite his threats including such text as, "I'm not going to rest until your body is a mess, soaked in blood and dying from all the little cuts," Elonis insists that his Facebook posts should be protected under the First Amendment, describing them as rap lyrics.[27] In his defense Elonis used the common argument that his statements should be evaluated based on whether he intended them as threats and not whether they were received as such. According to one article on the subject, "Elonis claims that you can't use an objective listener standard when you are dealing with the interpersonal and context-free conversation that takes place in the Wild West of social media."[28] In this view not only should we ignore threats unless the abuser says he's serious, apparently we should also regard social media as divorced from offline context, even when that context includes a restraining order.

In this instance the Supreme Court did not uphold the ruling of the lower courts. However, that does not mean the Supreme Court sided with Elonis. The Supreme Court overturned Elonis's conviction—not on the grounds of his speech having been protected but because the instructions given to the jury were incorrect. Because the ruling was not based on Elonis's actual defense, the case was handed back to a lower court, rather than decided on in its entirety. Justice Samuel Alito spent a great deal of time in a separate opinion sharing his thoughts on the actual content of the things Elonis had posted and for which he was arrested. "Statements on social media that are pointedly directed at their victims, by contrast, are much more likely to be taken seriously," he wrote. "To hold otherwise would grant a license to anyone who is clever enough to dress up a real threat in the guise of rap lyrics, a parody, or something similar. Threats of violence and intimidation are among the most favored weapons of domestic abusers, and the rise of social media has only made those tactics more commonplace. A fig leaf of artistic expression cannot convert such hurtful, valueless threats into protected speech," he concluded.[29]

As the historian and student activism advocate Angus Johnston points out, not only did Justice Alito come out strongly against Elonis in his separate opinion but the Supreme Court's primary decision also "said that a threat counts as a threat under federal law not only if it's intended as a

Types of Cybersexism

threat, but also if the writer knows it will be interpreted that way."[30] That is, while the Supreme Court did not make a decision about the Elonis case in its entirety, it did make some very strong statements about how we should regard threats sent via the Internet.

While the Supreme Court must still decide how to approach such threats under the law, current perceptions about how to decide whether an incident constituted sexual harassment should also be taken into consideration. For example, in personal, professional, and legal settings sexual harassment is largely defined by how the target viewed it, not how the person issuing the harassment viewed it. That is, a target's perception of the harassing words or actions is given more weight than the intent, if it is stated, of the harasser. Elonis can claim that his beliefs about social media mean that he's exempt from consequences for language that, said in offline space, would absolutely be perceived as an immediate and illegal threat; whether his targets and everyone else are required to agree with him is another matter entirely.

It remains to be seen what the long-term outcome of the Elonis case will be. The Supreme Court's decisions will likely have a huge effect on how and whether women are able to seek legal redress for online harassment and abuse. Legal solutions for dealing with online threats are currently ineffective at best. While cybersexist abusers are aware of and relying on the inefficiency of the legal system in reacting to their transmission of illegal threats, a decision from the Supreme Court will at least create a new framework for the discussion. At present, however, while people like Elonis can be arrested and jailed for using interstate communications methods to send illegal threats, it's a rare result and one that often offers little support for women, who often face threats from sources that are unknown and difficult or impossible to trace.

Although research on the number of threats women receive and how often they receive them is thin on the ground (in fact, there is significantly more academic research that's been done on online threats to banking and business, which says something about our priorities), most casual surveys of women who are online for any length of time reveal that they have received threats or know many other women who have.[31] One of the few pieces of research that deals with online discussions of violence only briefly addresses threats made to women online; it is focused instead on Internet discussions of domestic violence laws.

Although that research was specific to Romania, where it was conducted, the authors' comments describe common attitudes about violence that are expressed online, whether threats are made online or in a physical setting. "The prevalent discourse is focused on 'degendering the problem and gendering the blame,'" the authors note, "while [indications of] men as accountable for perpetrating violence against women are almost absent from the users' comments."[32] The concept of removing gender from discussions of violence is common in online conversations about threats against women: men get threats too, the reasoning goes, therefore there's no reason to discuss the specific ways in which threats are targeted at or affect women—and no reason to mention that men issue the majority of threats regardless of the gender of the target, conveniently erasing that dynamic from discussion. At the same time, blame becomes a space where gender is suddenly relevant: if a woman is receiving threats online—just as if she is attacked offline—she will be questioned about which of her actions could have led to the threat, as though such activities must have been provoked and therefore partially deserved.

A Pew Research Center study indicates that men and women report receiving threats in roughly equal numbers, but the study never addresses the frequency with which those threats are received. Casual observation and self-reporting across various platforms reveals that women tend to receive threats more frequently than men and to receive threats that are closely tied to the fact that they are women. One revealing statistic provided by Pew is that young women, particularly those between the ages of eighteen and twenty-four, are at the highest risk overall for stalking and sexual harassment. "In addition," concludes the report's author, "they do not escape the heightened rates of physical threats and sustained harassment common to their male peers and young people in general."[33]

Despite frequent attempts to ignore gender as a factor in attracting online threats, it cannot be ignored that women receive a significant number of threats and that those threats are often explicitly linked to gender,

Types of Cybersexism

as well as race and LGBT identity. Threats of rape are the most obviously gendered threat aimed at women; such threats play on offline rates of sexual assault to create an environment of intimidation and fear. However, threats of physical domination or abuse and death threats often contain explicit mentions of gender as a factor, usually taking the form of gendered stereotypes and slurs being incorporated into the text. Anita Sarkeesian, a feminist media critic and host of the *Feminist Frequency* web series, published a list of harassments she received during the course of a single week. Words such as "bitch," "whore," "cunt," "slut," "twat," and "ho" appear in nearly every comment, along with multiple racial slurs, encouragement for the target to commit suicide, and threats of rape and death.[34]

Online threats of violence seem to have a very simple purpose: they are intended to act as a reminder to women that men are dominant, that women can be attacked and overpowered if men choose to attack, and that women are to be silent and obedient. Many threats contain ultimatums: if a woman doesn't stop engaging in activities that the men issuing threats find undesirable, she will be punished with physical violence or even death. The intent of threats is to establish offline patterns of violence against women in online spaces.

From there it becomes convenient for cybersexists to deny the seriousness of such a threat—or even deny that it happened at all. This denial becomes a form of gaslighting, a type of abuse in which abusers attempt to make targets doubt their own memory of something that happened to them.[35] The attempt to cast doubt on women's experiences is intended to frame women as unreliable, attention-seeking, or lying, thereby reinforcing the silencing impact of the threat in the first place. Calling women's accounts of threats into question is particularly common during cyber mob activities, such as Gamergate (a hate movement discussed in chapter 5).

As mentioned in chapter 1, the impact of a threat is not necessarily in whether it will be carried out. For women who have been on the receiving end of threats, the message goes beyond the text of the threat itself. While the threat itself is often frightening enough, the larger purpose of threats is to remind women that the violence can be enacted at any time, that the persons sending threats have access to their targets, and that there is no good means of redress. The point is to attempt to force women into the identity the one sending the threats has chosen—to force women to reconsider every post, every online and offline activity, and every new face they encounter. In an environment where threatening behaviors typically go unpunished, a threat is a reminder to women that cybersexists have the power.

Doxxing and SWATting

Although death and rape threats cross the line from abusive into illegally abusive, there are forms of online abuse that go even further in exposing targets to offline danger. While death and rape threats sent online can and sometimes do result in physical attacks or attempted attacks offline, the majority of threats receive no follow-through (it should be noted that this low incidence of follow-through does not reduce the seriousness of such threats—indeed, as discussed later, not knowing which threats to regard as an immediate danger can heighten the fear and stress they cause). However, doxxing (also spelled doxing) and SWATting (or swatting) attempts very often have offline consequences.

Doxxing is the process of—legally and illegally—gathering personal information on a target, centralizing it in an archive location or other post, and distributing it to a harasser or harassers. The term, according to *Wired*, comes from an "abbreviated form of 'dropping dox,' an old-school revenge tactic that emerged from hacker culture." It is a strategy designed to make anonymity impossible or to make an already public target even less safe in their offline persona.[36]

Once individuals have been doxxed, information such as their email address, home address, place of work, phone numbers, Social Security number, credit card information, offline name, and more can be exposed to the entire Internet. If that occurs, anyone who wishes to harm a target has immediate, easy access to information that can be used to wreak incredible havoc on the individual's life. The effects of doxxing can be as seemingly mild as having a bunch of pizzas show up at a target's house to as terrifying as having people show up outside their place of work, take

Types of Cybersexism

photographs of them as they enter and leave their home, or attempt to engage or attack them.

Doxxing is also used as the backbone of swatting; once a harasser has a target's information, such as a home address, harassment and abuse can be escalated. The FBI defines swatting as "making a hoax call to 9-1-1 to draw a response from law enforcement, usually a SWAT team," and the bureau emphasizes the dangerous nature of the activity—swatting is typically done under the guise of a prank or as a form of revenge.[37] swatting calls typically reference a hostage situation, potential suicide, or other life-threatening event that would require an immediate police response. Such calls take up police time and could lead to a lack of resources in the event of an actual emergency, and they are expensive, wasting taxpayers' money. Additionally, there are no guarantees that the police will not be overzealous in their response, potentially leading to injury or death. Indeed, hope of injury or death is often the point of engaging in a SWAT attack.

Gamergate, the online hate mob devoted to harassing anyone who is perceived as engaging in critiques of video games and technology, used swatting on a number of occasions. In one notable incident roughly twenty police officers were sent to the former home of a female game developer, leaving the current residents frightened and confused.[38] No one was injured, but the event was not only violent; it also raises the issue of collateral damage in these situations: the abusers sent the police, who could potentially cause injury or death, to the home of people utterly uninvolved with the online vendetta—people who had no way of knowing they were in the line of fire.

swatting is dangerous enough for targeted people who have the time, ability, and technological know-how to track when they've been doxxed and can take steps to protect themselves, and abusers offer no justification or defense for engaging in threatening activities that end up harming those with some tangential connection to their target. Cybersexism is not only dangerous to its immediate victims but can have a ripple effect that leads to damage in ever-expanding circles.

In mid-2015 the UX designer Caroline Sinders wrote an article for *Narratively* that described such a ripple effect. When she started writing about

Gamergate, the mob sent a SWAT team to her mother's house. Sinders had "tried to come up with more advanced filter settings than 'public' or 'private' for Twitter and other social media sites" by watching Gamergate and associated mob activities.[39] Someone was watching her, despite the precautions she took.

When her mother's house was targeted, "the caller, a male, said he had shot his girlfriend, barricaded himself in the house, was heavily armed, and his girlfriend's daughter was in the house with him, currently alive. He was planning to shoot any police who approached the house."[40] Although her mother wasn't harmed, Sinders felt guilty and responsible for the fact that someone else had attacked her family. The SWAT attempt was a reminder to Sinders that being a woman online is a risky proposition, even (or perhaps especially) for someone who works in the technology industry.

Doxxing and SWATting are made easier by the wealth of information that is frequently stored on things like background check websites, which trawl the Internet for identifiable details and connect them to an individual's real name. These websites often manage to collect phone numbers, home addresses, places of work, and the names of individuals' relatives, all of which make it easy for those interested in doxxing and SWATting to plan their attacks and share the details. Many people are unaware of just how much of their information is readily available to anyone and everyone who takes the time to search for it.

Doxxing and SWATting are two forms of online abuse that rapidly spill into offline space. Someone who gains access to a woman's personal information and can call the police to her home at any time has a great deal of power. Many cybersexist abusers attempt to use this information as a bargaining chip—a way to control a woman's online and offline activities, with the threat of further releases of information or SWAT attacks as ever-present threats. The psychological toll of dealing with these abuses can be extraordinarily draining for women.

Fortunately, there are ways to remove most of this information from the Internet. Although doing so can be a time-consuming (and, at times, slightly costly) effort, most background screening aggregators have processes for removing an individual's information from their website.

Types of Cybersexism

Although the easiest solution for doxxing and SWATting is for people not to engage in those abusive activities, women who wish to increase their sense of security can visit such websites and ensure that their information is removed.[41]

INTERSECTIONS OF ABUSE

All of the abuses discussed thus far in this chapter can be used separately or, quite often, in tandem to create an environment of frustration, intimidation, and fear for women who try to exist in online spaces. It is critical to note, however, that they are far from the only types of abuse women experience online—the abuses outlined above are simply the shared types of abuse for most groups of women who use the Internet on a regular basis. However, women of color, women with disabilities, women belonging to religious minorities, and women who are LGBT experience all of those forms of abuse combined with harassment and violence that target other aspects of their identities.

As mentioned earlier, my identity and the privileges I receive as a result of it have the effect of exempting me from experiencing those specific forms of abuse. It is not my goal to use this space to speak for the many brilliant women already addressing these issues but to acknowledge that the issues exist, to affirm that I cannot fully understand them, and to connect them to the overarching themes on the abuse of women discussed in this book. With that said, I do want to outline the various types of abuse that affect women along intersecting axes, with an eye to broadening the understanding of anyone who has not seriously considered the varying types of online abuse. For example: a woman of color is going to experience the forms of cybersexist abuse already described in this chapter. On top of that she will also receive racist abuse—typically a combination of both cybersexism and cyberracism. Racist abuse online takes the form of attacks by white supremacists, outright ethnic and racial slurs, microaggressions from white people (including white allies), and a lack of support when such attacks occur.

Additionally, women of color are dramatically underrepresented in discussions of cybersexism, despite being among the primary targets for it. Most articles about online abuse focus on a small group of conventionally attractive white young women, leaving everyone else's experience unexamined (or deliberately erased). The tactics used by Gamergate, for example, were tested on women of color, primarily black women on Twitter in early 2014. These abusers created hashtags such as #EndFathersDay, #freebleeding, and #bikinibridge to target black women and feminists, exposing them to abuse for perceived association with the hashtags and in the event that they criticized them.[42] The harassing activities received almost no media fanfare or discussion at that time and are still widely unexamined in probes of the cyber mob's activities, despite the direct links between abuse from the spring of 2014 and Gamergate.

LGBT-specific abuse is also common in online spaces. Homophobia is common, and transphobic threats are frequently issued to transgender women. At the axis of multiple forms of oppression, transgender women of color experience a disproportionately high level of abuse that includes sexism, racism, transphobia, and more. As discussed in chapter 1, transgender women of color experience a high rate of offline violence, and the same pattern exists in online spaces.

Disabled women are regularly excluded from feminist discussions, which is, in itself, a form of erasure that must be addressed. In addition to erasure, casually ableist language is a feature of online life.[43] The opinions and thoughts of people with disabilities are often dismissed out of hand on the basis of the individual's disability. Mental illness in particular is stigmatized as the cause of much violence against women (see, for example, the immediate speculation that Isla Vista shooter Elliot Rodger was mentally ill), even when mental illness isn't a definitively diagnosed factor in the eventual threats or violence.[44] In fact, people with disabilities are at much greater risk of being the target of violence rather than being the perpetrator.[45]

Women who belong to religious minorities—especially Muslim women in the post-9/11 era—are subjected to online harassment and abuse along that axis of their identity as well. From overt Islamophobia and threats of violence to the sheer number of articles that erase Muslim women from their own experiences of, for example, wearing hijab, the Internet can be an extraordinarily hostile place. Many women in religious minorities face racist, xenophobic, sexist, and religiously based abuse across all social platforms, in addition to the risks of dealing with the same behaviors in offline spaces.

Finally, there is the issue of women abusing other women—often, unfortunately, under the guise of feminism. Distinctions of race, class, ability, sexuality, and more are frequently used as excuses for stealing or repurposing other women's work, without permission or attribution, and using it as the basis of articles for popular publications or academic papers. When these articles are criticized, the typically educated, middle-class, cisgender white women who have engaged in such abuse have a tendency to rely on racist stereotypes, painting themselves as the victims of vindictive bullying.

Academia, too, allows for similar abuses. Women unaffiliated with academic institutions regularly find that their online work has been consumed, repackaged, and used for conference presentations and as the basis for articles and books and their online profiles assigned as reading for college classrooms. This unpaid labor within feminist and academic spaces represents a form of exploitation that nearly always falls along the lines of race and class.

While in part a problem that reflects problems within certain feminist discourse groups online, the issue of typically white and cisgender women using privilege to deflect blame for harmful behaviors is neither new nor uncommon.[46] Many of the types of abuse outlined throughout this chapter can be found occurring among women online as well, including gaslighting, double standards, harassment, and even threats.

Intersectionality, a term coined by the theorist and law professor Kimberlé Crenshaw, describes the need to acknowledge, consider, and address oppressions that occur along multiple facets of an individual's identity, including race, gender, and class. While Crenshaw's initial work focuses on the experience of black women in liberation movements, the concept of intersectionality applies to multiple identities and axes of oppression. Acknowledging the intersectionality of abuse in online spaces is key to understanding the remainder of this book.

Generalities like "all women" have a tendency to erase the specific intersectional forms of violence experienced by the women mentioned above, as well as any woman who doesn't fit the expected ideal of femininity. When reading the remaining chapters, pay close attention to the kinds and types of statistics that are available on cybersexist abuse. The majority of generalities deal solely with women as a group, failing to take intersecting abuses into account.

Research on the combined effects of cybersexism, racism, Islamophobia, fat-shaming, homophobia, transphobia, ableism, and other intersecting forms of abuse is practically nonexistent. In the absence of research, it is up to us to listen to the experiences of women dealing with these forms of abuse, take them seriously, and understand that abusers have a tendency to target those they think lack the social power and support to fight back. As you continue reading, especially if you are in a position of privilege, complicate your notions of who is likely to be attacked, how, and along what axes of their identity.

[3] DON'T FEED THE TROLLS
Why Advice about Cybersexism Fails

One of the most common experiences a woman has when discussing online abuse is either receiving advice about how to handle it or being condemned for handling it "incorrectly." This advice is sometimes well intentioned but often delivered in the form of a mansplaining response to a woman who is pointing out that cybersexist abuse has been directed her way. The advice may be meant in a nice enough way, but it's offered with no thought to women's actual experiences, no consideration of the consequences of following the advice, and no evidence that what is proposed would even be effective for reducing future instances of abuse. In this chapter I lay out the most common types of advice given to women who are experiencing cybersexism and explain why they are typically not just unworkable but also unwelcome.

While men are the ones who can be relied upon to dispense this advice to women, they are by no means the only responsible party. Most of the advice in this chapter will be immediately familiar to anyone who's spent time online; the content of each statement is presented as a truism, despite the failure of most to think through their advice to its logical conclusion. The consequences of following these frequently offered forms of advice regarding online abuse are my primary focus in this chapter. It's critical to understand why our current methods for dealing with abuse do not work before we can find true solutions.

"Don't feed the trolls" has been an Internet refrain for so long that it has basically become a tautology in any discussion about online abuse. It doesn't need to be said, but it's one of the first things anyone will say—almost always without thinking about what that statement actually means. The idea of not feeding the trolls dates back to the earliest types of online interactions, which were largely message board conversations populated by groups of people who may or may not have known each other in their offline lives. "Trolling" started as an attempt to disrupt those conversations—to redirect board participants' attention to a troll's intentionally inflammatory bad arguments and derail the original topic of discussion. In that context, ignoring a troll could be good advice: if you don't let a troll take over the message board, they are, effectively, powerless.

Trolling of that type still exists—there are many people who get a kick out of ruining an otherwise interesting conversation, irritating people by making bad arguments in bad faith, and generally being annoying and getting attention for it. Ignoring people whose presence serves only to interrupt a discussion—not feeding that particular troll—can be an effective strategy, so long as such trolls are few in number and easily deterred when they don't get a response. The trolls who can be defeated by being starved of attention are generally not those engaging in cybersexist abuse, however; a person who interrupts a conversation with a random or off-topic statement is sending a different message than someone whose opening remark is to call a woman a cunt.

However, in the age of social media, when people are connected on multiple platforms and conversation can be distributed, nonlinear, and wide-ranging, "don't feed the trolls" is more often a way of saying, "Stop making everyone uncomfortable by pointing out abuse." Too often, invoking the call not to feed the trolls is really meant to tell women, specifically, that we should stop acknowledging the trolls' existence—and our experience with them—at all. Feeding the trolls, in today's parlance, can be construed as nothing more than acknowledging that abuse exists, and women are regularly told to stop talking about how cybersexist abusers act and how such actions affect women. On the Skepchick site the attitude was sarcastically described as follows: "Suffer in silence. Read those emails about what a fucking cunt you are and then quietly delete them. Go lay in bed and cry until you don't necessarily feel better but can at least pretend like you feel better so that we can all continue our lives blissfully ignorant of anything bad ever happening. The abuse will continue to come, because they don't want attention—they are bullies."[1]

Many people still insist "don't feed the trolls" can be applied to cyber-sexist abusers just as they might when dealing with the merely annoying: starve them of the attention they crave, and they'll go away. As Whitney Phillips has put it, "Under this logic, trolls are like great white sharks and their target's reactions like chum: the more you throw, the more worked up the shark will get," and the more likely you are to be bitten simply for being in the vicinity.[2] However, as Phillips points out, the context in which "trolling" exists has changed. Not paying attention to a troll is rarely a deterrent, and the type of behavior encompassed by the term trolling has changed drastically since 2000.

While ignoring individual trolls whose goal is only to disrupt a conversation may dissuade them, ignoring a cybersexist abuser using trolling as an opening method can also escalate a single comment into a torrent of harassment, abuse, and threats. And, given the ease with which online interactions can be dominated by mobbing behaviors, simply ignoring a troll sometimes means becoming incapable of participating in online conversations and activities due to the influx of abusive and reactionary comments.

As with street harassment, many cybersexist abusers feel entitled to women's time and attention, and the failure to understand this aspect of women's experience undercuts the effectiveness of not feeding the trolls as a strategy. Under the guise of trolling, these harassers demand that women listen and respond to them, and ignoring these cybersexists frequently backfires on the original target by giving the abuser a perceived excuse to escalate their behavior in hopes of receiving a response.

Ignoring trolls in a message board in the late 1990s meant that their comments, no matter how annoying, would quickly be erased by the flow of conversation; ignoring a troll on Twitter, Facebook, or a blog today can mean multiple comments on any given post and increased levels of harassment; abusers may begin responding to everything a woman says or posts and may create new accounts or use anonymous comment features to avoid being blocked. With different forms of online interaction come greater possibilities for harassers to make their presence felt, and many women have experienced this type of cross-platform harassment.

Not feeding the trolls has another component as well, and it's one that most people giving the advice haven't considered: ignoring the behavior of a troll (whether a cybersexist abuser or a troll in the original sense) validates their activities by allowing them to continue engaging in harassment without being noticed by anyone but their target. Avoidance isolates the target, telling her the only appropriate way to deal with unwanted interaction is to silently ignore it. In the case of cybersexism, following the advice of "don't feed the trolls" frees the harasser to continue his activities unabated and without consequence, even if done openly, publicly, and under his real identity. Trolls and abusers may want attention, but beyond that what they really want is the ability to harass and abuse freely, without facing any sort of censure. Ignoring abusers doesn't make seeing their comments and not responding to them any easier, and it certainly does nothing to actually end the harassment.

Current discussions of "trolling" still rely on an old definition of the activity that no longer fits the new context in which the activity occurs. If the abuse women received was merely a mild inconvenience—which is what the label "trolling" would imply—then there would be no need for these discussions. However, women are having their livelihoods ruined, being driven from their homes, and being subjected to violent threats that have a variety of negative impacts on their ability to work, socialize, and interact online. "Trolling" is no longer the right word for what women are experiencing online, which is something closer to gendered terrorism by men (and more than 80 percent of defendants in cases brought by the FBI's Communication and Information Technology Unit were men), and yet use of the term "trolling" persists.[3] If we must continue to refer to online cybersexist abuse as trolling, and to those who abuse women as trolls, then it is imperative to define exactly what we mean by these terms, each time we use them.

I'll close this section with a personal example of how ineffective "don't feed the trolls" can be. It's 2015 at the time of this writing, and for more than a year I have received periodic rape and death threats from one anonymous individual, always on Twitter. I have reason to believe I know who it is, but his accounts are usually deleted or suspended too quickly for Twitter to track. It wasn't until March 2015 that, after a year without me responding to him directly, he escalated the behavior, publicly posting what he believed was my home address on the Gamergate hashtag and inviting people to come rape me. Shortly after that he posted an additional rape threat accompanied by a photograph taken of me when I was in the eighth grade.

At that point I felt I had just cause to go to the police and file a report that would be taken seriously. Keep in mind that I had been "not feeding" this specific "troll" for more than a year, and yet I still had amassed a file with more than sixty different threats he sent me. Unlike many women I know who have had to involve the police, I was lucky enough to be assigned a younger officer who had some familiarity with online harassment and abuse and who understood the gravity of the situation. While I had to explain Gamergate and SWATting to him, and while I had to walk him through the process of filling out Twitter's law enforcement form, he was considerate, concerned, and serious about it.

Entirely too many police departments are untrained in dealing with online harassment, violence, and stalking, and women are often laughed out of the station. One woman I am close to reported the potential for a SWAT attempt to her local sheriff. The man on the telephone responded gruffly, "Anyone can call in an emergency; we aren't going to take the time to verify if it's real before sending out a response team," even when she was specifically requesting it in order to save them time and resources should her home be SWATted. Many women—particularly black women, sex workers, and women from other marginalized groups—have a variety of valid reasons for not being able to trust the police to deal with the online violence that is being directed at them, which is an issue that I address in a later chapter.

In my own case I was fortunate enough to be believed, get a report filed, and (after five hours) get my "troll's" latest account taken down. Even with that, however, I am still not confident that anything can be done about it. Without an IP address to trace, the police and Twitter are relatively powerless to find the person whose hobby is to find creative new ways to threaten me; additionally, my local police department is not likely to expend a lot of resources getting a warrant or engaging in online searches to positively identify him—if they even know how.[4]

From the perspective of the people this abuser targets, however, he has a number of patterns that identify him and alert me to the fact that he has returned to begin threatening me again. He always uses an anonymous account that follows almost no one and generally has no followers. The account is usually named in a way that refers to his past accounts or one of his targets. For a while he would use video game–related avatars or a picture of Christian Bale as Patrick Bateman from the film *American Psycho*; he has since used only the new account egg avatar provided by Twitter. He often makes reference to past threats or repeats them verbatim, or he simply varies them in some way. All of his tweets are threats, and all of his threats to me are rape threats, sexualized death threats, and threats aimed at my family members and friends. He targets an ever-widening group of people but always starts with a handful of specific long-term targets, including me.

I have responded directly to him on only a few occasions, toward the beginning of his harassment. Back then, responding to his threats— whether with anger or humor—did nothing. Responding to his threats by indicating my willingness to take legal action did nothing; like many online abusers, he is aware that legal remedies are almost nonexistent. Simply posting screenshots of his tweets to me and including Twitter's various support accounts in hopes of getting their attention did nothing, either on Twitter's end or on his, beyond encouraging him to taunt me over the lack of support I was receiving.

Long before he had escalated to posting addresses and asking people to rape me, I decided to stop "feeding the troll." Obviously my responses were only encouraging him to keep coming back, right? And if I stopped

Don't Feed the Trolls

acknowledging him, maybe he'd get bored and move on, right? It's been more than a year since then, and every couple of weeks, like clockwork, I get another threat, or two, or three. He sets up an anonymous account, or two, or three, and proceeds to tweet out a series of rape and death threats, reaching between five and thirty tweets on each account before abandoning or deleting them, allowing those that survive to be taken down by Twitter's spam filters or support team. (Incidentally, it should tell us something that, despite Twitter's regular acknowledgment of their inability to deal with abuse and desire to do better, it's still more effective to report threats via their spam filter than through their actual reporting mechanisms.)

I have not "fed" this troll in a year, nor have many of his other targets. I keep my discussions of his activities limited primarily to taking screen-shots of each threat he sends me so that I have a record and exchanging private messages with some of his other targets. And still he comes back, over and over again. He's threatened me in incredibly specific ways; he's threatened me in ways that, should he have said these things to me in person, would almost certainly have resulted in him being arrested for threatening and stalking me. And he has escalated his harassment in new and frightening directions by attempting to doxx me. But according to the "don't feed the trolls" advice, my ability to endure constant graphic threats to my bodily autonomy and life in near-silence should have deterred him from continuing these behaviors—so what gives?

What "don't feed the trolls" misses is that, for these online cybersexist abusers, it doesn't matter whether or not a woman responds to their abuse. The payoff for these types of "trolls," as mentioned earlier, is the ability to say horrendous things to women and never face real consequences for doing so. How a woman reacts is beside the point: we can fight back, mock them, ignore them, report them, call the police, and ask our friends to monitor our accounts. None of it makes a difference if the victory is being able to send the threat in the first place, know that the intended victim has seen it, and never face any consequences. The only thing that compounds the success, for these trolls, is the ability to use "don't feed the trolls" advice to make sure women don't seek out support and to occasionally drive a woman away from online spaces entirely.

Telling women that they shouldn't feed the trolls ignores the real problem of abusers who get off on their ability to abuse. The Internet facilitates such activities in unprecedented ways, while simultaneously downplaying the seriousness of receiving that abuse and scolding women who talk about the effects it has on their lives. "Don't feed the trolls" is advice that doesn't work, but we keep hearing it, because acknowledging that abusers enjoy abusing presents us with much more difficult questions. How do we create an Internet that has fewer incentives for abusers? How do we reach the people who take pleasure in causing pain? How do we develop effective consequences for abusers without gutting the ability for people who truly need anonymity to be anonymous?

Telling women not to feed the trolls is much easier than actually seeking answers to those questions, but it will never make the abuse go away.

EVERYONE GETS HARASSED

When women discuss the specific, gendered forms of harassment and abuse often experienced in online spaces, we can safely assume that a straight white man will appear within a matter of minutes to remind us that everyone gets harassed online and that we're just being overly dramatic about it. While it is true that nearly every person who spends time online will, at one point or another, experience harassment, rolling women's particular concerns under the umbrella of "everyone gets harassed" erases the specific experiences and intersections of abuse that characterize cybersexism.

Sexism, racism, ableism, homophobia, transphobia, and discrimination against religious minority groups, among other factors, all characterize and complicate the idea that "everyone" gets harassed online and what that harassment looks like. Straight, cisgender white men are often able to point to an example of harassment they have experienced—heated conversations, flame wars, and harassment in gaming situations are common. Also common, however, is the fact that such harassment rarely makes note of their identity as a straight, cisgender white man as the problem; more often they can expect to be targeted for a skill error or a difference in opinion, and this will frequently take the form of sexist or homophobic slurs ("pussy" and "faggot" are particularly widespread insults lobbed at

Don't Feed the Trolls

straight white men, in order to establish a form of dominance by positioning those men as approximations of someone from an oppressed group: women and gay men).

What they miss, then, in listing these forms of harassment as equal to sexist, racist, and other discriminatory forms of abuse is that the harassment these men experience is not aimed at the men's identities and beings in and of themselves but consists of attempts to deny them that identity and label them as part of a hated group: typically, women. It is also critical to note that such harassment almost universally comes from other men. While women are certainly not innocent of engaging in harassing behaviors, men are far more likely to be harassing one another in these scenarios. Women do engage in online abuse, but that abuse is often along other axes of oppression; racism, homophobia, transphobia, and other types of harassment are commonly engaged in by white, straight, cisgender women. Online, as offline, however, women have little power to do significant damage to men, and "attacks" on men from women are more likely to be in response to a man's sexism than the first overture in deliberate abuse of men.

Men of color, however, are at significant risk of dealing with racist online abuse from white people of any gender. Black men are subjected to threats from white supremacists and other racists, and online forums and groups devoted to antiblack hatred are, unfortunately, common. A much larger discussion around the issue of racist harassment in online spaces needs to be had—including the intersections of race and gender in the harassment of black women and other women of color. It is important to remember that when men are abused online the attack is most likely originating in another factor of their identity; being a transgender or queer man, a man of color, a fat or disabled man, or a man from a religious minority increases the likelihood of experiencing online abuse and harassment.

Men absolutely experience harassment and abuse online, but such abuse often relies on the same principles of cybersexism that lead men to attack and threaten women. When straight, cisgender men experience abuse online, they are being compared, primarily, to women. Straight, cisgender white men are not attacked for those factors of their identity;

the goal of harassment is to separate them from their identity by comparing them to groups seen as "lesser," and comparing them to women is a frequently used strategy. Women (and, indeed, any man who doesn't fit the above categories) can expect to be attacked solely on the basis of *not* being straight, cisgender white men, and often in seriously damaging ways.

Another flaw in the idea that harassment is equally applied to everyone online is a failure to appreciate the frequency with which that harassment occurs and how quickly it escalates into violent (sexualized) and threatening behaviors. One frequently cited study is used to support the idea that "everyone gets harassed." Mention of this study is usually deployed as an attempt to stop women from talking about our experiences as individuals dealing with sexism and as a group dealing with the effects of patriarchy. The Pew Research Center released this study about online harassment in the autumn of 2014, and it is almost a guarantee that statistics from it will be used any time "everyone gets harassed" is the argument of choice.[5]

The most commonly cited statistics from the Pew report are that men and women are roughly equally likely to be called offensive names, purposefully embarrassed, and physically threatened or to endure sustained harassment.[6] Indeed, in a couple of categories men are more likely to report experiencing such forms of online abuse. The categories that are conveniently ignored, however, are stalking and sexual harassment, where women dramatically outpace men—especially women between the ages of eighteen and twenty-four. While Pew identifies women in that group as being more likely than any other to experience online harassment, that conclusion is typically left out of the "everyone gets harassed" argument.

While Pew does excellent work at collecting a large volume of data, I find a number of methodological issues with the study, especially with how it has come to be used to argue that men and women experience harassment in a roughly equal way. For example, Pew uses "offensive name-calling" as a category of harassment but never defines the actual nature of such name-calling. In many cases, men have told me that using the term "men" to describe men, a group that possesses social, political, and economic privilege, is offensive name-calling—often while referring to me as a bitch, a slut, or a cunt, which are words with significantly greater

Don't Feed the Trolls

social impact. I am far from alone in this experience. The failure to define what "offensive name-calling" actually is strikes me as a serious problem with Pew's results, especially since gender-based and racial slurs play a role in maintaining harmful stereotypes and social inequality, while few if any such slurs exist that are solely aimed at men.

Even more problematic, however, is that Pew never addresses the frequency with which online harassment occurs for the groups under study. While "everyone gets harassed" online is true, the regularity with which women experience such harassment is on an entirely different scale from most men's online lives. For example, one study that collected research about online harassment across a period of eight years found that 72 percent of people who reported experiencing online abuse were women.[7] Another study set up a variety of male- and female-identified usernames and tracked the number of harassing and sexually explicit messages each set of names received. Women's names received more than twenty-five times as many such messages as men's did.[8] Other reports show that women of color "faced cyber harassment more than any other group, with 53 percent reporting having been harassed online"; in contrast, "the group least likely to have been harassed was white males."[9] Report after report shows that women as a whole are more likely to be on the receiving end of abuse in online environments and that race, sexuality, and other factors play a role in how that abuse is expressed.

A casual survey of your acquaintances will probably reveal similar results; women report experiencing abuse on a daily or weekly basis, whereas men may go weeks or months without receiving negative comments that rise to the level of harassment, much less abuse. Indeed, as noted elsewhere in this book, women sometimes change their avatars on social media websites to pictures of men or even an inanimate object or cartoon, solely to reduce the frequency abusive comments are sent to them.

As Jamie Nesbitt Golden puts it, "Being a white dude on Twitter has its advantages." In her article for the website *xoJane* she described the difference in interactions once she changed her profile picture: "The number of snarky, condescending tweets dropped off considerably, and discussions on race and gender were less volatile. I had suddenly become reasonable and level-headed."[10] Men who choose the opposite path often report that the type and amount of harassment they experience undergoes a dramatic shift in the opposite direction. Men who use a female avatar for such experiments often find themselves unwilling to commit to the entire period of the experiment because of the unpleasantness of the responses.

While it is challenging to account for all variables in research, any study that proposes to examine online abuse must take volume into consideration, along with the way abuse changes depending on the identity of the target. In all large-scale research that has been conducted (small though that pool may be), women report being abused in gendered ways, as well as abused and harassed at a much higher frequency than men. Failing to include this aspect of online interactions skews the results in a serious way. Gamergate provides a valuable example of this disparity. A single target of the hate mob's wrath—almost always a woman (or a man of color)—could expect to receive hundreds or thousands of negative, abusive, harassing, and threatening comments across various social platforms in the space of a few hours. Not only is such harassment impossible to keep up with, but any response in the face of it will be insignificant in comparison.

While the Pew study is often upheld as demonstrating the validity of the statement that "everyone gets harassed," I have far too many reservations about what information is missing from that study to accept that conclusion. Additionally, the Pew study examines only men's and women's experiences; while there are a couple of areas that address racist abuse, such analysis is missing from the rest of the study. Online abuse occurs not only due to gender but also as a combination of factors that include race, gender, gender identity, physical or mental disabilities and illnesses, sexuality, religion, and more. While the Pew study's results give us a good starting point for discussing online abuse, they are certainly not the final word on who experiences harassment and what that harassment looks like.

"Everyone gets harassed" is a misleading argument that attempts to paint women as hysterical or overreacting to abuse that "everyone" experiences. Research, however, shows repeatedly and conclusively that women are abused more often than men and solely on the basis of being women. Attempting to ignore the causes that lead to these types of abuse is not an

Don't Feed the Trolls

effective strategy for reducing online harassment or making the Internet a safe place for women—or, indeed, for everyone. Only by paying attention to the specific types of abuse that occur can we ever hope to find solutions.

IT'S JUST THE INTERNET

Another common scenario when women discuss experiencing abuse is hearing men say, "It's just the Internet." Insisting that women's experience of online abuse is simply a function of being online is often accompanied by also telling women that everyone experiences abuse on the Internet, and that's simply how things are. Harassment, in this scenario, is framed as an environmental hazard that must be weathered or prepared for and one that is equally experienced by all users—rather than what it really is, which is a deliberate activity engaged in by people who deliberately choose particular targets to abuse. As we've seen, while everyone does experience some level of harassment online, the harassment women receive is greater, more frequent, and more targeted; this harassment is further compounded by race, sexuality, disability, religious beliefs, and more. Saying "it's just the Internet" erases women's specific experiences and excuses the behavior.

Talking about the Internet as though it's a level playing field for all users is a common tactic for dismissing women's concerns as trivial or uninteresting. This argument has been around since the creation of the Internet and still gets bandied about as though repeating it will make it true. The level playing field argument rests on an idealized image of the Internet, where everyone has equal access to resources and an equal platform from which to speak; this ideal was particularly prominent during the early years of public Internet use, as discussed at other points in this book. As the Internet grew, however, particular sets of norms were quickly established, and those people and opinions that are closest to what was originally seen as a "normal" Internet user (typically a straight, cisgender white man working in academia or a white-collar tech job) were given precedence.

Despite the idealistic notion of an Internet where, if there is harassment, at least it's universal harassment, women experience more harassment, more violent harassment, and more specifically gendered harassment than men do. Men continue to be positioned as the default Internet user, giving women a lesser status. Indeed, women are often portrayed as interlopers encroaching upon men's "natural" online habitats, and women who are gamers have even been called "colonizers" of the hobby, which is an inaccurate statement on multiple levels. Part of the disparity in treatment rests on the assumption that anyone who hasn't identified themselves as someone other than a white man is a white man, given the assumption that the default Internet user tends to be one.

"It's just the Internet" is also used as a derailing tactic and as a way to position women's claims as unimportant, unnecessary, selfish, or hysterical. A common formulation of the argument is, "You're getting upset about mean words on the Internet, while children are starving, women are being *really* oppressed, wars are going on in foreign countries." Whatever form the latter half of the argument takes, it can be practically guaranteed to reference a country or a developing nation that the speaker knows nothing about and an issue on which they are doing absolutely no work themselves. The goal is to tell women that what they are complaining about doesn't matter and that true oppression only exists in far-flung parts of the world for which the speaker doesn't have to feel in any way responsible.

While being abused by cybersexists is not identical to offline abuse, the mistake this argument makes is assuming that women who experience online abuse don't also experience harassment, abuse, and violence in their offline lives. For the women who deal with cybersexist harassment, it is often an extension of the everyday types of sexist harassment that are part of being a woman in the world. "It's just the Internet" is an attempt to decontextualize women's online experiences from the global experience of sexism and to pretend that women can't possibly care about more than one issue.

This version of "it's just the Internet" also erases women from those very nations the speaker wishes to use as a tool of argument, and many women around the globe use the Internet to discuss their lives and deal with cybersexism as a result. In Pakistan, for example, throughout 2014 online harassment and abuse of women who had a visible online presence regularly spilled into threatening and violent actions in offline spaces. "There

Don't Feed the Trolls

have been more than 170 complaints of cybercrime against women this year in Pakistan's most populous province of Punjab," noted one report.[11] One individual there noted that getting abuse to be taken seriously by social media websites such as Facebook and Twitter seemed to be more difficult for them than it was for women in the United States or in Britain. For all women who experience online abuse, however, it's not "just" the Internet, and the people sending that abuse know it.

Trudy Gregorie, writing for the National Center for Victims of Crime, noted that "[online] harassment and threats are just as frightening and distressing as off-line harassment and threats" and that cyberstalking and sexist online harassment are prevalent online but in no way solely confined to the Internet.[12] In one example given by Gregorie in her article, a woman who had never even been online had been impersonated by a stalker in various chat rooms and forums; her stalker wrote multiple posts containing her personal information and claiming she fantasized about being raped. As a result, multiple men came to the woman's home and offered to rape her in response to posts she had never made and, to that point, did not know existed. For her, that experience was not "just the Internet" or threatening words on a screen. As has been the case for far too many victims of cybersexism, the abuse spilled over into the offline spaces in which women also deal with threats and sexism.

Further, talking about harassment and abuse as though it's an inevitable part of the online experience has a tendency to kill conversations about seeking solutions before they even get off the ground. The framework of the argument ignores the specific situations women face while describing online life as inherently abusive. Accepting that the Internet is a place where abuse must simply be taken, rather than a space where people live, work, interact, play, and converse, implicitly tells women that such abuse is the cost of entry to participation in all online activities. Even while the men who use this argument face comparatively less abuse, they assume the abuse they receive is the norm for everyone and regard women who speak out as hypersensitive, attention-seeking, or overly dramatic. After all, if "it's just the Internet," women who complain must not be able to handle online harassment the way men can, right?

Acting as if abuse is inevitable and women should simply stop whining and deal with it erases how women experience online abuse, excuses abusive behavior as an acceptable or expected activity, and does nothing to curb harassment or help people who have been targeted by harassers. No one should have to endure Internet abuse, but trying to silence women who discuss it only ensures that the Internet remains a space where the message that abuse must be tolerated will continue to flourish. "It's just the Internet" enforces the status quo, rather than offering workable advice for dismantling, avoiding, or preventing abuse.

Finally, "it's just the Internet" positions online abuse as separate from offline abuse—it creates a false impression of the two spheres of existence as being completely unattached. In the 1990s people could simply walk away from online life if they had to; today that is no longer an option. More and more people work online, we hang out with friends online, meet loved ones, and play, write, create, and interact with individuals around the world. Most people carry an instant connection to the Internet in their pocket. The boundaries between online life and offline life are increasingly blurred, and what happens in one space has effects in the other. Seeing abuse online doesn't mean that the abuse has no power to affect someone offline, and merely walking away does nothing to prevent the abuse or stop it from continuing. The Internet is what we make it, and an environment where abuse is tolerated can no longer be acceptable.

JUST BLOCK THEM

A corollary to "it's just the Internet"—"just block them"—is a frequently used argument and one sometimes used by the harassers themselves in the form of a taunt. While ostensibly a good idea, as it removes the immediate visibility of harassment from the target's Twitter mentions, blog comments, or Facebook page, just blocking an online abuser isn't enough to prevent abuse. On many websites, Twitter particularly, creating a new account to continue engaging in harassing behaviors takes only a few seconds. Blocking such harassers can quickly become a full-time social media experience, especially for those targeted by cyber mobs, as many Twitter users saw and continue to see with Gamergate.

Don't Feed the Trolls

In any online situation where the barrier to entry and interaction is low—where it's easy, fast, and typically free to join and interact—just blocking a harasser simply ensures the same person can immediately return and continue their abuse under another name. On Twitter particularly, many women report these types of throwaway accounts being used to engage in relentless harassment, which sometimes lasts for years on end. In a 2014 article the writer and legal analyst Imani Gandy describes two years of racist, misogynistic harassment by someone calling himself Assholster, who created up to ten new accounts per day for the sole purpose of harassing Gandy and other women of color.

"I've done all the things you're supposed to do when dealing with assholes on the Internet—all the victim-blaming advice that Twitter has to offer," Gandy writes. "I didn't respond to Assholster. I've blocked at least a thousand of his accounts over the past two years. I've reported him using Twitter's 'Report Abuse' form. . . . Nothing worked and the harassment got worse."[13] Gandy's experience with Assholster, whose identity was eventually revealed and whose real account was suspended, was not unique. Thousands of online harassers use the same strategy on Twitter, on blog sites, in YouTube comments, on Reddit forums, and more to find their targets and find ways to harass them. As Gandy and other women know all too well, blocking them doesn't help.

"Just block me" is often used by harassers themselves, identifying their behavior for what it is and challenging their target to respond in some way, even if it is just by blocking them. The statement indicates to the target that the abuser is deliberately overstepping a boundary and that it's up to the target to force them to stop. If blocked, such people often go on to say they've been "censored." Cybersexists, as mentioned previously, regularly employ DARVO—deny, attack, reverse victim and offender. When blocked by someone they are abusing, the strategy often involves claiming that they have been victimized in turn.

"Just block me" also clearly demonstrates the problem with "just block them" as a type of advice: the burden of dealing with harassment is placed squarely on the shoulders of those being targeted. Advising women to block their harassers puts women in a permanently reactive stance, assumes again that abuse is inevitable, and offers no strategy for helping to reduce the abuse in any meaningful way. Much like the victim-blaming rape prevention advice women often receive (don't wear short skirts, don't go out alone, don't drink), the responsibility is placed on women's shoulders, rather than targeting the people engaging in the abusive behavior.

Further, people who have been blocked are not prevented from continuing to talk about their target in public ways that can damage their reputation. Indeed, someone who has been blocked may rally their own supporters and ask those individuals to continue harassing a woman, dragging the original abuser back into the target's Twitter mentions, Facebook feed, blog comments, or email and forcing her to contend with additional comments and more abuse. Blocking harassers can sometimes be taken as a response that encourages escalation, not acceptance of a plainly stated boundary.

As women are disproportionately targeted for such harassing behaviors, the time spent on blocking represents a disproportionate burden on women's ability to freely and fully interact online. Many women quietly exit their online communities or delete their profiles entirely. During Gamergate's heyday developers such as Brianna Wu often reported hearing from young women who had been interested in game development as a career but were so horrified by the abuse they saw that their interest was killed before it could flourish. The visible harassment and abuse of women does not become ineffectual if individual women block individual harassers.

While occasionally blocking one or two people for harassment doesn't seem like much, being forced to block multiple harassers across every platform on a daily basis for years at a time is beyond exhausting. Such work contributes to women burning out on specific online communities and reducing their discussions and output. Many men have trouble understanding the disparate burden of "just block them" as it applies to women's online experience due to the infrequency with which they receive those levels and types of abuse.

Additionally, blocking a harasser requires a harasser to have appeared and engaged in behavior that is damaging or threatening, and blocking doesn't undo whatever damage occurs as a result of that behavior. All

Don't Feed the Trolls

blocking can do, often and only temporarily, is remove the harassing content from a target's sight and no one else's. What blocking cannot do is prevent harassment, defamation, or abuse from being visible to everyone else online, often preserved there for years to come. Just because a target no longer immediately sees the abuse doesn't mean it has stopped happening.

Further, blocking people still requires the target to see what was said in the first place. Harassers and online abusers deliberately make their abusive comments as upsetting as possible; crude sexual overtures, death and rape threats, and other forms of harassment are common from people whose goal is to "just" get blocked. "Just block them" doesn't prevent a target from having to see the initial abuse that occurred, and that abuse can leave long-lasting personal damage, as discussed at other points in this book.

Autoblockers have become a common tool on Twitter, where the Block Bot, Block Together, and Randi Harper's Good Game Autoblocker (aimed at Gamergate harassers) all help to reduce the influx of trolling and mobbing behaviors that women often experience. That these tools are user-created and maintained, often without compensation, should raise alarm bells. Online tools and women's strategies for using them are discussed in detail in a later chapter.

Women who are already being targeted for harassment, threats, doxxing, and swatting are receiving almost no support from major Internet companies with the resources to provide it and so must create it themselves. While these tools are a testament to the ingenuity of women, the need for them is a sad comment on how women are regarded as users and consumers of the Internet. While Twitter insists, for example, they are making strides in cutting back on harassment, progress is slow, and these user-generated tools remain the most effective way to avoid certain forms of abuse.

Another factor to consider is that such blocking tools are effective only on the sites for which they are created. When harassment spills over into other areas of the Internet—from Twitter into email harassment, Facebook abuse, DDOS (distributed denial of service) attacks, and more—women are still put into the position of having to react to the abuse. Autoblockers on Twitter provide women with a running list of blocked accounts so they can decide whether to check those profiles to track harassment; anywhere else, women are still exposed to the abuse first and must then find ways to respond to it.

"Just block them" is far more complex than people who offer this advice assume, and it ignores the problem of the abuse itself. Acting as if uncomfortable discussion about online abuse is worse than the abuse itself and suggesting that abuse can be avoided if women would just block abusers and stop talking about it do nothing to help women who are being targeted. "Just block them" places blame on the wrong person and demands an after-the-fact response from targets while letting harassers off the hook for their behavior.

IT'S A PUBLIC FORUM

Telling women who have been harassed that the Internet is a "public forum" and therefore we have no business discussing or being angry about how we're treated is an especially common argument. It typically comes from people who regard blocking as a form of censorship and who believe free expression involves only the right to speak to anyone at any time—and not the right to determine personal boundaries for conversations or to respond to such speech. The public forum argument simultaneously insists that women be receptive, welcoming, and passive in the face of harassing comments while it excuses harassing behavior and suggests that it's an acceptable part of public discourse.

Framing online discussions as part of a public forum often goes hand in hand, ironically enough, with silencing: "the Internet is public, so if you didn't want responses, you shouldn't have said anything." The implication is that harassment is an acceptable response to women having and expressing opinions or existing online, and abuse is therefore women's fault for having spoken up in the first place. Laurie Penny counters this notion by asserting that the Internet is, in fact "public space, real space; it's increasingly where we interact socially, do our work, organise our lives and engage with politics, and violence online is real violence."[14] To Penny the Internet's role as a public forum makes cybersexism a bigger problem, not a lesser one. While insisting that the Internet is public and therefore

Don't Feed the Trolls

women should expect abuse is perhaps unintentionally revealing of someone's beliefs regarding women's role in spaces that are regarded as public, this advice serves no purpose beyond shifting the blame of harassment onto those targeted by it. The right to send an offensive or threatening response is made unquestionable where a woman's mere existence is seen as the root of the problem.

Acting as though abuse is a normal, acceptable, and expected part of public discourse, especially when women are affected, is yet another strategy that excuses abusive behaviors. It also relies on a fundamental misapplication of free speech principles, especially when the First Amendment is cited. Often the phrase "it's a public forum" is used to defend harassment as an expression of free speech and to frame attempts to avoid or curb harassment as censorship. Any response from women in the face of abuse is likely to be seen as women censoring men's free expression. That women's presence—from speaking in the first place to blocking people who are harassing them—is protected free expression itself never seems to enter the picture.

In describing this attitude Sarah Jeong has written, "Platforms that claim to uphold 'free speech' are actually proactively engaged in moderation models that are not just mildly inconsistent with, but deeply averse to, the freedom of speech"—that is, the interpretation of free speech as an "anything goes" mentality is just not working for the Internet. Often, she notes, the commitment to free speech that websites like Reddit, Twitter, 4chan, and others claim they have is actually "a punting of responsibility" onto moderators and report systems that were added on after the websites went into use and with little thought as to their effectiveness.[15] As a result, abusive speech that crosses the line from vile but legally protected speech and into speech that is threatening and illegal is common across multiple platforms.

Both Twitter and Reddit have shown signs of realizing, however, that their acceptance of the harassers' version of the public forum argument has ended up stifling free speech by creating spaces where abuse and harassment run rampant. Dick Costolo, the former CEO of Twitter, released an internal memo on his frustrations with the way the platform handled its problems. "We suck at dealing with abuse and trolls on the platform and we've sucked at it for years," he stated, making a pledge to change things for the better and start kicking abusers off more quickly.[16] Some changes have occurred, although abuse is still alive and well on the site. In the summer of 2015 Reddit began closing down white-supremacist subreddits that had long been deemed abusive, noting that they seemed to be used "solely to annoy other redditors, prevent us [the Reddit team] from improving Reddit, and generally make Reddit worse for everyone else."[17] Acknowledging that members of these subreddits frequently invaded other subreddits to post racist, sexist, and other abusive content was a first step in improving the site. Abuse is still common on Reddit, as is the case on Twitter, but changes are happening.

Aside from the fact that social media websites, blogs, and other sites are not violating the First Amendment by creating and enforcing acceptable forms of engagement or terms of service (since the First Amendment applies only to restriction of speech by government bodies), individuals deciding what types of conversations they want to have in online spaces are expressing their equal right to free speech and free association. Jeong notes that "the language of First Amendment jurisprudence is thrown around without much regard for [its] actual use in case law," further pointing out that "the First Amendment does not apply to online platforms."[18] Because websites such as Twitter, Facebook, and YouTube are privately owned entities (even when publicly traded), their restrictions on user speech do not rise to the level of government censorship, which is where a First Amendment concern would be relevant. An individual blocking another user or a website deciding to terminate a user's account due to their abusive behavior is not censorship in any legal sense. Further, the global nature of the Internet and its users means that applying a U.S.-centered standard will have, at best, limited applicability.

Danielle Citron also points out that "cyber mobs and individual harassers are not engaged in political, cultural, or social discourse. . . . Defeating online aggressions that deny victims their ability to engage with others as citizens outweighs the negligible contribution that cyber harassment makes."[19] As Citron views it, cyber harassment actually impinges upon others' free expression by limiting their ability to engage in online life and discussions: "Along these lines, Professor Cass Sunstein contends that threats, libel, and sexual and racial harassment constitute low-value speech of little First Amendment consequence."[20] As Jeong notes, threats do not have First Amendment protection and do not have to be factual in order to be considered a "true" threat—that is, a threat is true "because it makes the recipient fear serious violence and is intended to make them afraid."[21] Such speech does not deserve and should not receive protection under the First Amendment.

The public forum argument therefore fails on multiple fronts in that free speech violations are not in play when one blocks harassers (or when websites ban them and their forums), and among individuals, choosing not to engage with harassing or abusive content is itself an aspect of free expression within a public forum. Further, much of the speech cybersexist harassers, abusers, and mobs engage in would not be legally protected speech even if a question of the First Amendment were to truly arise.

Abusive men are not prevented from speaking elsewhere about their disagreement with or dislike of a particular woman after she has ended the conversation in whatever way she sees fit; the very nature of a public forum means that there are multiple outlets to use for the purposes of communicating. Being blocked from mentioning someone on Twitter, commenting on their blog, or posting on their Facebook wall does not restrict their free speech in a legal sense; those individuals are still completely capable of continuing to discuss the topic with other people in other venues. Free speech is not a guarantee that individual people will receive whatever platform they choose—it does not give people the right to force a conversation with an unwilling participant, even when that participant is in public. Free speech and the right to free association also encompass the ability to opt out of talking to another individual—something that those who like to insist the Internet is a public forum prefer to ignore.

The public forum argument also insists that abusive speech should be an anticipated and acceptable risk for, specifically, women. Indeed, one Facebook post about the threatening and violent responses to Dixie Chicks singer Natalie Maines's criticism of George W. Bush asked if such a reaction was "too extreme? Or was it the price of free speech?"[22] Framing death and rape threats as the cost of entry for women to participate in online spaces sets a dangerous precedent and makes it all the more difficult to support women who are targeted in these ways. The argument also makes the common mistake of ignoring the reality that threatening to kill or assault another person is not, in the legal sense, an expression of free speech; such threats are legally actionable and, depending on the state, could result in a variety of civil penalties and criminal charges.

When abusers target women online, we often hear that entering the public forum of the Internet brings with it the possibility of encountering hostile behavior. If we accept such logic, it follows that if women wish to avoid such reactions to their online presence, the only options are to be silent and invisible or to speak solely in ways that appease the men who react violently to women's opinions. Calling the Internet a public forum is done to invoke a conceptualization of the Internet in which all expression is seen as valid and worthwhile. However, in reality it frames abusive comments as suitable online behavior while vilifying any attempt to make online spaces safer for everyone interacting in them. After all, if the only way for women to avoid abuse is not to talk, whose free speech has actually been affected?

JUST TURN OFF YOUR COMPUTER

Telling women to just give up and leave online spaces is often a last-resort argument for people who don't want to deal with the abuse itself: after all, if there are no women to abuse, that sort of solves the problem, doesn't it? This advice is addressed particularly often to women who are experiencing sustained harassment, and it is offered as a way for women to protect themselves from seeing the abuse. "Just turn off your computer," according to this logic, if you don't like how people are reacting to your presence. Abusers are never, in this construction, held responsible for their own abusive behavior; all of the responsibility falls to women who are being targeted.

The End to Cyber Bullying organization, although focused primarily on in-group teenage harassment conducted through the Internet, responds

Don't Feed the Trolls

strongly to the idea that targeted individuals should just shut off their computers. According to its website, "Why should a victim be required to interrupt an online experience because of someone else's maliciousness? It is not appropriate to blame the victim for another's aggressive actions. No one should have to turn off his or her computer due to harassment received online, just like no one should avoid going to school because of school bullying." The organization notes further that "cyber bullying can continue regardless of whether the target is online."[23] In those few sentences, the End to Cyber Bullying group gets to the heart of the problem with "just turn off your computer" as advice: that notion blames the victim for having been online in the first place, which is an unhelpful and stigmatizing response. On top of that it fails to end abuse in any meaningful way. The absence of a target does not persuade abusive people to stop looking for one.

As the anticyberbullying organization notes, walking away from online spaces doesn't just fail to curb the abuse; it also is often not possible for women to simply shut down their online lives and leave while still maintaining a career and personal connections. Women work and exist online in increasingly large numbers, with many of them building their entire careers in Internet spaces. Simply walking away from the Internet would mean lost personal connections, a destroyed livelihood, and isolation from support networks in the face of abuse. Turning off the computer can mean ending a career, and for many women that's simply not an option.

Not only that, but walking away from the Internet doesn't mean the abuse will stop or be erased. Anyone else still online has the ability to see, share, and participate in the abuse or have their opinion shaped by it, and if the targets are no longer online to counter the impressions left by abusive comments their absence can have long-lasting effects on job searches, new personal connections, and more. Just because the target doesn't see the abuse doesn't mean it isn't there. A target who shuts down her visible web pages can still be named, shamed, and abused in other areas of the Internet, and that ongoing abuse may have repercussions for years after she returns and even if she never returns.

Employers, for example, use social media and Internet searches to assess potential candidates when looking to fill a job. According to Jobvite, more than half of recruiters have reconsidered candidates based on their social media presence, and almost two-thirds of those reconsiderations are negative.[24] A woman who has been the target of extensive cybersexist harassment and abuse will have unpleasant things show up in search engine and social media results, which may affect employment opportunities and more. A woman who has walked away from the Internet to avoid the immediate impact of harassment has no presence or writing of her own to counteract the abuse, leaving her reputation even more vulnerable to abusers.

Further, harassers often celebrate forcing a woman to lock down her account or briefly leave a specific space by amplifying harassment, not ceasing it. Women who take steps to get away from online abuse are told they're putting themselves into echo chambers, and abusers often take steps to find new ways to abuse their target. Such steps can include starting to harass that person's remaining online friends and family, posting about how they drove a woman off the Internet, and seeking ways to take online harassment into offline venues.

Even if a woman does walk away from online spaces, whether temporarily or for a longer period of time, the harassment still might include activities such as doxxing and SWATting. For a woman who has been told to turn off her computer, doxxing and SWATting attempts would be a mystery until the offline abuses began occurring—and finding ways to mitigate the damage would be significantly more difficult. Leaving online spaces prevents women from developing self-defense tactics that respond to the abuse, such as tracking their abusers' behaviors and taking preventive steps to make it harder for abusers to find their information. Even if a woman has a good online support network to monitor abusive behaviors, being isolated from a chosen Internet community can also be devastating for personal and professional reasons.

No woman should have that burden in the first place: women should be able to safely and freely interact in online spaces without fear that their personal information will be stolen or that unknown individuals will show up at their homes or places of work. However, turning off the computer in the face of abuse also disempowers women to take proactive steps in dealing with the harassment, makes them more vulnerable to offline attacks, and leaves abuse visible to everyone with no possibility for counterspeech.

"Just turn off your computer" tells women that their options for online existence are to put up with abuse or not to be online at all (and likely still deal with the effects of abuse). These options are not acceptable for any woman I know—all of us live, work, and play in online spaces and deserve to do so without the unpleasant task of facing constant abuse and being told we're handling it wrong. No woman I know would regard spending time in an environment of abuse or total silence and being absent from the Internet as acceptable alternatives for how we're expected to approach online life—and they are not acceptable outcomes to present to women.

FOCUS ON THE ABUSERS

If anything has become clear in this chapter, I hope it's that most of the advice women are given regarding sexist online harassment and abuse is worthless at best and can be actively harmful if followed. Much of the advice is aimed more at getting women to silently deal with the pain of frequent, violent abuse, because those who don't experience it are tired of hearing about it. A lot of this advice is also intended to erase women's particular experiences of cybersexism or to place sexism under the general category of online abuse and then ignore it entirely.

What such advice fails to do, however, is offer any concrete methods for reducing the frequency of abuse or ameliorating its impacts. And, as the next chapter shows, the effects of online abuse can take an unimaginable toll on women's livelihood, well-being, and lives.

4 | THE EFFECTS OF CYBERSEXISM
Professional, Psychological, and Personal

Cybersexist abuse is often framed as an evanescent phenomenon: you see a nasty comment, scroll on by, and that's the end of it. Even though cybersexists engage in harassment they know to be unwelcome, violent, and sometimes illegal, they maintain that their activities are all in good fun, that abuse is committed as a prank, and that cybersexism shouldn't be taken seriously. For the women on the receiving end of their insults, harassment, stalking, and threats, however, the experience is much less than fun—it's often downright terrifying. Women's experience of cybersexism is that of a constant negotiation between wanting to claim space online and having the right to exist in cyberspace at all, as well as figuring out which opinion is the least likely to generate harassment and how to minimize exposure to abusers. The cyberfeminist Donna Haraway might have argued that we are all cyborgs, but there are those who insist that some cyborgs are better than others.

Women are repeatedly told that online life must involve scrupulous monitoring of their online presence: they must either maintain constant vigilance, using enhanced privacy settings and keeping a low profile, or they have no right to complain when they are harassed, attacked, stalked, or threatened for simply existing as they wish. No thought is given to the price women pay for choosing either option. If the first, then women miss out on the full potential of the Internet. Hobbies, personal connections, professional networking, and more all become difficult or impossible if your presence online must be a locked and limited profile (all of which is even more moot if you choose to leave the Internet entirely for any period of time to avoid harassment, and stressful vigilance is no guarantee that harassment won't still happen). If the second, then women are harassed for being visible and blamed for daring to mention that they are the focus of harassers and abusers.

One of the most common methods for dismissing the effects of online abuse is to insist that the Internet is not a space that we should take seriously. In this approach the Internet is presented as an unreal or liminal environment that cannot have offline effects, because Internet harassment is not as "real" as offline harassment. Such an argument is like saying verbal abuse in offline spaces isn't real abuse because there is no physical damage; such reasoning ignores the important connection between verbal and physical violence and must pretend that words have no power to harm even when deployed in manipulative, damaging, and abusive ways.

The argument that the Internet is not real and therefore cannot be harmful is deeply rooted in the mindset attributed to the years of the early Internet, when there was an assumption of unfettered freedom to do or say anything, because there weren't many people around to hear it. The audience was mostly composed of other white men (or people presumed to be other white men) who were more likely to cosign stereotypes than challenge them. Today, however, the Internet is as real and as important for most people as offline life. From developing countries to industrialized nations, practically everyone is connected, and rates of Internet use continue to increase. The lines between online and offline life continue to blur, which means the lines between online and offline harassment also continue to blur—and the effects of both types of abuse are incredibly similar.

WHAT SETS CYBERSEXISM APART

The cybersexists aren't entirely wrong in saying that online harassment is different from offline harassment, although their understanding of that difference is typically flawed. Despite the similarities between both the content and effects of each type of harassment, cybersexist abuse has a number of qualities that set it apart and that can actually amplify its effects, giving it the ability to have a unique and even more lasting impact on women than offline harassment and abuse. Harassers offline must seek out targets physically; online, any woman anywhere in the world is just a click away, instantly, at all hours of the day, along with a potentially global audience. Harassers offline often work alone or in small groups; online, it's easy for one harasser to recruit many others to go after the same target or for a small number of people to use multiple accounts to create the impression of a huge and abusive, angry, anonymous crowd. Harassers offline can often be identified by sight, surveillance, or their relationship to their target; online, the relative anonymity of social media, email, and comment sections mean that a cybersexist could be anyone, anywhere.

All three factors give cybersexist harassers significantly more freedom to seek out and abuse women without consequence, which is often the ultimate goal for engaging in harassment. While the increasing interaction between online and offline life means more and more women do experience harassment from people they know in both contexts, it also means that women are significantly more likely to receive harassment from more people and strangers online than in physical spaces. The effects of online harassment tend to be increased by the nature of the Internet. The ease with which harassers can disguise their offline identity and recruit others to their activities means that incidents of online abuse and harassment quickly add up.

Some forms of online abuse can have longer-lasting effects than offline interactions. An incident of street harassment ends as soon as a woman can get safely away from her harasser (not that escaping it makes it any less awful or that the experience won't leave unpleasant memories), while a comment made online may be visible to everyone, forever, and turn up in search results connected to the target. Far from the presumption of a here-and-gone comment, the permanence of online spaces and archived information can have profound effects on women's livelihood and personal lives. While less likely to result in direct physical confrontation or attacks—although that does happen, and many women are stalked and abused online by people they know offline—online abuse has intense psychological and emotional effects on the women who are targeted.

Despite the claims of cybersexists that their targets are simply weak-willed or need to "grow up" or "grow a thicker skin," the damaging effects of cybersexist abuse will take a toll on even the strongest of women. Whether a woman reads a threat or has it shouted at her from the open window of a passing car, the physiological response is the same: fight or flight reactions, fear, and concern. Over time, continued exposure to such abuse has even greater effects on women, which can lead to depression, eating disorders, and other serious issues.[1] Whether a woman is "mature" or not is irrelevant; online abuse and harassment rarely have the effects of playful banter—and are rarely meant as such.

Cybersexists like to reminisce about the imagined "Wild West" days of the Internet when no one would fault them for saying repulsive things, reciting sexist stereotypes, or sharing abusive opinions and attitudes about and toward women and marginalized groups. There has always been online abuse that has been seen for what it is, however, and there has always been resistance to that abuse. Cybersexism has been a problem since the early years of the Internet, and its presence simply continues to evolve and endure in new online spaces. Evidence for the ways in which the Internet has become a space with unpleasant and even dangerous aspects for women is supported both by empirical research and anecdotes, which come from women and the abusers themselves.

HARASSMENT AND ABUSE

When not decrying cybersexism as nonexistent, online abusers frequently mention that everyone gets trolled online. Therefore, they insist, women are not special or deserving of particular consideration where harassment is concerned. Women just don't deal with trolling as well as men, the harassers argue; men can handle themselves in a fight, whereas women are being oversensitive drama queens. Although rooted in obviously sexist stereotypes about women's ability to deal with conflict or criticism (insofar as gendered harassment can be considered "criticism" at all), that argument is a convenient and believable-sounding reason to excuse cybersexism from serious examination: everyone, after all, has seen or experienced a flame war, an online fight, or a particularly nasty bit of trolling. Contrary

The Effects of Cybersexism

to the cybersexists' arguments, however, not all harassment is equal, and it's certainly not equally applied.

The nonprofit organization Working to Halt Online Abuse (WHOA) collects information about online abuse and who experiences it, offering resources and assistance to people who come to them for help. While the organization's work is focused mostly on stalking, it has produced statistics applicable to many areas of online harassment. Working to Halt Online Abuse research showed that between 2000 and 2008 nearly three-quarters of individuals who reported experiencing abuse online were women, and about half of them had no prior relationship with their attackers.[2] While there may be men who downplay any harassment of their own due to social pressure for men to avoid reporting it (since being seen as a victim often results in a loss of social standing for men), other studies that do not rely on self-reported data have found similar numbers in terms of which groups of people are singled out for harassment online.

Research continually finds race and sexuality are also likely to play a role in which women are targeted for abuse and harassment, although there has been very little research that focuses on the intersections of identity and abuse.[3] Studies of cybersexism and online harassment, while limited, have consistently found that the preponderance of harassing activities are aimed at women, lending credibility to women's claims that they are the primary targets for online abuse, that the cause is typically gender bias, and that the harassment primarily originates with men.

As mentioned in the previous chapter, while men do receive harassment online, it is rarely of an explicitly gendered nature the way it often is for women—that is, men are much less likely to be harassed for being men but are instead attacked on the basis of perceived skill, for their opinion or argument, or for not being "manly" enough. Women, on the other hand, report that much of the harassment they receive contains gendered components or is solely based on gender—that is, their skills and opinions are disregarded because they are women, or they receive completely random gender-based attacks just because they're there. Abuse increases for women of color, women who are queer, and transgender women; often such abuse is not one or the other but an amalgam of attacks on the basis of a woman's very being.[4] Although there has been little research focusing on multiple axes of identity and their relationship to online abuse, it is likely—and anecdotally observable—that women with disabilities, women who belong to religious minority groups, and many other minority groups of women also experience increased abuse and harassment in addition to being attacked as women.

For example, Mariam Veiszadeh, a Muslim human rights activist who lives in Australia, was viciously attacked by the Australian Defence League, an anti-Islam group. After taking to Twitter to criticize a bigoted message she saw in a store, Veiszadeh received a torrent of abuse. She was called a whore, a rag-head, and told to go back to her "sand dune country"—all insults that rested on a combination of misogyny, racism, and bigotry toward religious minorities. In this case some of the worst abuse came from a twenty-two-year-old white Australian woman and a man from New South Wales who began sending death threats to Veiszadeh. As the attacks continued, Veiszadeh said, her health "deteriorated rapidly. She suffered vertigo and anxiety." She expressed fear and frustration that some of the people sending her abuse might simply be "slapped with a fine and go back to everyday life."[5] Online harassment of women from racial and religious minorities, especially Islam, often receives tacit mainstream acceptance due to stereotypes about those groups and the sense that the abuse is justified by that acceptance. As a result, women from minority groups and religions are more frequent targets for cybersexist and other forms of online harassment and receive less support in the face of such harassment.

Sexual harassment is also a key feature of the online abuse many women report experiencing. The University of Maryland Electrical and Computer Engineering Department conducted a study on the subject of gendered sexual harassment. For the purposes of the study the group created a number of fake accounts for a specific online discussion system, and some of those fake usernames were easily identified as traditionally male names, while others could be easily identified as traditionally female names. The researchers allowed the accounts to collect communication from other users in the form of direct private messages and then analyzed the types of

The Effects of Cybersexism

messages that each username style generated. The results collected during the study will not be a surprise to most women online.

The researchers found that female-identified usernames received an average of 100 sexually explicit or threatening messages from men across the period of the study. Male usernames, meanwhile, got an average of 3.7 such messages.[6] Given that statistic, we can readily surmise that women who have a visible presence as women on multiple platforms, social media accounts, and other points of connection online are likely to receive even more sexual harassment and threats from men. But that's not all—in examining the content of the messages, the researchers also found that the threatening messages women received were rarely sent automatically. That is, few of the harassing and threatening messages women received were sent through the use of scripts or other code. Instead, men deliberately took time out of their day to send women messages containing sexual harassment and violent language, simply because the women were there and they felt like they could do so without facing any serious backlash or consequences.

As Danielle Citron explains, "examples of cyber gender harassment show that it routinely involves threats of rape and other forms of sexual violence. It often reduces targeted women to sexual objects and includes humiliating comments that reinforce gender-constructed stereotypes," such as telling women to get back in the kitchen, make the man a sandwich, or perform sex acts at his command.[7] These types of explicitly sexual harassment are conducted in order to re-create and reinforce male dominance in those online spaces; women are positioned as subservient and subjects—or objects, to be acted on only at a man's desire. Women's presence anywhere online is used as an excuse for ridicule, harassment, and abuse at the hands and keyboards of men.

Another study on the prevalence of Internet harassment, conducted by researchers at Ohio University, used online gaming as the basis for examining how sexist harassment functions on the Internet.[8] Online gaming platforms, such as Xbox Live, allow for the use of microphones and headsets that enable players to communicate with one another during real-time play. However, women who use microphones and headsets during online gaming frequently report that they are subjected to propositions and sexual harassment, as well as gendered verbal abuse and threats.[9] In addition, men sometimes deliberately log out of gaming sessions to avoid having to play with women in their group, reflecting the belief that video gaming should be a male-only activity and offering another example of how men find ways to ensure that women are excluded, sidelined, or marginalized.

To see if the anecdotes reported by many women held up under research conditions, the Ohio University group conducted a series of experiments to the test reaction of other gamers to the introduction of female players. The research team created a set of three recordings that would play during multiple rounds of a multiplayer online game—*Halo*—thus giving the impression of a real person talking (or not) during the game. Identifiably male- and female-sounding voices were used, along with a third—silent—gamer. Different people of varying skill levels played the game as the recordings were used, allowing for multiple gaming styles to be attached to the voices. The researchers found that when women's voices are not written but heard in online spaces, the same types of cybersexist interactions take place, with men engaging in negative commentary toward women who are perceived as encroaching on "male" spaces.

After playing eighty rounds each with the three recordings, the researchers found that the woman's voice received three times as many negative comments as the male or the silent gamer. Men and silent gamers also received more in-game encouragement than women, implicitly encouraging women to silence themselves and reinforcing the attitude that women in online game environments are not deserving of praise. Because gaming is perceived as a male pastime, even though industry studies show that nearly half of all gamers are women, women's presence is frequently seen as unusual and unwelcome.[10]

In addition to highlighting the abuse women receive online, the Ohio University study also reveals a fatal flaw in the cyberfeminists' erstwhile wish for disembodiment online as a way to avoid abuse. True disembodiment is made impossible both by the near ubiquity of personal photographs online (consider, for example, the phenomenon of selfies in addition

The Effects of Cybersexism

to the presence of websites and apps such as Facebook, Instagram, and Snapchat), as well as women's desire for active and full participation in popular hobbies such as online gaming. Women are denied the ability to completely engage in an event or environment if they must be silent to avoid harassment, while a voice that is perceived as belonging to a woman will receive significantly more harassment, regardless of skill level.

On top of that, the harassment of women through online gaming doesn't stop with aiming negative comments at women in real time. Women who play cooperative games online have also come to expect abusive private messages from other players. One blog, *Not in the Kitchen Anymore,* was built solely to document this phenomenon and give women a space to discuss the issue. Many of the posts come directly from in-game recordings and private messages sent to Jenny Haniver, the blog's owner, but submissions from numerous other women who game are frequently included. As with the study conducted by the University of Maryland Electrical and Computer Engineering Department, it seems likely that women in online game environments—such as Xbox, Playstation, or PC-based platforms—receive significantly more harassing messages than men do.

In one instance Haniver recorded her experience of having to deal with Xbox and Microsoft support following a rape threat she received from another player.[11] The interaction had begun with the more typical types of cybersexism: during the real-time game Haniver's attacker implied that Haniver was a lesbian, asked if she was on her period, and engaged in other gender-based attacks. Following the game he sent her a private message calling her a slut and sending further insults, to which she responded dismissively. As often happens when a woman pushes back against sexist harassment, the man escalated the abuse: he sent her a rape threat using a voice recording function.

Haniver immediately reported the threat to Xbox Live, which ignored the report for more than a month, despite her repeated attempts to draw attention to the fact that the player was still active. Even though he had clearly violated Microsoft's terms of service by sending an illegal threat, the player was allowed to continue actively gaming on Microsoft's platforms. In one post on this issue Haniver wrote, "I love gaming, but this sort of incident and seeming lack of response or concern about issues like this is really starting to wear on me. . . . At this point, the best I can hope for is maybe getting a notification that action has been taken on a complaint I filed."[12] At one point Microsoft customer support acknowledged the seriousness of the threat and suggested that Haniver file a police report—while still allowing the player to remain active on its systems. After a media storm Microsoft took action on the complaint, but it took repeated efforts on Haniver's part and the attention of the media to get anything accomplished.

Haniver's experience demonstrates the ways in which the Internet and online interactions are still built to favor the "anything-goes" mentality that pervades much online discussion. Her story also reveals the frustration and fear that many women deal with when attempting to take steps to protect themselves from such interactions. Companies' response times tend to be slow, subjecting women to increased opportunities for repeated attacks by the same individuals. When the "best" one can hope for is knowing that a complaint has even been heard and it takes the attention of the media to force a company to take action on their own policies, something is very wrong with how we handle cybersexism.

Despite the virulence of cybersexism in online gaming environments, gaming is an elective activity that is engaged in by a particular group of Internet users with the time and money to devote to it—although I would not be surprised if more women would decide to allocate their resources to it if cybersexist abuse was not such a prominent factor. While harassment in gaming spaces is, as with the rest of the Internet, assumed to be the norm by those who engage in it, the figures for harassment don't really change when examining more everyday Internet usage, such as blogging, social media, and other forms of communication. Sexual harassment, gendered abuse, and threats of violence aimed at women are common across all Internet platforms.

The use of sexually explicit and gendered insults to demean and objectify women serves more than one purpose. It is not that men don't know how to communicate with women and therefore resort to explicit sexual overtures, as is often hypothesized, or that they are merely bored and choosing to harass women. Cybersexism is also a way to assert dominance over women when they are perceived as having entered "men's" space or become too visible. Through cybersexist harassment, men attempt to re-create the offline conversational patterns they already dominate, enabling them to continue controlling online spaces as well. Sexist harassment is intended to intimidate women, silence their voices, or force them to conform to men's chosen conversational norms for a specific space. In many cases women are expected to be silent, deferential, and objectified for the pleasure of the male gaze—and any women who fail to meet those expectations are punished for it.

The enduring result of cybersexist behaviors is that men "(re)make women into a marginalized class" online, where their presence is limited, and any pushback on the part of women is seen as threatening to men and male dominance.[13] Cybersexism discourages women from working and writing online, increases their vulnerability to offline sexual and physical violence—especially through activities like doxxing—and reinforces sexist stereotypes about technology use that make it more difficult for women to make inroads into online environments or overcome sexist harassment to achieve a successful online career.[14] Cybersexism has psychological, professional, and personal effects on women, and thus far we haven't done a great job at finding ways to combat it.

PROFESSIONAL EFFECTS OF CYBERSEXISM

Imagine being a recruiter or hiring manager. You, like nearly 100 percent of other professional recruiters, have either connected with your chosen candidates on the networking site LinkedIn, found their blog, or looked them up on social media websites such as Facebook and Twitter.[15] Now imagine conducting those first Google searches and coming across blog posts that call your candidate a bitch, a slut, a whore, or a cunt or accuse her of causing problems in professional spaces, organizations, or social groups. Alternatively, you might see comments and altered photos left on multiple websites that suddenly make a stellar candidate seem like too much trouble to bring into your company. After all, a single individual's online reputation can affect your how your organization is perceived, especially if these comments have the potential to bring your logo or brand into their harassment.

While this scenario might seem far-fetched, a great deal of business research shows that companies frequently use findings on social media to reject job candidates. Although the legality of that decision has come under fire and is likely to be challenged regularly, women must currently monitor their online presence to help identify risk factors and mitigate potential problems in changing jobs or retaining a current position due to significant cybersexist harassment. In addition to creating and maintaining their own online profile, women have to keep an eye out for potentially damaging behaviors engaged in by other people on the Internet. This vigilance may include activities that expose women to more cybersexist harassment, such as having to read, record, or otherwise save evidence of the abuse they have received or that has been posted about them. While there are products and services designed to help professional women maintain their online reputations, they tend to be costly and may end up being an ineffective solution for women who are subjected to persistent harassment.[16]

It is also not uncommon for women to be driven out of a specific profession or position due to cybersexist harassment, abuse, and threats. While more prominent in heavily male-dominated industries such as tech and video gaming, cybersexism has the ability to ruin women's careers in practically any field. As discussed in chapter 1, a prominent woman in tech, Kathy Sierra, was the victim of deliberate cybersexist harassment, and it prevented her from blogging, speaking at conferences, and maintaining her career. Due to the severity of the threats and harassment she received, Sierra chose to put her life on hold—and leave the Internet—for years. Sierra is far from the only woman to deal with these kinds of abuse.

Jennifer Hepler, at one point a senior writer for video game developer BioWare, became the target of vicious cybersexist harassment over her position as a woman within a male-dominated space.[17] Although Hepler, unlike Sierra, did not completely leave the Internet to protect her own safety, the enormity of the harassment aimed at her was one of the catalysts for larger discussions of sexism and abuse in the gaming community. Due to an interview in which Hepler discussed enjoying the storyline of games more than the combat, as well as her work on BioWare's more progressive and gay- and lesbian-inclusive storylines, she was subjected to intense cybersexist abuse. For Hepler, limiting her online presence and the ability of harassers to access her was the immediate option she chose; doing so was a way to protect herself from direct exposure to the abuse, but as a result she had to close down her Twitter account and avoid reading articles about the issue that contained any of the threats or commentary, except those she was shown for security reasons.

Hepler was sent graphic threats of violence that were aimed not only at her but also at her children, "to show them that they should have been aborted at birth rather than have to have me as a mother," as she recounted in an interview about the harassment.[18] For Hepler, the outpouring of support became a larger factor than the abuse itself, because she had systems in place that allowed her to avoid seeing most of the harassment that was aimed at her and because she was already well established in her field. However, Hepler left BioWare after the abuse she received, and the experience has become part of her professional identity where gaming and writing are concerned. A quick online search of Hepler's name, or even just of video games and harassment, brings up stories about the issue. The abuse she experienced and the writing about it are likely to accompany her professional image for the rest of her working life.

Adria Richards was driven out of her job in tech after reporting two men, one of whom also eventually lost his job, who were making inappropriate jokes at a professional convention. Although they were in flagrant violation of conference policies, Richards herself was fired for posting a picture of the men on her Twitter account. In the years since that incident it is she who has become the target of the Internet's cybersexist rage machine.[19] As a result Richards has been driven from her home and to the margins of an industry she loves. She regularly receives death and rape threats and is still frequently framed as the villain of the piece for daring to point out that the men's behavior was inappropriate for a professional environment—especially one like tech, which remains fraught with issues of the underrepresentation of and discrimination toward women.[20]

Additionally, women who are small business owners are likely to be disproportionately affected by cybersexist attacks and harassment. Coordinated attacks by groups of people who leave fake negative reviews on websites such as Yelp can result in an immediate loss of business, and online hacking and other attacks can take down a small business website, causing lost ranking in search engines and customer dissatisfaction. Women whose careers depend on online exposure and connections are at a significant risk for losing their livelihoods over cybersexist harassment. Women who start online businesses are also much less likely to receive funding (only 15 percent of companies receiving venture capital funding between 2011 and 2013 had a woman on their executive team).[21] Whether financial support comes from venture capital groups or from government programs aimed at minority-owned businesses, women receive less money than men do and less support for the continuation of their businesses, and they have a higher level of turnover as a result. Women begin their online careers at a disadvantage, and cybersexist harassment can be the final nail in the coffin for women's online businesses.

PSYCHOLOGICAL EFFECTS OF CYBERSEXISM

Throughout Internet communities and especially on social media, where cybersexism is rampant, messages like these are common:

"I'm taking off for the day to avoid the harassment."

"I'm leaving for a few days of self-care."

"I'm signing off for a while—I need a break."

"I'm deactivating my account so I can get away from the abuse. I don't know if I'll be back."

"I can't deal with the abuse anymore. I'm done."

Women send out similar messages on a daily basis, letting their friends and followers on social media, blogs, and websites know that they're getting away from the cybersexism for a brief period or permanently leaving a particular space to protect themselves and, often, their families. Over time the psychological effects of dealing with cybersexism become overwhelming, and the only way to safely remain online is to temporarily disconnect. While advice to leave the Internet is given to

The Effects of Cybersexism

many women by cybersexists in an attempt to silence criticism of their harassing activities, it's important to note that women don't regard leaving the Internet as a solution to cybersexism. Instead, short- and long-term online absences are a way to relax, recharge, and regroup before returning with the knowledge that they will continue to be exposed to online harassment. Briefly disconnecting from online interactions isn't a solution. It's a survival mechanism.

For many women, dealing with the regular onslaught of cybersexist harassment necessitates time away from the Internet. Unlike men who advocate that women leave in response to harassment and regard that as the answer (instead of finding constructive solutions to dealing with the abusers), women are well aware of the costs of their breaks, as well as the price they will likely have to pay for not taking any respite. Leaving the Internet for even just a few days can cost women professional opportunities, result in lost online business, or damage their personal brands and relationships. However, staying online without a break from the abuse, violence, or threats presents its own set of issues, which can prove even more dangerous than not taking a breather at all.

Cybersexism is intended to wear women down, erode their individual defenses and confidence, and make the psychological cost of online visibility too high a price to pay. To achieve this result—to force women into disappearing from online spaces—cybersexists harass women from every conceivable angle. As with offline sexism, cracks about a woman's appearance are common. From come-ons to insults, a woman online can expect to be judged first and foremost by what she looks like. Taunts about a woman's sexuality or perceived sexual behavior are also used, positioning women's value as contingent upon male desire, which is often "revoked" in the face of women's resistance (similar to a street harasser who, once his advances are rebuffed, shifts from calling a woman beautiful to saying she's not that pretty anyway). Gendered stereotypes and slurs are a ubiquitous component of cybersexist harassment: being called a bitch or any number of other overtly gendered slurs is not an unusual experience for a woman who expresses opinions on the Internet. Substantive critique, on the other hand, is somewhat less common.

Other forms of harassment may include sending sexist stereotypes and jokes, demanding that a woman "debate" on the topic of the harasser's choice, wasting a woman's time by asking for "proof" of every point she makes and then disregarding it without consideration, employing mobbing tactics, "sea lioning" (discussed in depth in a later chapter), deliberately overstepping stated boundaries, and more. Tactics like flooding a woman's Twitter mentions, email, blog, Facebook, or YouTube comments with links, repeating the same negative comment over and over, or posting images (commonly memes, pornography, or pornography with the woman's face digitally added) are also common strategies.

Repeatedly and deliberately removing a woman's statement from its context and distorting it to appear as though she is saying something inflammatory, derogatory, or anti–free speech is also common. When an initial round of sexual harassment or other type of abuse does not elicit the desired response, an escalation typically occurs. For example, a woman who refuses to acknowledge a harasser may be accused of having a sexually transmitted infection, or the cybersexist may begin spreading that accusation elsewhere in hopes of gaining a response. As Danielle Citron points out, "falsely accusing someone of having a sexually transmitted infection, a criminal conviction, or an inappropriate sexual affair amounts to libel that does not require proof of special damages."[22] The escalation of abuse from "casual" sexual harassment, incessant demands for attention, or sexist stereotypes to libel and illegal threats can often occur within the space of hours or minutes.

When everyday harassment doesn't seem to be doing enough damage, dedicated cybersexists begin to issue threats. They may take the form of wishing for a specific and graphic ill to befall a woman and often cross the line into illegality and include a declaration of intent.[23] Threats have a tendency to escalate as more cybersexists get involved; the Internet allows easy recruiting of multiple individuals to harass one woman, and abusers seek to outdo each other in the vileness of their abuse. Over time the situation may evolve to include threatening emails sent to the target, public posts that include the woman's home or work address and phone numbers, and threats to family members, pets, and friends.

The Effects of Cybersexism

Citron describes one such incident, in which a young actor's fan website became a target for a group of harassers: "A poster . . . explained that at first, the comments seemed 'derogatory, though jesting.' Soon, however, the 'postings became increasingly bizarre and weird[;] it became apparent . . . that everyone was competing to see who could be the most outrageous.'" The escalation culminated in graphic threats of violence justified by a "desire for peer approval."[24] In addition to the seemingly consequence-free space in which the group could send harassment, the perceived social benefit of upping the ante was regarded as an acceptable reason to send more and more abusive comments. The effect of their behavior on their target wasn't taken into consideration until after the fact.

Even when individuals sending a threat say they never intended to carry it out in person, cybersexists deliberately expose women to the risk of having their personal information falling into the hands of someone who will, especially in cases of doxxing. A woman who becomes the target of a mob that seeks to outdo itself in the violence of its threats has the potential to be in physical, offline danger as a result. Additionally, physical harm is only sometimes the actual goal of sending an online threat to a woman. In many cases a threat is sent with the larger purpose of creating an environment of fear and intimidation. Threats are a reminder to women that their presence online is always at the mercy of men and that men can choose to harm them at any point. Women who are on the receiving end of violent threats online are left constantly waiting for the other shoe to drop.

The psychological impact of dealing with harassment and threats varies from individual to individual. Each woman handles threats in her own way, both internally and through external forms of attempting to control or stop the harassment. However, there are a number of patterns that have been observed in women who have dealt with online abuse. One factor to keep in mind is that research done with students demonstrates that "misogynist comments were seen as more harassing online than in traditional settings."[25] This finding may be due in part to the fact that such misogyny is often issued from anonymous sources; as many women report, lacking context for harassing and threatening comments can make the interaction more frightening rather than less. The research overall found that people tend to apply relatively equal standards for how they perceive online and offline behavior, although slightly more stringent standards were applied to the Internet. While cybersexists may argue that the Internet is a place where social rules don't exist, that does not seem to be the way most people approach online interactions.

Simply disapproving of online harassment is not the only reaction women have. Often reactions occur at a subconscious level—women are not choosing to be offended but are physically and mentally responding to harassment and abuse at a deep level that manifests itself in a variety of ways. Research has repeatedly shown that women "report more daily hassles" that are indicative of gender-based prejudice and bias than do men.[26] During a small-scale study in which participants were asked to record such incidents each day and the resulting reactions they had, the researchers found that sexist interactions "affected women's psychological well-being by decreasing their comfort, increasing their feelings of anger and depression, and decreasing their state self-esteem."[27] Across decades research has shown that the expression of sexist biases—and how women experience them—is often implicit.

Women react to sexism not just consciously but subconsciously: adjusting how to speak, walk, take up space, and interact with the world based on cues about how women's presence is being regarded and what sexist biases are likely to be encountered. Processing sexist incidents—from overt attacks to microaggressions and sexist interactions that might not even be intentional—causes women stress, increases the likelihood of anxiety and depression, and is connected to eating disorders, reduced personal goals, and more. Although women can shrug off a sexist comment consciously, it still contributes to her awareness of her surroundings and has an underlying effect on how she acts and feels in that space in the future.

As with offline harassment, although it too is often dismissed as juvenile pranks and complaints about harassment are judged to be an overreaction, "sexual harassment . . . has been shown to have long-lasting and severe effects on its victims no matter where it occurs."[28] Women cannot simply choose to ignore all harassment and abuse. While each woman internalizes the interactions differently, the damaging effects of cybersexist online abuse are all too common.

Women who have experienced sexual, physical, or emotional violence or other forms of trauma that lead to post-traumatic stress disorder (PTSD) often report that being exposed to violent and overtly sexist content online, frequently referred to as triggers, can result in panic attacks and other issues. Being triggered is an immediate and often debilitating psychological response to external stimuli, such as references to threats, descriptions of threats, or actual threats regarding trauma-inducing events. Individuals who have been triggered may experience panic attacks, depression, relapses into self-harming behavior or eating disorders, or suicidal ideations, among other reactions. Feminists often tag conversations with trigger warnings or content notes to help other people opt out of potentially damaging online experiences, while cybersexists sometimes try to provoke individuals by making specific references to triggering events and emotions, or they may downplay the need for trigger warnings at all and refer to those who use them as overly sensitive and anti-intellectual.[29]

However, not all of the issues associated with online abuse can be linked to past trauma. Women who are subjected to cybersexism and online harassment are at risk of experiencing a number of other adverse psychological effects as a result, including anxiety, fear, shame, depression, reduced personal and professional goals, significantly higher suicidal ideations and attempts, and more.[30] Many harassed women also experience feelings of undermined personal agency and additional physical and emotional harms in response to the abuse.[31] The effects of cybersexism are serious and sometimes deadly, despite the fact that cybersexism is seen as harmless because it exists online and because perpetrators are depicted as young pranksters. There are many factors of online sexism that contribute to harmful psychological outcomes of Internet abuse, such as the availability of women to target, the anonymity, and the challenges to reducing, preventing, or stopping cybersexist harassment.

One young woman, Alyssa Funke, committed suicide after becoming the subject of intense online harassment.[32] At nineteen Funke was a straight-A student struggling to pay her way through college. To help cover the costs she agreed to appear in a porn film. When the movie was discovered by people from her former high school and community, the online abuse began almost immediately. Funke was called a slut and was sent additional harassing and threatening messages across both Facebook and Twitter; shortly after the harassment began Funke killed herself. While she left no note and the high school she had attended denies having an issue with students participating in online harassment, it seems likely that the level and types of harassment Funke received were a contributing factor in her decision to end her own life.

Despite the explicitly gendered nature of the abuse aimed at Funke, the online abuse she received is most often referred to in the media reports about her death as cyberbullying rather than cybersexism. This word choice corresponds to the denial of cybersexism as a serious issue; all harassment online is presumed to be a form of bullying, and the role that gender stereotypes play is largely ignored. The label was likely also applied because most of Funke's tormenters were themselves young. While the effect and intent of the harassment was specifically to engage in sexist abuse, the youthfulness of all of those involved gives the cybersexism the appearance of mere fighting among children and teens.

Although the instigators in this instance were teenagers, one study showed that "the lowest levels of verbal and sexual harassment, flaming, and cybserstalking were found in the youngest group of participants."[33] Although the nature of much online harassment tends to make it difficult to get a good grasp of the demographics of cybersexists, organizations such as Working to Halt Online Abuse attempt to track this information. Across a fourteen-year period 47 percent of abusers in reports to the organization could be reliably identified as men. In contrast only 30 percent of harassers could be reliably identified as women, with an additional 23 percent of harassment occurring in groups or being perpetrated by unknown harassers, which is a figure that likely contains a significant percentage of men hiding their identity, given the limited amount of other research conducted.[34] During the same period of time 72 percent of people reporting abuse to WHOA were women, regardless of the gender of their harasser.

The Effects of Cybersexism

Across that fourteen-year period only 27.7 percent of people who reported online abuse to WHOA were people of color. As with most research reports, WHOA does not break down race and gender statistics in combination, so it is not possible to tell how many women among the 72 percent of people reporting abuse were women of color. Given anecdotal evidence, however, it is likely that many people resisted reporting their abuse to any organization and that women of color were far more likely to experience abuse than white women. Although there are limitations to the data that WHOA is able to produce, the organization tracks information only on adult reports, and the detail available from the reports they receive and collect is worth considering.

Given the limited availability of data on reported online abuse, it seems that teens tend to be much less likely to engage in the cybersexist behaviors that affect women's lives most prominently, leading to further questions about why adult men are primarily responsible for cybersexist behaviors and why so much abuse is committed by and against adult users of the Internet. The lower levels of harassment from younger users could be related to attitudes about gender that are less prominent in more recent generations; alternatively, it may reflect younger Internet users' greater awareness that online behaviors are easily tracked and monitored, as evidenced in the attempt by Alyssa Funke's former school to deny its students' responsibility for her harassment.

Suicide is not the only adverse effect of cybersexism, however. Eating disorders are another common issue amplified by experiences online, including body-shaming, harassment, and constant exposure to manipulated images of thin women's bodies, which has been linked to reduced self-esteem and more. While direct cybersexist harassment itself may not always be the cause (although there is a great deal of gendered harassment and abuse aimed at women for their weight), sexist attitudes about women's bodies pervade the Internet. Photoshopped celebrity photographs in various publications are not the only source of distorted ideas about the ideal female form; pro-anorexia websites, often referred to as pro-ana sites, abound.[35] These are websites where young women share tips for or encourage one another to develop eating disorders.

On such websites anorexic bodies are held up as an ideal goal for women, the ultimate achievement in a society that regards thinness as one of the pinnacles of beauty. Eating disorders are one of the most common mental illnesses among young women and have the highest mortality rate among mental illnesses as a group.[36] The promotion of and support for deliberately engaging in self-harm, along with cybersexist harassment around women's weight and appearance, make the Internet a breeding ground for the development of severe and unhealthy body issues.

Cybersexist harassment, as usually intended, leads to sensations of worthlessness for women who are targeted; additionally, dealing with sustained cybersexist harassment is simply exhausting. Many women who become the victims of dedicated campaigns of cybersexist abuse find that dealing with the harassment takes too great a toll on their emotional well-being. Many women give up on personal and professional goals as a result of such harassment. Cybersexist abuse does not merely target women's psychological well-being; it also has immense effects on their personal lives.

PERSONAL EFFECTS OF CYBERSEXISM

While psychological damage is about as personal as an outcome of abuse can be, there are other factors of personal damage that result from the online abuse and harassment of women. "Although cyber harassment substantially harms women," Danielle Citron notes, "many view it as a benign part of online life that should be tolerated. This is perhaps to be expected—we often overlook harms to women."[37] The act of overlooking the distinct and long-lasting effects of cybersexism is part of a tradition of ignoring the behaviors and attitudes that injure women in gender-based ways and one that stretches far beyond the Internet. Citron has noted the reluctance to classify domestic violence as a crime, for example, as well as a cultural disregard of gender-specific harms, which makes it harder for women to exercise bodily autonomy and seek redress when that autonomy is violated—whether in person or through something like the nonconsensual sharing of private photographs.[38] Further, the Internet is a place where people such as men's rights activists (MRAs) argue that marital rape isn't possible, as they insist ongoing consent to sex is part of what it means to be married.[39] The refusal to consider online abuse a serious issue for women is itself an example of sexism: women's reports of abuse online and offline tend to be disregarded, ignored, or presumed to be exaggerations so as to garner attention. Despite that, women's experience of cybersexism is one that includes damaging effects experienced on an individual level.

Women experience not only professional but personal limitations online, as they self-limit their Internet activities to avoid experiencing cybersexist online harassment. Limiting online hobbies might include refraining from blogging on certain topics, commenting on specific websites, or visiting particular forums. Women might turn down connections with other people for fear of exposing themselves to harassment and abuse, or they might limit all online interactions by heightening their security features to reduce the likelihood that they will become a target.

Online safeguards continue to be a concern for women, who often want to reduce the amount of personally identifiable information about them that is available. While most people make some attempt to keep their online and offline activities at least partially separate, 64 percent of women versus 54 percent of men feel that it is not possible to be completely anonymous online; this divergence may be due, in part, to the online harassment and abuse undertaken to expose women's personal information.[40] A Pew report from 2005 also tracked an 11 percent decline in women's commentary on chat rooms, which it blamed on "menacing comments" aimed at women.[41] To avoid harassment, women may make attempts to disguise their presence or even remove themselves entirely from certain online spaces.

Women are also significantly more likely to be concerned about the use of online resources that use offline location-based tracking than men are; while apps such as Foursquare and others make it easy to form offline connections with online companions, they also make it simple for stalkers and other harassers to find out where a woman goes and when.[42] Women, who are at a greater risk of stalking than men, have good reason to be concerned about the use of apps, websites, and tools that offer public access to their location-based information, even as the trade-off means they might miss out on valuable personal or professional connections with other people.

Even online dating, while rosily portrayed in ads as a safe, comfortable way to meet potential mates, dates, or friends, can be a fraught experience for women. Women of color and transgender women in particular are subjected to fetishistic interactions in which men send demeaning private messages to them about their perceived race or ethnicity or ask invasive questions about their bodies. When rebuffed, these men often resort to overtly sexist, racist, and transphobic attacks. A Tumblr blog called *Creepy White Guys* was set up specifically to collect and display these types of racist and sexist interactions.[43] The Instagram account "Bye Felipe" accepts submissions of particularly atrocious online dating interactions, which are often horrendous both on the basis of their content and how familiar they are to women.[44] Almost every woman who has an online dating profile has a story about a man who went from attempting to woo her to calling her any variety of racial or gender slurs the instant he is told "no."

While serving as a source of solidarity and humor for people who got to see firsthand the messages that women chose to share, that Tumblr blog, Instagram account, and others like them are also reminders of what can and often does happen in online dating and therefore act as potential deterrents for women who are considering going online to meet potential partners. The rapidity with which men move from claiming they want to date or sleep with a woman to calling her ugly, threatening her, or encouraging her to commit suicide is sometimes humorous in its sheer absurdity but can be terrifying to experience firsthand.

Few online dating platforms have adequate safety measures in place for women who are repeatedly harassed or stalked, and online dating sites and social media alike offer various ways for cybersexist harassers to engage in other forms of sexual harassment. Common strategies include such activities as tracking women across multiple online profiles, repeatedly messaging them—often with increasingly angry sexist, racist, and violent overtones—and even sending unsolicited nude photographs of themselves (entire Twitter accounts exist that are nothing but, most often, white men sending pictures of their penises to random women). While invasive and abusive, this last occurrence is relatively common.

Unsolicited pornographic photos are an unsubtle way for men to assert dominance in an interaction. Women are being forced to unexpectedly look at a man's genitalia; these photos are thus the online equivalent of offline flashers. Often, men will use temporary chatting applications like Snapchat to send the pictures, which makes it difficult for women to document their harassment because the app deletes the content after a brief window of time. On other forms of social media, men use their unwanted and unasked-for nude photographs as a way to sexually harass women without consequence and to provoke women into interacting with them, subsequently using feigned outrage at women who mock them—all to attract more attention to their behavior. As a form of sexual harassment, sending nude pictures is particularly overt. It is also closely connected to another form of online abuse of women, one often referred to as "revenge porn."

So-called revenge porn is the act of taking once-consensual nude photographs of a woman—often an ex—and posting them online after a divorce, a breakup, or a fight. While it is most commonly referred to as revenge porn (most web searches for it under any other name don't even bring up the relevant news results), here, for the purposes of this discussion, it will primarily be called the nonconsensual sharing or posting of women's photographs.[45] "Revenge porn" as a term lends itself both to the continuing stigma associated with actual and consensual pornography, as well as to blaming the victim of these invasions of privacy by insinuation: many people who discuss the problem of the nonconsensual sharing of women's photographs of themselves suggest that the women in the pictures should not have taken the pictures in the first place.

However, faking photographs and hacking women's emails and computers to find compromising photos, or taking nonconsensual pictures of women, are also common strategies for developing these kinds of images. Entire websites have been devoted to hosting nonconsensual photographs of women, and they often include the targeted women's phone numbers, email addresses, contact information, and offline locations. Some websites allow commentary on the women featured, and such comments are often cybersexist in the extreme. Being featured on these websites has cost women their jobs, friends, and the support of their family members; women are sometimes permanently linked to such images, which can have a long-lasting effect on their personal and professional success.

A damaged personal image is not the worst that has happened due to the nonconsensual sharing of these images, however. At least three young women have committed suicide after having nude photos of them circulated online. Audrie Pott, at fifteen, killed herself after being sexually assaulted at a party and after photographs of that night subsequently circulated throughout her school.[46] Rehtaeh Parsons had a nearly identical experience, one that also resulted in her suicide at the age of seventeen. Amanda Todd, at twelve, was photographed by a stranger via webcam; a year later that image and her personal information were used to coerce her into taking further photographs for his use, which resulted in a physical assault. Shortly before she turned sixteen, Todd also killed herself.[47] Nearly half of women who have private photographs circulated on "revenge porn" websites or throughout their communities report considering suicide.[48]

Perhaps the most famous example of a website where men were encouraged to share nude images of women without the women's consent was the site Is Anyone Up?, the owner of which, Hunter Moore, became the target of an FBI investigation.[49] In early 2015 Moore entered a guilty plea on multiple counts of identity theft for which he faced several years in prison.[50] Although legislation taking any action on revenge porn itself has not been passed, hacking is illegal, and Moore relied on hacking women's computers to help populate his website with pictures. Among the "legitimate" submissions to his site, such as they were, he also added another layer of invasion to the practice of sharing images of women without their consent: paying other young men to hack women's computers, find any compromising photos of themselves they had, and putting them online. Charlotte Laws, the mother of a young woman whose computer was hacked in just that fashion, was instrumental in identifying the men engaged in the hacking and getting Moore's website taken down. However, dozens of copycat websites still exist, and many women fear becoming a target

The Effects of Cybersexism

of an angry former partner or spouse and facing the resulting cybersexist harassment.

Increasing numbers of U.S. states are implementing laws that make the nonconsensual sharing of nude images illegal. In 2015 Kevin Christian Bollaert, the owner and operator of a website like Moore's, was sentenced to eighteen years in prison after being convicted of twenty-seven different felonies.[51] These crimes included identity theft and extortion, as he would charge women between $250 and $300 to have the pictures taken down from the website. During the time his site was running there were more than ten thousand pictures of women featured on it. The nonconsensual posting of women's private pictures represents a massive financial opportunity for the unscrupulous, and many states are considering the options they have to prevent these predatory individuals from harming women.

Social media websites such as Twitter, Reddit, and Facebook have also implemented policies that prohibit the posting of nonconsensual images and that include penalties such as having an account shut down. While such policies are an encouraging if shockingly belated step in the right direction, much of the burden of reporting nude pictures that are shared without the subject's consent still falls on the target, who must know that the picture was posted, find where it was, file a report, and then wait for the review process. In the time that it takes to accomplish that and wait for the website to review and take down the photos, they can be spread widely across the Internet. Damage to a woman's reputation and livelihood can already have taken place, and no mechanisms exist to prevent the photos from being saved and then reposted on new accounts by other individuals.

One of the only ways a woman can successfully file a DMCA takedown notice on a nonconsensually posted nude photograph that is uploaded to such a website is to prove to the website or its service provider that she is the copyright owner of the picture.[52] In some cases doing so can involve requiring the woman to take further nude photographs of herself to send to a government copyright office in order to prove that the body in the picture is hers, thus exposing her to even more strangers and increasing the risk that more photographs may be acquired and circulated without her consent. This procedure is clearly an unworkable long-term solution.

Few if any penalties are put in place for the men who are submitting these photos to the websites in the first place, whether they are social media sites or "revenge porn" hubs. Even when "the Fappening" occurred—a harassment campaign in which thousands of nude photos of actresses were posted online after having been illegally accessed—it took the threat of significant lawsuits to bring down the pictures.[53] Women, whether or not they have the benefit of celebrity, are often left to fend largely for themselves in the face of these abusers' actions, and websites that host the images are still a dime a dozen. The coming years will probably result in even more lawsuits and criminal cases around this issue, and women will continue to deal with the fallout of men posting their private photos in public places.

A key initiative for helping women will be finding preventive measures for addressing these behaviors and ensuring that women are able to maintain their livelihoods and lives in the face of this abuse.[54] Germany has taken steps to protect people from the possibility of having their private photographs exposed to the public, having ruled in favor of a woman who demanded that her former partner delete all naked photos he had of her at the end of the relationship. "Consent to use and own privately recorded nude pictures, the court stated, could in this instance be withdrawn on the grounds of personal rights, which are valued higher than the ownership rights of the photographer," the *Guardian* reported.[55] While similar initiatives would have to be created in line with in-country laws, steps like the one taken by the German court ensure that people have an active say in how private photographs can be used.

Also at issue is the fact that a woman's nude body is still regarded as a shameful, titillating object. Countering repressive attitudes about sexuality, ensuring that the subjects of private photographs have control over those images, and ensuring that resources are in place when exploitation occurs are all essential steps to reducing the impact of publicly released private images.

SAFETY MEASURES

Many women take a number of steps to help reduce the likelihood that they will be subjected to cybersexist attacks—whether it's a serious attack, nonconsensual sharing of images, or the more everyday types of harassment most women have come to expect from the Internet. Women's strategies may include not linking social media accounts together to prevent people from finding them on different platforms, refraining from engaging in online discussions or only doing so anonymously, closing down comments on their personal blogs, or adopting a neutral or masculine username and profile picture in the hopes of staving off abuse.

Employing more security features, such as using autoblocker tools, locking accounts, and screening all new friends and followers, is also used to help reduce cybersexist abuse; many women adopt this strategy if they become the target of coordinated abuse, in order to help limit their harassers' access to their accounts. As noted at other points in this book, each of these decisions comes with a cost: while only marginally effective at reducing online harassment and abuse, these strategies also make it more difficult for women to form meaningful personal and professional connections in online spaces.

Women may also change their online behaviors to more closely adhere to male norms for a specific space. Doing so may include increasing the aggression of their interactions, downplaying attributes like compassion, and even engaging in cybersexist harassment themselves as a way to put the focus of sexist abuse on another individual.[56] Even within feminism, white feminists and trans-exclusive radical feminists are known to engage in racist or transphobic attacks on other women and then claim they are being harassed when the response to their behavior is negative.

Antifeminist women in particular are comfortable engaging in the same types of cybersexist harassment as men, positioning themselves as allies to men's rights activists and other misogynist groups. These behaviors may be a form of self-defense in which one redirects the wrath of certain groups at an easier target and reduces negative attention aimed at oneself; however, such activities are also useful for building a reputation within various spaces, including online publications and even academia. Such activities also have the effect of creating an environment of mistrust among women and reducing the possibility of forging positive relationships.

Identity disguise and altered behaviors in the face of the pressure exerted by male norms and harassment can also be damaging to women. Contrary to the hopes of the cyberfeminists, who thought that shedding identity online would be beneficial for everyone, most people using neutral and masculine usernames are just presumed to be white men. Although this presumption comes with some limited benefits, which may include less harassment and more genuine consideration of stated opinions, pretending to be someone you're not is a difficult task. Continuing to use a false identity can create a sense of alienation from one's actual self and over time produces feelings of shame or self-loathing.[57] It is uncomfortable to act like someone else, to take on the characteristics of the dominant voices in online spaces. Role-playing in video games is one thing, and often fun and exciting, while a consistent denial of your own identity can eventually become exhausting, emotionally draining, and ineffective.

THE BURDEN OF CYBERSEXISM

Each day when I wake up and get online, I have a routine. Read the news, check my email, glance at Facebook, read my Twitter mentions, review the readership of my latest articles or check my blog stats—all pretty normal stuff for anyone who spends time online. I check my blog and article comments, just in case something has gotten caught in the spam filters; sometimes, I find some harassment. Then I look up the accounts that have sent me rape threats recently: are their profiles still active? Has my report been received and reviewed? After that I scroll through the tweets and Facebook posts and blogs of the people and groups who are dedicated to stalking and harassing women online, including groups that stalk a few of my online friends and occasionally me; sometimes there's advance warning if they're planning on ramping things up. Once in a while I'll let friends know that they've appeared on certain websites used to coordinate harassment, or they'll let me know if I have. I spend some time preemptively blocking Twitter and Facebook accounts that are engaging in cybersexist harassment in public forums, a practice that continues throughout the day. All of this, too, is normal—for women online.

The Effects of Cybersexism

Not every woman deals with cybersexist harassment but enough do to make my personal routines part of the norm, and it's a norm that is shaped by the awareness and expectation of being on the receiving end of gender-based abuse. And while not every woman receives cybersexist harassment, there are many women whose daily activities involve dealing with significantly more abuse than what I see in a month. For them, too, it is routine: wake up, get online, begin dealing with cybersexism.

This routine might sound depressing; it is. It's also annoying, and occasionally scary, and it puts an additional burden on women's online presence that men just don't experience. The effort of dealing with cyber-sexist abuse takes time away from women's hobbies, positive interactions both personal and professional with other people, and is a contributing factor in making women feel that the Internet is not a welcoming space for their presence. Cybersexist abuse goes beyond just sending a nasty comment to a woman online. It also encompasses all of the extra work placed on women as a result of those comments. The emotional and psychological labor of reading online abuse and deciding how to deal with it—How many people will I have to block today? Should I shut down comments on my blog? Is this threat serious enough to report?—is exhausting, and it sometimes leaves women with little energy for other online activities. In many ways that's the true purpose of cybersexist abuse: to wear down individual women so that they give up and leave the space to the men.

Many people still refuse to believe that cybersexism is a serious issue. Despite the many studies that "have demonstrated that gender roles remain in effect online, prescribing the rules of acceptable behavior, [and] allowing for the harassment of women," it is entirely too common for women to be told that we're taking the Internet too seriously—that cybersexism is only a burden because we burden ourselves with it and that we receive harassment because we did something that invited it.[58] Of course, women are told the same things offline when the conversation turns to talk about street harassment, interpersonal violence, and sexual assault. It's much easier to downplay the harassment and abuse aimed at women as an issue of how women are behaving or responding and to put the onus of dealing with the issues on women instead of examining the social structures offline that have been imported to the Internet and that allow cybersexist behavior to flourish.

In an article on online comments about domestic violence, researchers have written, "Not surprisingly in a culture of violence, the man as the abuser is rather absent from users' statements: the process of blaming the victim is obsessively focused on *her* behaviour, *her* fault, *her* decision to stay."[59] The same attitude is often extrapolated to women who discuss times when they experience online abuse; even though the true problem is the abuse itself, the focus shifts to what women did to "deserve" it, why they didn't just leave, and other equally useless victim-blaming comments.

Not only do these types of arguments avoid dealing with the source of online harassment and abuse (the abusers), they also make women responsible for bearing the additional emotional burden of being blamed for the abuse they experienced. When it comes to cybersexist harassment, women are often told that it's their labor that must be employed to deal with the abuse: not only must women read and deal with the initial comments, but they are also told they are responsible for the fallout and must either find ways to protect themselves or stop talking about it.

Women are thus forced into a reactive stance where cybersexist abuse is concerned. There are few structures in place that exist to prevent cyber-sexism from occurring and little support for the women who are targeted. When women do speak up about the abuse they receive, their experience is often trivialized, and women are blamed for making up a problem where none exists. "Commentators dismiss [online abuse] as harmless locker-room talk, characterizing perpetrators as juvenile pranksters and tar-geted individuals as overly sensitive complainers," Citron notes.[60] Women, therefore, have to take on the burden of receiving the abuse, deciding how to deal with it, seeking solutions, and engaging in self-defense—all while also facing demands to prove the abuse exists in the first place and being told that they're overreacting. Many women with significant online platforms deal with threats on a daily or near-daily basis; most women online receive at least some cybersexist harassment regularly. Each time harassment occurs, this cycle repeats itself.

The Effects of Cybersexism

The extra work that individual women must do in order to make being on the web possible and sustainable is a burden that results from the actions of cybersexist harassers, but that burden is increased by the reactions to women's stories. The excuses made for cybersexist harassers (as discussed in chapter 3), the victim-blaming, and the silence of men who don't participate in cybersexist abuse all enable its presence and its continuing effects. On top of the personal, professional, and psychological effects of cybersexism alone, dealing with the backlash can be exhausting. It's no wonder that so many women feel the need to temporarily disconnect from Internet life, even with the cost of doing so, and that so many women regard the Internet as hostile.

The prevalence of cybersexism is not wholly disheartening, however. Many of the positive things people say about the Internet happen to be true—it is a space where the rules aren't yet set in stone, and it has the potential to become a more level playing field than its current, unequal state. The same factors that enable online abuse to persist can be used to combat it, and the fluctuating, constantly changing culture of the Internet means that we don't have to accept cybersexism as an inevitable part of online life.

5 MISOGYNIST MOVEMENTS
Men's Rights Activists and Gamergate

The previous chapters have featured discussions of online misogyny from a variety of angles but focused primarily on the everyday abuse women receive solely for being women online. That type of abuse is the most common—it is the background hum of the Internet, a persistent whine in women's ears, and one to which most men are deaf. What makes news headlines, however, are the targeted movements, the hate mobs, the truly dedicated groups of harassers and misogynists who devote their online time to making women's entire lives miserable. Men's rights activists (MRAs) and Gamergate are two of the most prominent examples of this phenomenon from recent years, although Gamergate itself was merely the largest explosion of a previous series of similar attacks.

This chapter examines both movements, including the core beliefs behind them and the misogyny that underpins their activities. These movements seem extreme, and they are, but it is important to keep in mind that the sexism they rely on is different from everyday sexism only in its expression and scale. The beliefs are exaggerated and the activities engaged in are more violent and threatening, but the foundational beliefs about women and women's role in society are the same.

THE CREATION OF A HARASSMENT MOB

A critical aspect of understanding how MRAs and Gamergate came to be requires the understanding that neither group is unique or unprecedented. In size, scope, and longevity Gamergate is perhaps unusual, but harassment mobs and coordinated groups of abusers are far from uncommon in online spaces. The abuse tactics used in Gamergate were first practiced through 4chan under Operation Lollipop and others—and aimed primarily at black women—to far less fanfare and media attention than Gamergate received.[1] Hoaxes such as the Twitter hashtag #EndFathersDay began on 4chan, specifically targeted black mothers, and relied on stereotypes about black family life to aim harassment at women on Twitter, who have less support in the first place. Such abuses went almost unnoticed, except by a handful of mainly feminist websites, while the hashtag itself received some credulous mainstream coverage.

The tactics that rocked social media spaces in the form of Gamergate were practiced and refined primarily on black women. Although Gamergate began as an incident of domestic violence that spiraled into a vicious attack on marginalized voices in video game spaces and nerd culture more broadly, many of its participants were already primed for perpetrating abuse by prior abusive activity. Fake accounts are often created and reserved for the next round of harassment, whatever form it may take. Each time a hoax or harassment incident was carried out prior to and then during Gamergate, the efforts had been planned in plain sight, and the successes, failures, and response were discussed on the same forums used to launch the attacks. Due to the sexism, racism, and misogynoir that characterizes so many online spaces, these behaviors went unchecked.

Understanding the mentality that leads to the harassment mobs led by Gamergate and MRAS requires a grasp of not just what they say they're doing but also the underlying psychological reasons for their behavior, which may be unknown to the mobbers themselves. Deindividuation theory goes a long way toward explaining how harassment mobs develop and why they spiral so far out of control. According to a paper from 1998 by M. E. Kabay, deindividuation is common among anonymous online users. It involves a reduced sense of self-awareness, lowered inhibitions, and poor impulse control. In essence, deindividuated persons lose their sense of individual identity and, as a result, any idea that they have individual responsibility for their actions.[2] While anonymity is an essential

Misogynist Movements

component of online life for many, the presence of mobs that rely on the effects of deindividuation to do harm must be taken into consideration.

In her paper Kabay notes that research on anonymous groups finds that unidentified members of a crowd show a reduced inhibition to antisocial behavior, as well as "increased irritability and suggestibility. One wonders if the well-known incidence of *flaming* . . . may be traceable to the same factors that influence crowd behavior."[3] Deindividuated users are more likely to feel that their personal identity is subsumed to a group identity and that responsibility for their actions can be transferred to the group, rather than assigned to individual actors on the basis of their actions. When examining the mobbing behaviors that emerge from sites such as 4chan, 8chan, and Reddit, an overarching identity—Anonymous, Gamergate, /pol/, and the like—is seen as the responsible actor, and criticism of individual actions is rejected as nonsensical or irrelevant. The occasional figurehead seems to wield immense power over the activities of the group and can direct members' actions to a series of targets.

Further, Kabay connects what are called "autotelic experiences" to the harmful outcomes of deindividuation. Autotelic experiences involve "the loss of self-awareness that can occur in repetitive, challenging, feedback-rich activities" such as gaming, coding, or even scripted and structured patterns of harassment.[4] Autotelic activity usually involves engaging in the same action repeatedly, escalating certain aspects of it, and receiving environmental responses that encourage certain behaviors and discourage others. In the parlance of a video game an autotelic experience might be created by an in-world environment in which a person plays a character that must repeatedly fight similar but progressively more challenging enemies and in which each success or failure is rewarded with points, money or progress, or death, the last requiring the player to start over at a previous point in the game. The combination of feedback for each activity, the repetition of movements to achieve success, and the subtle increases of difficulty work to keep a player's attention on the game and can result in a feeling of timelessness or intense focus that leads to playing a game for hours without realizing it.

Online harassment mobs generate a similar repetitive experience that provides members with self-defined patterns of feedback and rewards. Harassment and abuse may be scripted or shared language patterns will emerge; the group will reward more and more flagrant abuses and encourage more invasive types of attacks (leading to things like doxxing or hacking); feedback is given in the form of in-group encouragement and other reactions. Any response to the harassment is interpreted as "feedback," whether it's encouragement from other abusers, being blocked or berated by targets, or having an account reported and deleted. When the sense of timelessness comes into play with harassment, the result is hours and hours of planning "raids" and engaging in hacking, doxxing, and abusing. The nature of Gamergate's abuse was often described as a game by its proponents, and treating it like a game enhanced the sense of timelessness and focus that characterizes autotelic experiences.

Deindividuation and autotelic experiences are a potent brew and, when experienced in tandem, are repeatedly connected to increased aggression, a willingness to commit illegal and abusive activities, and a reduction in the capacity for self-reflection. Kabay and others theorize that deindividuation may be akin to an altered state, wherein engaging in high-level self-reflection becomes impossible, aggression is more keenly felt, dehumanization of a target becomes significantly easier, and the likelihood of having one's behavior externally influenced is increased. As Kabay puts it, "These people may not be [the] permanently, irremediably damaged human beings they sometimes seem; they may be relatively normal people responding in predictable ways to the absence of stable identification and identity."[5] That is, those participating in harassment mobs are not mentally ill, as is sometimes theorized (a stigmatizing attitude that harms people who actually have mental illnesses). Instead, abusers are people who are reacting to their environment in an abnormal but contextually logical way.

The presence or addition of an authoritative figurehead, such as Gamergate's Mike Cernovich, Christina Hoff Sommers, or Milo Yiannopoulos, thus also creates predictable patterns. Deindividuated people are more open to suggestion and have less impulse control; during Gamergate a

Misogynist Movements

single mention from any of those individuals was more than enough to turn the mob's attention to a particular target for hours, days, weeks, or months. Similarly, those targeted by Paul Elam and other MRA figureheads can expect to receive waves of harassment from their followers. Everyone involved, from the figurehead to each individual harasser, is able to diffuse responsibility for the abuse among the group, claiming abuse was always committed by "someone else" and thus was not the concern of any one member, regardless of their own actions. The dehumanization of their targets makes it that much easier to engage in harassment without ever characterizing it as such.

While deindividuation theory is a necessary component of understanding how cybersexist harassment mobs form online, it is not a complete explanation for the behavior. Targets are not chosen at random by unthinking mobs. Instead, a complex set of sociocultural factors comes into play, including the demographics of both the mob and the targets, how easy it is to access the targets, and what types of support and recourse targets have in the face of abuse. It is for these reasons that mobs typically attack women of color, and particularly black women, before expanding their harassment to white women, women with a high-profile online presence, and eventually men, especially men of color. Harassment mobs are acting on the beliefs they hold—consciously or subconsciously—about their role and the role of their targets in specific cultural situations. Understanding how cybersexism and deindividuation interact is essential for understanding how hate mobs come to exist and for considering ways to circumvent or stop future mobs from forming.

MEN'S RIGHTS ACTIVISTS

Men's rights activists or MRAS are disparate groups of men who ostensibly work to support men's needs in what they often describe as a matriarchal or misandrist culture.[6] Common issues raised by MRAS include women disproportionately receiving custody in divorce, domestic violence aimed at men, high rates of male suicide, and false rape accusations. Their primary mode of activism is writing angry forum posts about "sluts" and "bitches" and something called the "cock carousel," which women apparently ride on for free until about the age of twenty-five, at which point they lose all sexual appeal.

Today's MRAS exist in a wide variety of overlapping and contradictory groups with few common goals, but most profess a shared belief that it is in fact women who hold social power and men who are oppressed. Despite the many variances within MRA thought and organization, many of them trace a loose history back to Warren Farrell, the closest thing they have to an intellectual leader. Farrell, the author of *The Myth of Male Power*, among other works, is a proponent of the idea that heterosexual men are powerless when confronted with an attractive woman (specifically, an attractive woman's attractive posterior) and that this imbalance gives women the upper hand in every aspect of society. His work often veers into the ludicrous and downright frightening; he has on more than one occasion engaged in victim-blaming rape survivors.[7]

Today MRAS can be found on a variety of websites, online forums, and, increasingly, college campuses. A Voice for Men is the largest MRA website, serving as a central hub where MRAS can gather and converse. Paul Elam, the owner and one of many writers for the site, is the most likely MRA to fill Warren Farrell's shoes as the leader for a new generation of MRAS. As he does not lay claim to academic status the way Farrell does, Elam relies on polemic and fundraising to keep his website afloat and his causes in the periphery of public consciousness. He has hosted one men's rights conference, in 2014, and had plans to host such events on an annual basis, although the 2015 event fell through. Several withering articles were published about the 2014 conference and its attendees on a variety of popular media platforms, including *Time, Vice,* and even GQ.

MRAS can be found in many forums on Reddit, the social media and news website, including men's rights–specific subreddits, as well as within the Pick-Up Artist and Red Pill communities. Pick-Up Artists are men who use and teach one another to use manipulative tactics for hitting on women, with the goal of getting them into bed. Such tactics are often indistinguishable from sexual harassment and include activities like "negging," or casually insulting women in the hopes of garnering a defensive reaction that continues the conversation. Red Pill groups, named after the red

　　　　Misogynist Movements

pill in the 1999 movie *The Matrix*, are devoted to discussing the moment members decided women have all the power in society and complaining about this injustice.

There are often deep divisions between Pick-Up Artists and Red Pill forum members—Pick-Up Artists want to attract and use women, while Red Pill proponents often want to have nothing to do with them. Failed Pick-Up Artists often move to the Red Pill camp. Men Going Their Own Way (MGTOW) are yet another subset of MRAs; these are men who say they want nothing to do with women or the institution of marriage and yet spend a great deal of their time complaining about and harassing women in online spaces. An MGTOW, without provocation or response, once harassed me on Twitter almost nonstop for twelve hours.

While MRAs claim to have lofty goals and to support men in a society that is weighted against them, the reality is very different. An MRA is far more likely to be involved in harassing and abusing women than he is to be genuinely supportive of other men or working to solve the issues MRAs claim to care about so deeply.[8] In my interactions with MRAs I have often noted that they are capable of identifying problems but incapable of figuring out the source of them or developing any actual solutions—or are merely unwilling to do so. Instead, MRAs will find any excuse to blame the issues they raise on women and, specifically, on young or feminist women.

Before moving into examining the ways MRAs dedicate their time to harassing women online, it's worthwhile to look at some of the issues they claim to care about and to explore more of the logic that underpins and informs their activities. In each of the major issues they raise MRAs begin with an existing problem and then completely misattribute the cause of the problem to women's supposedly nefarious influence in society. No amount of factual information is sufficient to cause an MRA to reevaluate the belief that women are the root of all male suffering.

For example, a prime complaint of MRAs is that mothers receive child custody more often than fathers do in cases of divorce. While true at first glance, the argument ignores a significant number of mitigating factors and fails to examine the reasons that mothers more often get custody. The stereotype that women are natural caregivers and nurturers is an old one, and it still influences situations in which decisions have to be made regarding the custody of children. The assumption that a woman's "true" role is as a mother is a core part of the reason mothers are granted custody more often, even when the father might be a better choice. Courts still regularly decide that a man's work outside the home is more important than child-rearing, with the implicit assumption that the father will be better able to provide financial support, while the mother should be more focused on the children themselves. Far from being the devious work of women to keep fathers from their children, this attitude is rooted in old-fashioned sexism.

The doctrine that led to this belief, often referred to as the "tender-years" doctrine—an assumption that mothers are the more suitable parent for children under seven—was abolished by the majority of U.S. states prior to 1990, yet sexist attitudes in assigning custody persist. However, they lack the weight that they once had, and attitudes about parenting continue to shift. What MRAs fail to acknowledge is that much of this change is due to the work of feminists. In asserting that women's work is valuable both inside the home and out and that fathers can be and should be equally good parents (and in supporting the rights of people of all genders to parent children), feminists continue to work to make sure that primary custody is given to the parent best suited in each individual case, not according to gender.

MRAs often frame their activism as "fathers' rights" activism and focus most specifically on the issue of custody. A Voice for Men places a great deal of emphasis on women as child-stealing villains, and a whole host of fringe groups, websites, and forums feature men doing little more than bitterly complaining about their ex-wives. MRAs often discuss parental alienation syndrome as a key factor in their loss of custody. "Parental alienation syndrome" was a term developed by the psychiatrist Richard Gardner; it describes a supposed disorder that causes a child to withdraw from, insult, or dislike one parent during a custody dispute. The assumption is that the child has been coached or conditioned by the other parent (often, according to Gardner and in most MRA discussions, the mother) to help guarantee victory in court.

Misogynist Movements

Despite the popularity of Gardner's coinage, the disorder itself has been soundly and frequently discredited by legal and mental health experts alike. Gardner's initial estimate was that parental alienation syndrome appeared in nearly all divorce cases—a claim he made without providing any supporting evidence. One scholar, in assessing the impact of Gardner's work on divorce cases, stated, "The overwhelming absence of careful analysis and attention to scientific rigor these professionals demonstrate, however, is deeply troubling. . . . This carelessness has permitted what is popularly termed junk science (pseudo science) to influence custody cases in ways that are likely to harm children."[9] Although all reliable research notes that parental alienation syndrome is not a diagnosed or recognized disorder, a cottage industry has sprung up around it. Websites devoted to raising awareness—and, of course, money—are a dime a dozen, and more than a few books have been written by those looking to capitalize on the fury of divorcing parents.

One of the most troubling offshoots of the concept of parental alienation syndrome is a tendency for those who believe in it to deny or discredit children's claims of parental abuse. MRAS often assert that women force their children to falsify accusations of abuse or molestation to guarantee their fathers will lose custody—any discussion of the actual rates of child abuse is unsurprisingly absent from these conversations. A Voice for Men writers regularly refer to parental alienation syndrome as though it is a legitimate disorder that has been taken into account by the medical field, and the comment sections of these articles are littered with furious anecdotes about lost custody. Stoking the rage of these men by relying on a widely discredited and unsound concept is profitable.

One such article on A Voice for Men has a plethora of comments that refer to "the woman's viper tongue," noting that "women can be quite vicious with spreading propaganda everywhere," asserting that "this act of abuse (i.e. causing parental alienation syndrome) has been a ratio of 100/1 [sic]. That is 100% the bloody alienating mother against the father."[10] One person who was banned for posting articles and comments critical of Gardner's theory received this comment from the moderator who banned them: "All-purpose bitch."[11] Aside from the sole person raising concerns about the validity of the diagnosis, all of the comments confidently assert that not only is parental alienation syndrome real but that it is a tool primarily or even solely used by women.

In one post on divorce on A Voice for Men, Elam first described himself as a pacifist and then went on to describe his dream for divorce court: "The day I see one of these absolutely incredulous excuses for a judge dragged out of his courtroom into the street, beaten mercilessly, doused with gasoline and set afire by a father who just won't take another moment of injustice, I will be the first to put on the pages of this website that what happened was a minor tragedy that pales by far in comparison to the systematic brutality and thuggery inflicted daily on American fathers by those courts and their police henchmen."[12] The calmer, more academic-seeming articles about parental alienation syndrome on A Voice for Men provide at best a smokescreen for this violence and anger, which lurks just below the surface. Those attitudes don't stay confined to the website, either; A Voice for Men adherents can be found using similar arguments to harass women in all corners of the Internet.

Beyond their violent fantasies, MRAs miss the mark about divorce in yet another significant way. What they repeatedly fail to mention is that the number of fathers who win custody changes dramatically for those men who actively pursue custody of their children. A full 50 percent of fathers who seek custody in a divorce case receive it.[13] Since men who seek custody of their children have the same odds women have of receiving it, it's hard to fathom what MRAs' actual issue with the courts truly is and where the alleged "thuggery" Elam mentions comes from, other than being a convenient way to accuse women of stealing an ex-husband's children and repeatedly painting women as abusive vipers. Men who are less likely to receive custody are those who simply don't make any effort to get it, but the odds of hearing an MRA acknowledge that are slim to none.

The other issues so frequently raised by MRAs follow a similar pattern: the identification of a problem, followed by deliberately obscuring its true causes, presenting skewed information or outright dishonesty, and ignoring the complex web of factors that play into the reality of the situation.

Misogynist Movements

Nowhere is this pattern more obvious than in the insistent focus MRAS place on the specter of false rape accusations.

Men who are falsely accused of rape, according to MRAS, are at risk of having their lives ruined, while women can freely accuse anyone they like without facing any serious consequences for doing so, despite the illegality of filing a false report of any kind. While the lives and careers of known rapists such as Jimmy Page, Mike Tyson, Roman Polanski, and many, many others have been at best minimally affected, MRAS cling to the idea that being falsely accused of rape is a scarlet letter that will haunt a man for the remainder of his life. Women, according to MRAS, can rely on spitefully accusing a man of rape to ruin him and often do.

In reality the rate at which rape is reported is already dramatically lower than the number of rapes that occur—nearly 70 percent of sexual assaults go unreported, and 98 percent of all accused rapists never spend even one day in jail.[14] In the face of those numbers false reports are barely a blip on the radar. Despite that, MRAS are given to grossly exaggerating the number of false rape accusations that are made, insisting that close to half or even the majority of reports are false. To support this assertion they often cite a decades-old study from an unnamed small town in which more than 40 percent of reports were determined by the police to be false; in contrast, the number used by the FBI is roughly 8 percent—a figure that is in line with false reports for all other crimes.[15]

What is misleading about the statistics favored by MRAS is that the criteria for establishing that a report was "false" includes everything from a woman withdrawing the report due to trauma, to other or lesser charges being filed, to the opinion of the police officer taking the report in the first place. In mid-2015 a woman who was assaulted in a bar's restroom reported that the police interviewing her in the hospital said, "Maybe you're a party girl. You know regrettable sex is not the same as rape."[16] Despite the fact that she had been hospitalized and was visibly injured, the police continued to insist that her report was not convincing. Police officers who don't believe that a woman's initial report is true are unlikely to pursue it, leading to a report being marked as false based on nothing more than their initial assessment.

The assessment made by police is often skewed by poor training on how to respond to and understand the initial reaction to a trauma such as sexual assault; many people who have been assaulted react in ways that seem strange, such as displaying no emotion at all or even laughing.[17] Many people are also unable to recall details of the attack, or they may only begin remembering details later. These factors can lead police to believe the person is submitting a false report, despite the underlying trauma responsible for such behaviors.

One study conducted in Britain by the Crown Prosecution Service (CPS) found that during a seventeen-month test period in which 5,651 reports of rape were prosecuted, only 35 of those cases were the result of someone making a false allegation.[18] And yet CPS also discovered that many people believed the rate of false accusations was much higher than it was, leading to a tendency to discount reports. Of the 159 total claims that were believed to be false, the majority still contained evidence that a crime of some kind had been committed or resulted in lesser charges being filed as part of a plea bargain. Again, however, even if charges were filed for another crime, the initial report of rape would be listed as false.

What all of these details tell us is not that false rape accusations never happen but that what gets counted as "false" is far more complicated than MRAs would like to imagine. It's much easier to drum up anger and fear about false accusations without examining the many reasons that a report can be discounted and the ways in which true reports get misclassified. Instead, we hear again and again that women are malicious liars who seek to ruin men's lives, without any evidence that such a false report actually does ruin said lives. As with all of the issues they raise, MRAs acquire only a surface-level understanding of the concept and proceed to concoct a variety of reasons that the problem is, somehow, women's fault. From there they continue to turn that anger on women in public and often dangerous ways.

A Voice for Men repeatedly posts and publishes inflammatory and hateful screeds about women. For years the website hosted the text of Thomas James Ball, a man who set himself on fire outside a courthouse and encouraged other men to bomb courthouses and police stations in a

Misogynist Movements

revolt against the supposed war on men. Paul Elam himself wrote a piece, later described as satirical, encouraging people to make October "Bash a Violent Bitch Month." In the piece he gleefully advises beating a woman and forcing her to clean up the resulting "mess" as self-defense against a world that he believes unfairly punishes men for domestic violence.[19] In an article in which he described his refusal to take down a website that he and others would use to stalk and harass women, Elam wrote to a feminist that "the idea of fucking your shit up gives me an erection."[20]

In another incident so convoluted as to almost defy belief, A Voice for Men placed a bounty on a photograph of a professor at Kennesaw State University, where the MRA site's main campus activist, Sage Gerard, had enrolled. In this incident a complaint was made about Gerard after he posted a video of himself placing stickers in various campus locations, including women's restrooms, which he entered by posing as a member of custodial staff. At one point in the video he audibly fantasizes about putting one of the stickers over a feminist's mouth to shut her up.[21] The professor who filed the complaint referenced this video, as well as Gerard's cartoons, which include drawings of guns pointed at feminist symbols, stating that these factors contributed to a hostile work environment. The professor also said she feared retribution from Gerard or other MRAs. The complaint, along with the professor's name, was then passed along to Gerard.

Kennesaw State University took no action against Gerard, noting that his speech was protected, and merely requested that he stay out of women's restrooms and avoid the professor's department to prevent an escalation, which would in fact constitute a hostile work environment. In response, Elam and Gerard took to the platform of A Voice for Men to retaliate against the professor. Elam offered $100 for a clear picture of the professor in question and issued a series of threats, starting with a demand that she apologize to Gerard or face an escalation of harassment with the goal of ruining her career. He went on to encourage his readers to contact her via her academic email address, warning her that they would notice if her contact information was deleted.

The escalation of the harassment continued on through a series of five articles collectively titled "Interdisciplinary Shaming Dept." on A

Voice for Men. The fifth article, posted in early 2015, included a photo of the chairperson of the Interdisciplinary Department at Kennesaw State University—not the original target—and a similar group of threats aimed at her career should the group's demands not be met.[22] The requested photo of the original professor who made the complaint was, apparently, never delivered, but Elam's language reflected someone who had become increasingly incensed throughout the writing of the series of articles.

It is important to remember that the entire harassment campaign was in response to Gerard being found innocent of wrongdoing but being asked to leave the professor and her department alone. In response, MRAS encouraged one another to repeatedly contact the professor and other members of her department and threaten to ruin their careers if the women they were targeting did not capitulate. In other words, they did exactly what the professor had initially said she was worried about them doing.

David Futrelle, owner of the blog *We Hunted the Mammoth*, has dedicated his online presence to tracking the activities of MRAS and presenting a compelling and thorough opposition to them. In a post about the harassment of Kennesaw State University professors he included a list of other harassment campaigns mounted by A Voice for Men. The list includes, but is certainly not limited to, starting a website called Register-Her in order to track, dox, and harass feminists; launching harassment campaigns against individual campus feminists and feminist groups; harassing and libeling the feminist activist and writer Jessica Valenti (in fact, A Voice for Men's social media director, Janet Bloomfield, has had multiple Twitter accounts permanently suspended for her unceasing abuse of Valenti); coordinating with Gamergate to attend and disrupt Calgary Expo, a comic and entertainment convention, in 2015; making a number of false accusations of threats and rape; and much more.[23]

In another post Futrelle offers a succinct list of the ways in which contributors to A Voice for Men specifically, but MRAS generally, target women in online spaces. These methods include threatening or attempting to damage women's professional careers, offering money for their targets' personal information, creating and inciting harassment mobs on social media, participating in such harassment, engaging in DARVO—deny, attack,

Misogynist Movements

reverse victim and offender—to paint themselves as the target, blackmail, doxxing, and more.[24] All of these methods play out well in online spaces because it's so easy to engage in online abuse. Harassment is made simple by the ease of creating new accounts on most websites, and MRAS can rely on the reality that their falsehoods about women will stay visible for long periods of time; women who are targeted often spend years dealing with the fallout.

And of course such fallout is precisely the point. Jack Barnes, a frequent contributor to A Voice for Men and cohost of an affiliated radio show, once tweeted that the MRAS' harassment "will continue and accelerate. We're not going to stop until no one will openly admit to being feminist"—a far cry from the supposed human rights activism A Voice for Men and other MRAS claim is their primary goal.[25] This apparent contradiction, however, is just part and parcel of MRA behavior: their goal is, in fact, to harass women into silence, to restore and maintain open misogyny as a positive trait, and to reinforce gender roles that appear to have been ripped from an imaginary version of the 1950s. Men's human rights, under MRA descriptions, require the subjugation of women.

A Voice for Men is far from the only hub of such harassment and abuse, however. Another MRA website, spearheaded by a man named Peter Andrew Nolan, doxxed a sophomore named Rachel Cassidy who was attending Ohio University, accusing her of falsely accusing a man of rape—except the woman he doxxed was not the woman who had submitted the report.[26] Nolan's website listed the young woman's name, address, social media accounts, and the name of her sorority; she was so thoroughly deluged with threats and harassment that she deleted all of her social media accounts and told reporters she was afraid to leave her home.[27]

Nolan's website, Crimes against Fathers, features lists of other women who have been doxxed by stalkers and exes. Women who wish to have their information removed from the website are charged a fee. As noted in another chapter, a similar website hosting nude images of women shared without their consent saw its owner hit with a lengthy jail sentence for extortion; no such action has yet been taken against Nolan, but the site is less and less active as time goes on.

Return of Kings is a combination MRA and Pick-Up Artist haven. Run by Pick-Up Artist and self-professed rapist Roosh Valizadeh, the site is a haven for overt and toxic forms of misogyny.[28] Some sample articles on the website include such gems as "Protein World Enrages Feminists Who Hate Female Beauty," "Why I Am Proud to Be Called a Misogynist," "How to Game a Hot French Girl," and "Why Most Women Didn't Want the Right to Vote." Writers for the site have composed pieces on the supposed inability of women to write, think, remain faithful in a monogamous relationship, or successfully achieve anything of note without having it handed to them by men; they have released screeds on why women are to blame for the mass murders committed by angry young men (because women won't have sex with them). Article after article is devoted to criticizing women's appearance, including offering "warning signs" to men who might be foolish enough to think there are more important things than what a woman looks like.

One Return of Kings contributor, Blair Naso, who got drunk at a White Power conference (the 2015 American Renaissance event), harassed a group of women at a nearby bar, and was summarily ejected from it, subsequently wrote a long post about quitting the "Manosphere" (MRAs often refer to their various websites and forums in this way).[29] With Naso at that event was Matt Forney, another Return of Kings contributor, who also acts as the editor for Reaxxion, Valizadeh's contribution to the Gamergate debacle. The overlap between MRAs and active participants in Gamergate is extensive.

Forney has written such charming things as "girls with tattoos and/ or piercings . . . are slags who fall in and out of guys' beds at moment's notice. . . . A girl who willfully disfigures herself [by getting a tattoo, piercing, or short haircut] . . . will generally be a moody, unlikable cunt."[30] Such assessments are not uncommon within MRA circles, and any woman with short or dyed hair or visible tattoos or piercings in her online profile picture can expect to have it used against her by MRAs. In another unsurprising bit of overlap between MRAs and Gamergate, adherents of Gamergate also regard any nontraditional self-expression by women as a fatal flaw.

Return of Kings provides a safe space for these ideas, emboldening its readers and writers to go out into other online spaces and repeat them or to harass women who diverge from the MRAs' ideal woman. As the ideal woman for an MRA would have to be an eternally youthful white woman with absolutely no mind of her own, any woman online can expect to come under fire if she happens to be in the wrong place at the wrong time.

In an incident in which MRA beliefs extended into physical space, a woman writing for *xoJane* recounted the story of going on a date with someone she discovered was an MRA. He then assaulted her. The man had asked for her number while she was at work, and although she was taken aback at how forward he was, the two agreed to go on a date: "Many of the texts focused on how excited he was for our date, as well as comments about my body. He would punctuate mildly explicit comments by stating how honest he was. Honesty, he would tell me, was his favorite quality."[31] During the date the man described himself as a member of the Red Pill community; when he went to the restroom, the woman looked it up online and discovered the forums, subreddits, and blogs devoted to Red Pill discussions.

At that point she chose to end the date. As she walked away, the man grabbed her arm hard enough to leave nail marks and attempted to force his hand under her shirt. It was only after she punched him that she was able to get into her car and escape; at that point she started receiving text messages: "It was him, asking why I was playing hard to get. I ignored it as I did the following texts where he called me a bitch, a slut and a tease."[32] While she was able to get away from him and share her story, the comments section of the article is filled with arguments about whether what she experienced was "really" an assault at all, with commenters blaming her for his behavior and insisting that feminism was responsible for her experience. Self-identified MRAs flooded the comment section with harassment, abuse, and even graphic pornography.

In addition to causing dates to go seriously awry, MRA rhetoric led to a female student at Queen's University being attacked outside her home. She had been speaking publicly in defense of women's rights and protesting an MRA event that was being held on campus. The student noted that she had received "multiple threatening emails related to her involvement" in the protests, and a few days later she was assaulted. Her attacker knew her name and punched her multiple times in the face, resulting in significant bruising and a chipped tooth.[33]

As with the *xoJane* article, the article reporting the attack on the Queen's University student received numerous comments (on a now-closed platform) calling feminism a "bigoted, reverse-sexist, female supremacist hate movement," accusing the victim of lying about her assault (despite the photo of the woman that she took in the aftermath of the event), doxxing the victim, and more. One of the people leaving such comments used the name Fidelbogen, the username of a longtime MRA who dedicates his online presence to harassing feminists. In one post on his own blog he insisted that "anybody who claims to care about men, but doesn't savage feminism pretty harshly on a regular basis, is either a damned liar or a lazy, muddled fool with his head up his ass."[34] MRAs might claim to care about men or human rights, but their actual activities will always betray their true motives; Fidelbogen is simply more honest than most.

What MRAs have in rage, harassment, and violence against women, they lack in actual activism. MRAs regularly complain about the lack of support for male victims of domestic violence and the scarcity of shelters for men in that situation, yet A Voice for Men—which regularly conducts fundraisers to keep itself running and Elam's pockets lined—has done nothing substantial to create or support such a shelter.

In fact, a quick search for the term "shelter" on the site returns fewer than 800 results (many of which are complaints and very few of which contain any actual information on how men can find, create, or support shelters for other men). In comparison, a search for the term "bitch" or "bitches" returns more than 3,000 results. Search for "cunt" or "cunting" (a favorite neologism of the site's writers) and you'll get 1,600 results, while "whore" and "slut" return nearly 1,500 and 1,200 results, respectively. Such results do not give A Voice for Men's claim to be engaged in human rights activism a lot of weight.

In 2012 the Southern Poverty Law Center (SPLC), an organization dedicated to tracking, explaining, and combating hatred and bigotry, released an in-depth report on the misogyny and violence of the men's rights movement.[35] A Voice for Men receives a prominent mention as a leader of the violence and abuse promoted by MRAS. The SPLC makes strong connections between the online diatribes of MRAS and the offline violence committed by those who connect themselves with the ideology espoused on sites like Elam's. The hatred that underpins MRA writing and harassment campaigns is visible to everyone but those engaged in it, who continue to portray themselves as crusaders for a righteous cause—not unlike the proponents of Gamergate.

GAMERGATE

In August 2014 the Internet blew up—or so it seemed to many people. A geyser of hatred that had been building mostly below the surface of various online communities finally broke through, and the explosion has yet to come to an end. While the initial earthquake of abuse has passed, its aftershocks are likely to continue for years. Gamergate is one of the most chilling and obvious examples of how everyday misogyny can spiral into something much uglier in online spaces.

It all started with what has become known as the "Zoe post," a continuation of domestic violence that became the springboard abusers used to enact violence on as many marginalized people as possible. Written over a period of weeks about video game developer Zoe Quinn by Eron Gjoni, Quinn's former boyfriend, it is an inflammatory piece: more than nine thousand words long and filled with a mixture of hyperbolic accusations, personal information, and outright lies. It is exactly the kind of narrative angry and reactionary misogynists enjoy latching onto when looking for an excuse to harass and abuse a woman. Gjoni crafted the post to elicit precisely that reaction. He posted the screed in the comments sections of various game-related websites, most of which deleted it. Then, he created a Wordpress site solely for the post, and it ended up on 4chan.

4chan, and more particularly 4chan's /b/ and /pol/ boards, has long been a repository for the worst of the worst examples of online harassment. Despite being a source of many popular memes that spread across the Internet and even make it offline, 4chan and /b/ have been home to Anonymous as well—that amorphous group of unknowns who might as easily hack a corrupt government website as harass a teen past the point of endurance "for the lulz." The forums on the site, which rely on semianonymous posting, are a haven for gore threads, misogyny, racism and white supremacy, homophobia, transphobia, violent fantasies, and those who refuse to acknowledge that engaging with and promoting such content can have serious consequences.

The Zoe post was right at home on 4chan, and the rage that it sparked spilled over into other areas of the Internet like an uncontrollable wildfire. In his writing Gjoni asserts that Quinn had multiple affairs during their brief relationship, referring to her as "burgers and fries," after the popular burger chain Five Guys Burgers and Fries. In the early days of Gamergate the hate mob that was forming used the hashtag #burgersandfries. Harassment of Quinn began immediately. Quinn, who developed the award-winning video game *Depression Quest*, has been a target for sexism and harassment in video game circles. Her game eschews popular video game staples and places a greater emphasis on empathy and experience over graphics and gameplay; this fact alone was enough to make her a target for those who can only understand the hobby of gaming through mechanics and frame rates. Her success has been a thorn in the side of gamers who believe their hobby should have a "no girls allowed" sign hung at every possible entrance.

But when Gjoni's post went live, the low-level whispers of harassment became a roar that drowned out everything else. In an article about the history of the event Quinn recalls the first night: "[Her] phone began buzzing uncontrollably. Angry emails from strangers flooded her inbox, calling her a 'slut' and linking to a blog she'd never seen before. . . . Within minutes, a friend warned Quinn that someone had altered her biography on Wikipedia. It now read, 'Died: soon.' . . . The next day, the real horror began."[36] Gjoni's post was out in the world, and the face of Internet harassment was about to change.

Gamergate didn't get its name immediately following the release of Gjoni's first overture in the harassment. Adam Baldwin, in fact, gave Gamergate the name it retains to this day. Best known for his roles in *Full Metal Jacket* and as Jayne in the popular but short-lived television show *Firefly*, Baldwin used his Twitter account to promote a variety of right-wing viewpoints and to argue furiously with anyone he sees as an opponent. He still reminds people of Jayne, just without any of the occasional charm or heart his character could muster. On Twitter Baldwin linked to a YouTube video about the Zoe post, one that repeated the accusations Gjoni made, and his tweet included the hashtag #Gamergate. That became the rallying cry, and it is one that continues to be used.

Anyone who is familiar with Gamergate has become familiar with what is simultaneously a joke, a tired refrain, and an acknowledgment of the lies on which the mob was built: "Actually, it's about ethics in games journalism." From its initial burst of misogynist harassment, forums immediately began looking for ways to spin the abuse and hide it beneath a veneer of legitimacy. The burgeoning mob seized on an accusation of Gjoni's that seemed to imply Quinn had slept with a video game reviewer when he was reviewing *Depression Quest*. Doing so, they felt, was an obvious breach of journalistic ethics: Quinn was sleeping with people for good reviews!

This story is not at all an uncommon one in tech circles, including gaming. The popular notion is that women who get ahead must be engaging in something underhanded to do so, because tech is a white man's world (even as they will then describe it as a meritocracy of the best kind). Any successful woman can expect to be accused of sleeping her way to the top. It also provided further excuses to deny *Depression Quest* any legitimacy as a game, satisfying the long-held grudge within the circles where Gjoni's words had found a home. The Zoe post continued to fuel the most retrograde and sexist fears men in gaming hold about women.

Most notable, however, is the fact that the story they felt they had—that Zoe Quinn had slept with a reviewer to get more attention for her work—just isn't true. While Quinn and the games journalist, Nathan Grayson, did have a relationship at one point, he never actually reviewed *Depression Quest*, and the brief paragraph he did write about it was published before the two were more than professional acquaintances. This information, however, is irrelevant to Gamergaters (who are often referred to as "gaters" or "gators"): they have their narrative, and the narrative is all that matters. Even today this lie is circulated despite all available facts to the contrary, including a statement from the editor-in-chief of the site where Grayson's work was published. As conspiracy theorists do, Gamergate's adherents see opposing facts as indications of collusion and scheming, rather than evidence that they might be wrong.

For the next several months the harassment was unceasing. It targeted not just Quinn but anyone who so much as hinted that Gamergate might be more about finding excuses to abuse women than about ethics. Aside from women, Gamergate's other major targets are men of color who are critical of the racism they experience and the sexism and other issues they see in gaming spaces. The harassment escalated from calling women sluts and whores to sending rape and death threats, doxxing, SWAT calls, and stalking, both online and off. Thousands of new Twitter accounts were created for the express purpose of engaging in this abuse, with their users swarming to attack each new target, and more were built to take their place after each new account was suspended. As Gamergate continued to grow, the abusers sought excuses to justify their behavior and women scrambled to find ways to cope.

"Actually, it's about ethics in games journalism" became the immediate and fervent reply to anyone discussing Gamergate's harassment of Quinn. As she fled her home in the face of horrifically detailed death and rape threats that included her address and other personal information, those watching in shock were repeatedly told that Gamergate did not condone harassment. A Gamergater on Twitter might politely assert the "actually" line in one set of conversations, while simultaneously saying in another set that Quinn or another target was a slut who should kill herself. This campaign continued through the identification of new targets and the broadening of the harassment from Quinn to anyone critical of Gamergate. The split between even-keeled if clearly scripted conversations and frothing, misogynistic hatred was apparent to everyone but those engaging in it, who would invariably pretend to be affronted when such discrepancies were pointed out.

Exaggerated politeness often signaled an oncoming mob. One person would include the Gamergate hashtag, and more and more of them would appear to insist that, actually, they were concerned about ethics in games journalism and that a dozen or fifty or a hundred such messengers arriving in your Twitter notifications could not possibly constitute a harassment mob, because look how polite they were being. This form of mobbing eventually got its own name: sea lioning.

The webcomic *Wondermark* features a black-and-white image of a man and a woman conversing, with the woman saying, "I don't mind most marine mammals. But sea lions? I could do without sea lions," and, immediately, one appears behind the pair. "Pardon me, I couldn't help but overhear . . . ," he begins, and he never lets up. The remainder of the panels feature the invariably polite sea lion invading every part of the woman's life in an attempt to force her to discuss her dislike of sea lions.[37] The comic strip so perfectly captured the behavior that this mode of harassment will now always have a name.

In addition to the outright falsehood that Gamergate is concerned about ethics in games journalism, a few other things about Gamergate's attitude toward journalism itself are worth noting. Gamergate has, at best, an entry-level grasp of what journalistic ethics encompass; when asked what ethical standards they would like to see, adherents are more likely to post a link to the Society of Professional Journalists code of ethics page than they are to offer their own argument, cogent or otherwise. What Gamergate has never noted, however, is that games journalism is enthusiast press—it is not held to the same standards of reporting that the AP, the *New York Times*, and other traditional media must adhere to. Games journalism is not required or even expected to be objective— another favorite request of Gamergate's—and game reviews, specifically, are subjective by their very nature.

Gamergate's ignorance about actual standards of ethical journalism and how or even if such standards should be applied to the enthusiast websites and organizations they favor would have been laughable, if the expression of their outrage had not taken the form of attempting to destroy the lives of women they disliked. And, further, one might wonder why the people so often mentioned by Gamergate as the worst ethics violators were so often women with a small presence within the games industry, rather than AAA game companies, the source of many actual ethical issues, such as companies purchasing reviews and providing incentives to websites or even the writers themselves.

Gamergate's true enemy is anyone the adherents describe as a "social justice warrior" (sɪw). Lofty claims about journalistic ethics aside, the true abuses they delivered were reserved primarily for feminists, especially women. An "sɪw" is anyone who critically analyzes society, media, or pop culture—particularly video games—and most especially anyone from a marginalized group engaged in that type of critical analysis. The merest acknowledgment that video game culture and video games themselves have focused primarily on the thoughts and feelings of cisgender straight white men and that perhaps diversifying protagonists and storytelling would benefit the industry and its many members who are not cisgender straight white men is enough to earn the label sɪw and therefore the hatred of Gamergate adherents.

To the Gamergate crowd the true issue has always been maintaining the status quo: a status quo in which appealing to cisgender straight white men should be the primary goal of anything related to video games. The push for gaming to become more inclusive of women gamers, disabled gamers, gamers of color, LGBT gamers, and more is perceived not as an attempt to help the industry grow but a way to oppress the "true" gamers and destroy their identity. Quinn, with her tattoos and dyed hair (both of which Gamergaters have a deeply misogynistic aversion to on any woman), her growing presence and acclaim in the industry, and *Depression Quest*, a game that challenges the standard notion of what a game should be, made an ideal first target.

A movement that was not about misogyny would have found a more realistic target than Zoe Quinn and the idea of sɪws, and yet the harassment just continued to ramp up. Gjoni spent months coaching Gamergate from behind the scenes—posting on forums, setting up a Twitter account, and feeding the harassers personal and private information they could use to destroy Quinn's life from the inside out. While Gjoni was eventually placed under a restraining order that prevented him from discussing Quinn publicly, much of the damage had already been done.

Misogynist Movements

While everyone seemed to be at risk of sea lioning and more violent forms of abuse, including doxxing and threats, Gamergate adherents did not shy away from selecting larger targets to use as sjw figureheads and scapegoats for their misogyny. A wave of harassment might come and go for a person on the periphery of the events, but for many women it is constant and unceasing. Brianna Wu, like Quinn, is a game developer. She became an additional and deeply hated target. In May 2015 she wrote an article on *The Mary Sue*, an online geek-focused news and entertainment source, about the ongoing harassment and whether or not the State of Ohio would take action against someone who had sent her a threat.

"I'm coming to your fucking house right now," says a man's eerily monotone voice on the recording Wu made of one of the threats she received. "I will slit your throat, you stupid little fucking whore. I'm coming, and you'd better be fucking ready for me."[38] In the article Wu describes her experience dealing with Gamergate: the threat quoted here is one of more than one hundred she received. She knows its origin is Columbus, Ohio. She knows it is legally actionable—Wu has an employee at her company whose sole job is researching and cataloging such threats, and she provided information to the FBI in August 2014, when it all began.

Wu's article makes a simple request: for law enforcement, which has been largely absent from responding to Gamergate except when falling for the latest swatting attempt, to do its job and discover who is sending her these threats. An update to the article revealed that Wu had spoken with prosecuting attorney Ron O'Brien and was hopeful that there would be movement on identifying the perpetrator. Remember that for many women, involving the police in their experience of receiving online threats, Gamergate-related or otherwise, is not an option. While moving through legal channels may be an appropriate response to certain forms of online abuse, women often discuss not being believed or assisted when reporting harassment and threats; additionally, many women have other, valid reasons for not wanting a police presence in their lives.

Another favorite Gamergate target, to no one's surprise, is Anita Sarkeesian. Creator of the *Feminist Frequency* series and the Kickstarter that produced *Tropes vs. Women in Video Games*, a YouTube series about feminist analysis of sexist elements common to video games, Sarkeesian's continued presence was a natural outlet for Gamergate's ire. Many of the same arguments used against her initial series continue to be used, including, bizarrely, that she is a fraud, despite having delivered on her Kickstarter and then some. This argument is offered amid the misogynist, racist, and antisemitic arguments that have been continuously leveled at her for years, including showing her face redrawn to look like a famous piece of Nazi propaganda.

At the height of Gamergate, in October 2014, Sarkeesian was forced to cancel a speaking engagement at Utah State University after the university received a threat that said, if she spoke, there would be "the deadliest school shooting in American history." The threat included a list of the various weapons—including a semiautomatic rifle and pipe bombs—the person claimed to have.[39] When the school refused to put any additional security in place or prohibit weaponry from being brought to the lecture, Sarkeesian felt she had no option but to cancel her appearance.

Gamergate supporters continue to send threats, harassment, and abuse to Quinn, Wu, Sarkeesian, and all of the people who voice their support for Gamergate's targets or their opposition to Gamergate's behavior, including academics attempting to study Gamergate or any form of online harassment. Even when those sending the threats identified themselves as adherents of Gamergate, people accused Sarkeesian, Wu, Quinn, and others of falsifying the threats themselves to gain attention. A favorite line of Gamergate's is that such women are "professional victims," who concoct elaborate schemes to create the appearance of harassment, up to and including fleeing their own homes, in order to garner news attention and, somehow, money.

"I am a professional developer," Wu said in one article, responding to these accusations. "The quickest way I could think of to end my career and destroy my credibility would be making something like this up and getting arrested for filing a false police report."[40] Nevertheless, Gamergate continues to assert that all harassment and death threats issued on the Gamergate hashtag and by Gamergate adherents are the work of the targets themselves or third-party individuals attempting to make Gamergate look worse than it managed to on its own.

Gamergate took multiple steps to create a smokescreen between its own activities and the impact on the lives of women it targeted. In a laughably transparent and failed attempt to act like their movement was not based entirely on harassing selected women, Gamergate forums began referring to their targets as "Literally Who" (as in, "literally who are you talking about?"). The references to LW1, LW2, and LW3 were consistently and obviously coded to denote which woman was being discussed. Gamergate apparently failed to realize that not using a woman's name to coordinate methods of harassing her is still harassment.

However, Gamergate supporters would rush to assure their detractors that they don't hate women. Why, their very mascot is a woman! How could they possibly be misogynists, they seem to ask, when their entire movement is represented by Vivian James, a cartoon character they created to espouse their viewpoints for them and whose appearance is partially based on a rape joke?[41] Where's the misogyny in that, apart from everywhere?

Vivian James is a ubiquitous presence within Gamergate: she appears in avatars, website headers, in the memes and cartoons sent in lieu of actual arguments, and, not surprisingly, in pornographic renderings. What good is an utterly malleable imaginary ideal girlfriend otherwise? Vivian James is the kind of woman Gamergate would accept into its ranks, should she exist: she is "not like other girls." The basic Vivian James template portrays her as red-haired, freckled, and green-eyed and wearing a green-and-purple hoodie and jeans. Her serious expression is often paired with Gamergate talking points about just playing the games, not stereotyping gamers, fighting corruption in games journalism, and women not being the "shields" of those criticizing misogyny in games and gaming. The irony of a group of men manufacturing a spokeswoman to make such arguments on their behalf was, apparently, lost on Gamergate.

While women do exist within Gamergate, few of them could live up to the standard set by Vivian James. Internecine fighting, transphobia, and misogyny drove many women out of Gamergate as soon as they questioned the methods, arguments, or goals of the group. Those who remained are those who conform most closely to Gamergate's ideal behaviors—a tactic discussed earlier in this book as a method women use to cope with hostile online environments. Many of the women who successfully gained a foothold in Gamergate were those who sexually harassed other women and participated in doxxing, sending threats, and other forms of abuse.

Gamergate's absolute favorite woman is unquestionably the antifeminist's feminist: Christina Hoff Sommers. In a move that reveals even more of the underlying beliefs about women within Gamergate, she became colloquially referred to by its members as "Based Mom."[42] Sommers is a resident fellow at the American Enterprise Institute, a right-wing, pro-business think tank. Her version of feminism rejects what she calls "gender feminism," or any type of feminism that acknowledges, points out, or counters sexism in everyday cultural or social environments.

This rejection made her an ideal mother figure for Gamergate: she offered them a soothing lullaby that convinced them they did not have to wonder if misogyny is, perhaps, present in many video games or in video gaming as a hobby, because, according to her, the only people who see it are those who are trying to portray themselves as victims. For weeks Gamergaters who had decried feminism as antithetical to logic, reason, and discourse suddenly became experts in Sommers's version of it and would flood their targets' Twitter mentions and comments sections with links to her videos and books.

Sommers's role as Based Mom resulted in some truly revealing commentary from committed Gamergaters, as they inundated her with tweets asking her to cook them dinner, read them bedtime stories, and otherwise perform the menial support roles they expect of a mother. Somehow this behavior was never seen as an indication of how the mob might treat a woman who refused to meet their expectations. Instead, Sommers saw an opportunity to use Gamergaters' unquestioning support of anyone who agreed with them and has produced a number of videos in defense of Gamergate, claiming that it is unfairly maligned.

Sommers is far from the only person to see Gamergate as an ideal outlet for gaining a personal online army. Anyone with a large enough platform who posted in support of Gamergate, regardless of any earlier

Misogynist Movements

comments they had made about gamers, was welcomed into the fold without question. Gamergate became their biggest supporters, their attack squad, and their bullhorn.

For example, Milo Yiannopoulos (who goes by the handle @Nero on Twitter) is a well-known right-wing columnist. He currently writes for *Breitbart* and has been embroiled in numerous controversies. He was once sued for failing to pay contributors to an online magazine he had cofounded, and in retaliation he threatened to release compromising information about and photographs of one of the contributors when that writer asked to be paid for contributing work.[43] His dubious past in the journalistic field might seem to make him an odd choice for a Gamergate hero, which purportedly cares about ethics in journalism, but Yiannopoulos is a Gamergate hero for his strong stance against the sjws.

While Gamergate raged against Leigh Alexander for writing an article that supposedly said gamers were dead (in fact, it said "gamers are over," in the sense that the gaming industry must, to survive, move beyond appealing solely to entitled squabbling white men who form online hate mobs at any sign of change—so you can see where Gamergate got confused), Yiannopoulos was, apparently, utterly forgiven for some of his own comments about gamers and gamer culture.[44] "Few things," he once wrote on Twitter, "are more embarrassing than grown men getting over-excited about video games"—a ringing endorsement for Gamergate, which is almost entirely composed of grown men and their heightened emotions vis-à-vis video games.[45]

Alexander has written passionately about and in support of video games for years and now writes for Offworld, a video game–focused website hosted by BoingBoing. Her critique of the toxicity of gamer culture, reflected perfectly by Gamergate's response to it, appears to be a worse crime than referring to gamers as "pungent beta male bollock-scratchers," as Yiannopoulos has.[46] The difference between them, of course, is that Alexander supports diversity and empathy and Yiannopoulos does not. Such double standards are a core feature of Gamergate activities. While they desperately searched for ancient forum posts and conservative viewpoints previously held by those who criticized Gamergate (and, in some cases, outright fabricated them), no malignant previous comment about gamers or gamer culture was enough to dislodge people like Yiannopoulos, as long as they remained supportive.

Yiannopoulos has long mocked gamers, but, like Gamergate, he is far more interested in harassing feminists than in practicing journalism. The sudden change in attitude was not seen as a cynical ploy for the unwavering attention of a highly gullible group of conspiracy theorists but a genuine shift worthy of respect and admiration. His first article on the Gamergate controversy was titled "Feminist Bullies Tearing the Video Game Industry Apart." From start to finish it echoed Gamergate's narrative of sjws "lying, bullying and manipulating their way around the internet for profit and attention," focusing particular attention on Quinn and Sarkeesian, what he refers to as "death threat hysteria," and positioning Gamergate adherents as the unsung heroes of the situation.[47] Yiannopoulos continued writing in a similar vein during the peak Gamergate period, and his unwavering support has ensured an audience.

The same pattern that started with Yiannopoulos held true with the "Based Lawyer" of Gamergate: Mike Cernovich. While Cernovich in the early days of Gamergate tweeted that he "had never heard of 'gaming media' until recently" and wished men would "put down the fucking video games," he quickly recognized that Gamergate was not about games journalism at all.[48] In the fervent desire to maintain a conservative environment dominated by straight white men, Cernovich did not see just an audience—he saw a market. From August to October Cernovich went from scoffing at gamers and games journalism to being a figurehead within Gamergate, milking it for all it was worth.

Cernovich is a First Amendment lawyer based in California. He is also a self-styled juicing proponent and author of an as-yet-unreleased book called *Gorilla Mindset*, which purports to be self-help for men. Cernovich's work has the flavor of a Pick-Up Artist salesman's tactics—lots of pithy catchphrases about masculinity, gaming women, and "a man's instinct," without much reference to supporting scientific evidence or even success stories.[49]

Misogynist Movements

However, Cernovich's description of his own dating tactics leaves a lot to be desired. "Have you guys ever tried 'raping' a girl without using force?" he asked on Twitter. "Try it. It's basically impossible. Date rape does not exist."[50] In another conversation Cernovich described his strategy for building a defense in advance of being accused of rape: "After abusing a girl, I always immediately send a text and save her reply"—definitely the sort of ethical lawyer Gamergate would love.[51] Like Yiannopoulos and Gamergate itself, Cernovich is far more interested in attacking women and feminism than anything else.

Cernovich's tactics within Gamergate have been among the most actively dangerous to the women targeted by the mob. He hired private investigators to dig into the lives of women such as Quinn and Randi Harper, who designed the Good Game Autoblocker that enabled people targeted by Gamergate to automatically block thousands of harassers' accounts. Cernovich began working with Gjoni after he received the restraining order that prevented him from continuing to coordinate harassment of Quinn. Cernovich and Gamergate regarded this restraining order as an attack on Gjoni's free speech. Remember from previous chapters that online abusers regularly regard any attempt women make to engage in self-defense as an attempt to stifle men's free speech; abusers do so not out of an actual concern for First Amendment rights but because of their desire to say anything they want online without facing any online or offline consequences.

Cernovich's reputation as a First Amendment lawyer, however, gave Gamergate fuel for the fire. Gjoni was not just the spark that lit the powder keg; he was now a martyr to the sjw conspiracy. Of course, these types of behaviors are anything but new for Cernovich. In an article on his history with Gamergate, readers could note that, "as far back as 2010, he was doxxing people . . . and often going above and beyond the duty of a criminal defense attorney . . . by actually defending the substance of what they [were] doing."[52] As Cernovich credulously repeated Gamergate's claims about the various women the mob sought to target, he offered his legal resources to the group, engaged private investigators, dug through legal filings, and generally bloviated about his plans to sue various people for various reasons.

As of 2015 Cernovich had filed no suits on behalf of Gamergate or in relation to Gamergate at all. The litigation he threatened a multitude of times did not materialize; instead, Cernovich uses his status as "Based Lawyer" to harass and intimidate those he sees as sjws, relying on the Gamergate crowd to be his personal attack dogs—and, of course, to be a built-in customer base for the lifestyle guides he is so eager to sell. At the height of Gamergate's existence, a mere mocking comment from him would be enough to inundate a target's Twitter mentions and online presence with hostility.

For example, I regularly discuss online abuse on my own Twitter account. During Gamergate any such discussion—regardless of whether or not Gamergate was mentioned—was assumed to be about that mob. Those making that assumption were almost always adherents of Gamergate, which says quite a lot about how they saw their own behavior. One such tweet of mine came to Cernovich's attention, and his screenshot, retweet, and comment were enough to point his hangers-on in my direction. I logged on to Twitter the next morning to find more than two hundred notifications, many of them referring to me as a stupid bitch, a pussy, and a cunt. On an ordinary night I get between twenty and sixty notifications; to get more than two hundred of them, and in the form of an apparently unending stream of hatred, was daunting.

Cernovich's strategy remained the same throughout much of Gamergate's heyday: repeat and support Gamergate's claims, no matter how ludicrous, provide dubious legal advice, and offer a constantly rotating platter of targets to harass. As of 2015 Cernovich was continuing these behaviors, identifying sjws and other individuals he believes are worthy of an online mob's attention, all the while hawking his upcoming book. While the Gamergate hashtag itself may have declined in prominence, the rage unleashed by it, and stoked by figureheads like Cernovich, remains.

Cernovich, Yiannopoulos, and Sommers all found a marketing opportunity in Gamergate: a constantly active audience willing to buy whatever it was they felt like selling that day. No matter what their stance had

Misogynist Movements

been previously, their support of Gamergate guaranteed that followers of Gamergate would hang on their every word. While Cernovich and @Nero were certainly responsible for coordinating a great deal of harassment, Gamergate also developed its own outlets for that activity. After being banned from coordinating attacks or even discussing Gamergate on 4chan, its members moved over to 8chan, a website built on the same principles as 4chan but without the modicum of humanity 4chan moderators have tried to enforce in recent years.

8chan and Kotaku in Action (KIA), a subreddit devoted to Gamergate and its pet causes, both became havens for organizing harassment plans, posting personal information on Quinn, Wu, Sarkeesian, and other prominent targets, creating defamation campaigns based on rumors, old forum posts, or outright fabrications, organizing SWATting, and more. Gamergate was responsible for multiple SWATting attempts on selected targets, and nearly all of those attempts were planned in advance on 8chan; at least one of them resulted in a SWAT team being sent to the wrong location.[53] 8chan itself was not only a home for Gamergate and its activities but is also a website that unabashedly hosts child pornography.

In an in-depth and damning article Dan Olson has offered the results of his research into 8chan and the unbelievable failure of the website moderators to eliminate such content from the website's message boards. "8chan hosts over a dozen boards dedicated to the trade of child pornography," he concluded, noting that site owner Fredrick Brennan, himself a major Gamergate supporter, and his moderators "float just out of notice, moderating themselves just enough that there's always a bigger fish to catch."[54] In a move that shocked many who felt Gamergate could go no lower, Gamergate adherents did not decry the website on which they had planned raids and tried to ruin women's lives; instead, they defended it. They circled the wagons around Brennan, accusing critics of his site's ethical failures of attacking him for being disabled, and many defended the child pornography itself as an issue of free expression.

KIA remains a major hub of Gamergate discussion where members continue to try to craft a narrative of caring about ethics in games journalism while fervently expressing their desire to attack and destroy the sjws they feel are a threat to their gaming hobby. An illustration of Vivian James graces the KIA header, in case anyone was confused about where the subreddit's focus is. A new thread was entered on KIA every hour or even more frequently throughout most of 2015, much more often filled with content about evil sjws than anything related to games journalism.

While Gamergate's actions spread across the Internet and into every corner of women's lives, its most visible harassment took place on Twitter. Twitter, which has perhaps the lowest barrier to entry of any social media site, enabled Gamergate adherents to create multiple accounts and engage in harassment with all of them—when one account was suspended, another one would pop up to take its place. This pattern of activity had multiple effects: ensuring that targets spent a disproportionate amount of time blocking and reporting new accounts, as well as giving Gamergate the appearance of being a much larger mob than it truly was. A study conducted by Women, Action, & the Media (WAM!) revealed a few notable things about harassment that occurs on Twitter and Twitter's dismal failure to respond to it.[55]

During the period WAM! studied, 12 percent of the reports of harassment, threats, and violence they pursued in partnership with Twitter could be directly linked to Gamergate. One estimate on the actual size of Gamergate found that there were roughly 17,000 accounts posting to the Gamergate hashtag, both for and against it, and that most of the pro-Gamergate accounts were under two months old.[56] Even assuming that all 17,000 accounts were individuals and not people using multiple accounts, and even assuming that all 17,000 accounts were Gamergate supporters, that still puts those accounts at a fraction of a fraction of 1 percent of all 302 million active Twitter users.[57]

Globally, more than 1.2 billion people play games, and yet at an outside estimate only 17,000 people actively posted to the Gamergate hashtag, whether in support or otherwise.[58] Despite the infinitesimally small numbers of overall users aligned with Gamergate, they accounted for more than 10 percent of harassment that took place on Twitter—a figure large enough to be noticeable to the WAM! researchers and certainly noticeable to those caught in the crosshairs.

Since August 2014 Gamergate has morphed into a variety of new forms, choosing a multitude of new outlets for its rage at women and other marginalized groups. Gamergate harassment campaigns have spread into areas that have nothing whatsoever to do with gaming and continue to focus specifically—as always—on anything that looks related to sjws. For example, in early May 2015 Gamergate attacked a Kickstarter project to make a deck of cards focusing on prominent feminists. A $10,000 pledge was added to the account; Kiva Smith-Pearson, the creator of the Kickstarter, traced the pledge to 8chan, where she found comments about the donation and gleeful plans to cancel the pledge during the last minutes of the project, with a goal of ensuring it failed to achieve the fundraising goals.[59] Kickstarter worked with Smith-Pearson to cancel the spurious pledge, and the attempt backfired on Gamergate further: the attention brought to the Kickstarter campaign helped to ensure that it surpassed its funding goal.[60]

A website called What Is Gamergate Currently Ruining was set up to track what the mob focused its attention on; many of the entries describe attacks on people, websites, and campaigns that are, at best, peripherally related to games or gaming. Just a few of the things Gamergate has participated in include creating a massive blacklist of journalists accused of ethical breaches, where the supposed breach was, more often than not, writing something critical of Gamergate; gaming the Hugo Awards, literary awards for science fiction and fantasy writing, to provide awards to a slate of selected writers; sending people to the Calgary Expo under false pretenses (and getting kicked out and banned for life as a result); and more.[61]

Gamergate as a massive tidal wave of harassment aimed at anyone and everyone has slowly come to something like an end. Although the Internet is still flooded with the detritus of Gamergate attacks and its adherents are still trying to make waves, its inescapable presence on social media has dropped down to a somewhat less intrusive new normal. Many of the original targets are still dealing with extensive harassment and threats, however, and Gamergate is unlikely to disappear entirely. While the harassment campaigns will continue to flare up and die down, one positive outcome of Gamergate has been a shift in awareness of the seriousness of online abuse, as well as attempts to finally, seriously address it.

[6] DEALING WITH CYBERSEXISM
Current Solutions

The earliest inhabitants of the Internet did not manage to predict that it would become a place where offline prejudices and attitudes would continue to be acted out, where harassment campaigns would spill from words on a screen to forcing women from their homes in the wake of threat after threat, and where women must anticipate daily cybersexist harassment as the status quo. Instead, for years we collectively imagined the Internet as a blank slate onto which we could draw a new existence for humanity and create a world in which all people were considered equal and treated equally well. Cyberfeminists in particular hailed the Internet as a place where offline prejudices and abuse could be negated and destroyed. Such analysis, while it produced interesting concepts and ideals to be realized, neglected to fully take into account that no tool is neutral and that people moving into a new space are unlikely to shed their old beliefs and habits— even the destructive ones.

Far from an innovative new environment where people would discard the limitations of physical humanity and become cyborgs, as Donna Haraway theorized, many people use the Internet to reify existing identities along the axes of race, gender, and sexuality. Instead of seeing the building an Internet based on collaboration and mutual respect regardless of identity, we have witnessed the evolution of an Internet that is largely dependent on everyone fending for themselves, with the assumption of regularly encountering hostility. When it comes to online harassment and abuse, women tend to feel very alone. Current solutions for dealing with cybersexism require women to adopt a reactive stance, and there are few true solutions that protect women from abuse or discourage cybersexists from engaging in it. This chapter examines how women are trying to deal with online abuse, what men can do to help, and why many solutions—including working with law enforcement—often fail.

WOMEN'S STRATEGIES FOR DEALING WITH CYBERSEXISM

To survive online, women have learned a variety of methods for responding to abuse. Few solutions can be truly proactive, as cybersexist harassment is so often spontaneous and unpredictable. Those characteristics of the harassment have had the effect of forcing most women to develop methods of responding to harassment after it occurs. Even in situations such as Gamergate, in which the aggressors visibly and publicly planned their attacks on websites such as 8chan, 4chan, and Reddit, there was little that women could do to prepare for the escalation of abuse.

Throughout years of online life, women find ways to cobble together different methods of creating safer spaces and ensuring that the response to their presence doesn't become too toxic to handle, with varying levels of success. Some of the strategies adopted by women who experience regular cybersexist harassment include fully utilizing existing functionalities across the websites they access (limited though they might be), developing new networks and technologies, and participating in backchannel conversations with other women.

Existing Functionalities and New Technologies

Since the advent of Gamergate much more focus has been placed on how websites—especially social media websites—allow people to filter out interactions they don't want to have. Note again that these functionalities are presumed to be responsive: abuse is still typically seen as an inevitable environmental factor of the Internet, and the emphasis is on dealing with it once it happens, not preventing it from occurring in the first place. While women, and particularly black women, have spent years pointing out the failure of profitable social media sites such as Twitter, Facebook, and

Tumblr to protect their most vulnerable users, it took coverage of extensive abuse and harassment aimed at prominent women, most of them white and working in gaming or tech spaces, to get any traction. Solutions that have been designed also frequently fail to take into account the needs of the most marginalized populations.

The ability to curate a positive online experience includes maintaining access to the things you're interested in, along with not seeing the things you don't want to see, such as abusive comments and harassment. Currently, the available functions on most websites require women to make a series of unfortunate choices about what and how much content to let through to their timelines, Facebook walls, or blog and video comments and what forms of interaction will be lost when they feel they need to take the most stringent precautions they can. As mentioned in earlier chapters, merely blocking people or setting an account to private doesn't stop harassment from occurring; such efforts just change how much of it a target can see and how easy it is to gain access to that target. Blocking and filtering, however, also restrict women's activities, force them to focus on the process of filtering as opposed to engagement and content creation of their own, and take an emotional toll on women through regular and repeated contact with abusive cybersexists.

The primary functions available to women for initially responding to online harassment are blocking or muting other users, increasing privacy settings, and moderating comments or groups. While each strategy has its benefits, the drawbacks to implementing various security features may be equal to the benefits or create even bigger problems, and such strategies often involve a time commitment that reduces one's ability to participate in other, more pleasant or productive activities. Women's online lives require navigating the fine line between wanting open interaction and conversation versus wanting to be safe from having to deal with the ever-present harassment cybersexist abusers are willing to dish out, since websites themselves have done very little to improve existing safety measures. The tension caused by this balancing act is itself part of the landscape of responses to online harassment.

Currently there is no good solution that enables women to use the Internet without risking exposure to harassment or closing themselves off to the point of losing the opportunity to interact at all in order to avoid it.

Blocking and Muting

Blocking and muting harassers and abusers are fully reactive responses, which are typically employed only after abuse has already occurred—whether it is aimed at oneself or one witnesses another user harass someone else. Preemptive blocking or muting is about as proactive as such a function can get and yet still often requires the target to have seen or experienced the abuse. As a result, blocking tends to be too little, too late. Abuse cannot be unseen, and most abusers—especially on websites such as Reddit, Tumblr, and Twitter—often rely on making their first overture as shocking, violent, or graphic as possible, knowing that their first statement might be the only one they get to make before being muted or blocked.

Forcing women into a perpetually reactive stance where online abuse is concerned gives cybersexist harassers much of the power in the interaction and places a burden on women to constantly monitor their profiles, comments, and notifications. Starting the day off by blocking harassers that appeared overnight is not an uncommon experience. The drawbacks of telling women to "just block" their harassers were addressed previously—be sure to keep that information in mind when considering that blocking is still one of the only marginally empowering methods women have for dealing with abuse online.

Most of the academic research that concerns blocking in online spaces deals specifically with censorship of social media and other content by government bodies, as well as copyright concerns. This area is one where additional research on individual blocking and one-to-one or mobbing behaviors is needed. However, the existing research focuses on the same fundamental questions as online abuse—namely, how to create solutions that do not place undue burdens on individual users or Internet service providers (ISPs) to monitor and report such content while also avoiding overregulation of the Internet that results in true infringements of speech and expression. "There are several regulatory options to remove illegal

Internet content. Solutions for blocking illegal Internet content usually require the substantial involvement of base level actors, such as private users and ISPs," write Katalin Parti and Luisa Marin, noting that such involvement is typically a barrier to success, since the time commitment is great and the tools for such involvement are limited.[1] While the illegal content referred to in their writing is the sexual exploitation of children, cybercrime, terrorism, hacking, and organized crime, cybersexist abuse that crosses the line between overt harassment and stalking or threats of violence would certainly fall under the same category of illegality in many countries.

Parti and Marin note that actions taken by a government body to regulate the Internet and protect its users can easily be used to disguise surveillance and other state activities that may be equally dangerous to freedoms and participation in online spaces, presenting another serious barrier to effective ongoing implementation. Anyone working in an office with a firewall has experience with top-down corporate filters, which often exclude legitimate content that is deemed not safe for work; top-down state or corporate filtering is often indiscriminate and based on criteria that will prevent access to useful and necessary material. It is in part for these reasons that support for top-down control of the Internet remains low.

As Parti and Marin put it, "domain-based internet-blocking technology, relying on blacklists and the concept built on it, are not proportionate to the envisaged goals. Due to overfiltering, it intervenes more drastically in the basic freedoms of citizens than the severity of the damage caused by the online behaviour."[2] The risk of implementing too many content filters to make the Internet usable is a serious concern, although such worries vary by demographic. Women, for example, tend to be more interested in content filtering as a solution to "objectionable materials," especially as they grow older.[3] While women and men are equally unlikely to favor content filtering before they reach the age of twenty-five, after that age there is a sharp divergence in the two groups, with women becoming more likely to desire top-down filters that enable them to avoid seeing, specifically, sexually explicit and violent imagery.[4] Overall support for such filtering remains a definite minority, but as women tend to be more regularly and unwillingly exposed to such content, it is perhaps not surprising that there is some level of desire to prevent it from ever reaching women's screens in the first place.

At present, top-down filtering of the Internet is an unlikely and in fact undesirable outcome; despite that, individuals and individual websites are therefore left to shoulder the burden of finding other ways to deal with abuse—ways that tend to be piecemeal, after the fact, and only marginally effective. A bottom-up model of reporting illegal content to an ISP or other authority still requires individual users to see such material and take the appropriate actions and to call for systems to be put in place that can adequately and swiftly respond to such content and the activities that are enabling or producing it. As any woman who has struggled with reporting abuse knows, using such systems is currently a hopeful gesture rather than an act that is sure to get results.

Neither top-down nor bottom-up models of blocking illegal or abusive content are wholly effective for protecting individual users and maintaining a free, collective online space. While Parti and Marin's work focuses more specifically on the blocking of websites, rather than one-to-one interactions, they note that nearly all blocking methods can be circumvented and conclude that "blocking measures do not represent a solution, in the sense that they do not contribute to the repression of most serious crimes."[5] Despite these issues, content filters and blocking individual users remain the most common methods of responding to one-on-one harassment in social media spaces such as Twitter, Facebook, and Tumblr.

Different methods exist on every website that allow users to control who has access to their profile page and written content, although cybersexist abusers exploit every possible loophole to continue gaining access to their targets and engaging in harassment. For each step toward a safer Internet, women must also contend with committed abusers seeking new methods of contact. For many women, however, the ability to remove visible harassment from a Facebook feed, Twitter timeline, or the comment section of a YouTube video or a blog is sometimes the only recourse available.

Muting, for example, is a capability of Twitter that is used to ensure a user will no longer receive notifications from another specific user in their main timeline or in the form of mentions, favorites, or retweets. Muting functions can also be accessed for specific hashtags and words from a variety of apps and browser add-ons. Many women opt to mute rather than block someone who is harassing them on Twitter, as blocking is intended to prevent the harasser from seeing their target's profile at all. Muting allows harassers to see and interact with their target, but the target no longer receives notifications of the interactions.

While neither blocking nor muting stops someone from continuing to tweet rude, abrasive, or abusive things at their target, and they do not prevent other people from seeing the harassment, muting sometimes has a slight advantage over outright blocking. As many women have experienced, blocked harassers will often find ways to respond to other people who have talked to their target or will get their friends to reply to the conversation, keeping them in the target's notifications regardless of being blocked. Muting is often regarded as a less confrontational response, as the muted user has no way of knowing that they have been muted beyond the lack of response from their target and may therefore be slightly less motivated to find other ways to continue visibly interacting with the person they were harassing.

On Facebook, muting or unfollowing a friended person's posts is one way to avoid content that is sexist, racist, or just plain boring. However, there are fewer ways to prevent a combative individual from commenting on other posts or engaging in harassment through private messages. In those instances many women opt to remove that individual from their friends list. In addition, blocking on Facebook tends to be far more effective than on most other social media websites. While logged in on Facebook, blocked users receive an error message when trying to find a target's account: it's as though the account no longer exists at all. Although that person can log out and access any public posts or content, they will be unable to interact with the target's account directly. In addition to that, their comments on the posts of mutual friends do not appear for the person who has blocked them; while responses from other people can then give the impression of a rather one-sided and confusing conversation, the blocked individual's replies remain unseen.

Tumblr, the popular blogging website, has add-on capabilities that can be downloaded to a browser or account and that give users the option to mute certain key words and tags. This move prevents potentially abusive content from entering a user's feed, although untagged images will make it through the filters. Tumblr itself allows users to "ignore" one another, which has roughly the same effect as blocking. An ignored user will not be able to see a target's posts or send them messages, and the target will no longer see their posts or their comments on other users' posts. This functionality helps reduce some of the abuse that occurs for users of the site, which has abusers that range from cybersexist harassers to those committed by a variety of white supremacist blogs and everything unpleasant in between. Ignoring such blogs, which often exist for the sole purpose of harassment, is a simple way to not have to see the abuses that are committed, even though they still exist. That websites such as Tumblr often fail to remove these blogs, despite the obvious and repeated patterns of harassment they exhibit, is a serious ethical breach and yet one over which individual users have no control. That is one area in which top-down moderation of website content must be taken more seriously.

Twitter, as mentioned earlier, continues to have a serious issue with the ineffectiveness of its blocking function. As with Facebook, any user who is logged out, or logged in on an alternate account, can see all public posts from a target. Even when blocked and logged in on the blocked account, however, the impact of blocking someone on Twitter is so poor that there are multiple ways abusers can continue to see their target's discussions.

While going directly to their profile page will inform individuals if they have been blocked, searching for their target's tweets by username or clicking on responses from other users who are not blocked both enable harassers to continue seeing and interacting with tweets from someone who has blocked them. A link to a tweet posted by another user also allows someone who has been blocked to see the content and even provides the option to retweet, favorite, or reply to that tweet, although retweeting and favoriting will bring a pop-up notice that the action cannot be completed. However, using these methods, people who have been blocked are given the ability to monitor their targets and continue engaging in harassment.

Additionally, this capability forces people who are being targeted to, in turn, spend time monitoring the harassers in order to be aware of escalations in abuse or threats that require further action.

As with muting, an additional problem remains. Blocking someone on Twitter does not prevent them from continuing to tweet at a target—it just prevents the target from seeing it. Someone who has been blocked can keep sending tweets with their target's username, unfettered, despite not being able to see their target's reactions or responses quite as easily. In cases of severe harassment, that feature can force a woman to monitor multiple harassing or threatening accounts in order to file reports or keep records of sustained harassment. In situations such as Gamergate such monitoring becomes an impossible task due to the sheer number of abusive accounts. Blocking someone also fails to prevent anyone else from seeing the abusive comments, especially if they include hashtags or are tweeted by popular accounts.

Essentially, all blocking does is make it slightly more difficult for abusers to see their target's account and for an abused user to track those who are hounding them. Nothing, however, prevents a harasser from finding those alternate routes and abusing them, often bringing more cybersexist harassers into the discussion. Blocking makes it more difficult for the target to monitor potentially threatening accounts by placing a reminder that the user has been blocked on the blocked user's profile page, which the target has to click to dismiss before being able to see their tweets. Simply not having abusive comments show up directly in a target's notifications is not a satisfactory blocking solution when such comments can still be sent and seen by others. The visibility of harassing comments can affect perceptions about an individual user, hinder her personal interactions, and damage her professional career.

Given all of these factors, blocking someone on Twitter is hardly an impediment to harassers and abusers. As recently as June 2015 Twitter announced a new functionality—the ability to export and share a block list.[6] While multiple external services already offer Twitter block list sharing, this feature is the first one developed and released by Twitter itself that enables users to block additional accounts en masse. Until Twitter fixes the bugs that undermine the effectiveness of blocking, though, it is little more than a PR measure designed to give the appearance of solving Twitter's ongoing problems with abuse.

There is another flaw in blocking on websites such as Twitter and Tumblr or on a blog: the ease of creating new accounts. As Gamergate showed, a significant factor in how much harassment occurred was due to the rapidity and simplicity of creating new accounts to engage in abuse. It takes next to no time to create a new email address and send a threatening email to a target, leave abusive blog comments, or build yet another Twitter account and start the cycle of harassment all over again. As Chris Plante wrote in *The Verge*, "existing on social media sometimes feels like a game of whack-a-mole where the moles spew a string of slurs before being banished into the dank hole they came from."[7] It is easy for cybersexist abusers to create a series of brand-new accounts to continue engaging in cybersexist harassment after an initial account is blocked or even suspended, and this pattern keeps women constantly on the alert for comments from new accounts.

The attempt to solve this issue generated new technologies, programs, and communities. The Block Bot, for example, is an opt-in Twitter bot that automatically blocks certain users based on varying levels of criteria, from a user simply being annoying to a user displaying patterns of abusive behavior. Blockers who volunteer to work on the team will review submissions and confirm or reject blocks; as with any human-run team, there are lag times and other issues of bias that affect the usability of the tool. However, many people have found the Block Bot to be an effective means of weeding out abusers.

Block Together is the closest to a preemptive blocking solution that exists on Twitter. According to Block Together's home page, the app "is designed to reduce the burden of blocking when many accounts are attacking you, or when a few accounts are attacking many people in your community."[8] It accomplishes this goal in a few ways: individual users are given automatic blocking options, allowing Block Together to filter out accounts that are under two weeks old and/or those that have fewer than fifteen followers. These two aspects of a Twitter account, while not a perfect filter set, do tend to indicate an account that has been set up for the sole purpose of abusing.

Dealing with Cybersexism

Once a user has signed up for the tool, Block Together also allows individuals to share their own block lists and subscribe to other users' lists. This capability can rapidly increase the number of blocked users without an individual user having to experience cybersexist harassment or other forms of abuse first. In the first eight months of 2015, for example, my Block Together account grew by more than nine hundred blocked accounts, including those that were later deleted or suspended; the only blocked accounts are those that have directly tweeted at me and were manually blocked or were caught by Block Together's filters. I regularly check my newly blocked accounts to weed out false positives and watch for upticks in harassment, which the tool enables me to track more easily. While false positives are always a possibility when blocking in large numbers (some people have blocked more than twenty thousand accounts), users are able to unblock individuals from their list or unblock and simply mute selected individuals or groups. The option to preemptively block harassers and potential harassers is one of a few ways that Twitter has been made marginally safer by third-party groups.

It was using Block Together as a foundation that Randi Harper, an engineer and developer, designed the Good Game Autoblocker, also known as the GGautoblocker. It has been used, and continues to be used, to block Gamergate's mobs and the waves of new accounts developed under Gamergate's aegis. The tool "compares the follower lists for a given set of Twitter accounts. If anyone is found to be following more than one of these accounts, they are added to a list and blocked."[9] By using a handful of known Gamergate ringleaders as the basis for the tool, the app was designed to preemptively block anyone who followed two or more of the accounts. As of August 2015 there were more than 10,600 accounts on the Good Game Autoblocker block list.[10] Using the tool spares women from having to deal with entire mobs of harassers—provided those harassers are following some of the selected filter accounts. As with the Block Bot, there is a process for being removed from the block list following review.

While tools like Block Together exist for websites such as Twitter, fewer preemptive solutions exist on individually run websites, blogs, or video channels. Many blog-hosting websites also offer the option for anonymous commenting, for example, and Tumblr in particular has opt-in settings that allow users to receive anonymous questions or comments. Anonymity and readily created new accounts mean that a harasser who is blocked on one front can simply begin leaving anonymous comments or create a series of new accounts with which to continue the harassment. The easy access to anonymity in online spaces is regularly connected to abusive behaviors (although, as anyone reading Facebook comments will note, even being connected to one's real identity is not a huge deterrent).

As a result of the reduced inhibitions created by anonymity and the ease with which people can create anonymous profiles for the sake of engaging in abuse, women end up spending a disproportionate amount of time weeding through abusive Twitter, Tumblr, or blog comments and blocking account after account—a process that quickly becomes tiresome and disheartening. This form of maintenance still requires women to read the comments and engage with the material; when the comments are left on a blog anonymously, there might not even be a way to block the account beyond deleting the original comment.

Cybersexist harassers also frequently attempt to set the terms of engagement with their targets, to force them to continue an interaction by putting them on the defensive. Blocking someone, especially on Twitter, is often framed as the blocker "losing" a game they never agreed to play, the rules of which are determined—and changed—at the harasser's whim. In the mindset adopted by such cybersexist harassers the one who "wins" is the one who remains in the conversation the longest and escalates the aggression the most; exiting an interaction is not considered a sign of disinterest or refusal to engage with someone who is disingenuous and abusive but is instead deemed a failure or an inability to defend whatever the target's original statement was. Recall from chapter 5 M. E. Kabay's discussion of autotelic experiences and the feedback loop created by engaging in online harassment as a type of game: such experiences inform the belief that being blocked is a victory in a game they are playing at everyone else's expense. Cybersexist abusers often create accounts solely for the purpose of sending women sexual harassment, threats, or argumentative abuse with a goal of getting blocked and declaring victory over them as a result.

Dealing with Cybersexism

Defensive reactions in the face of such a construction are common: no one wants to be the loser in an interaction like that, but neither is it possible for a target to win. By relying on an ethos that insists all conversation is valuable and must be treated as an individual discussion and never regarded as part of an overall pattern and by accepting that there is an implied burden of proof that women, specifically, are required to meet when sharing stories even about their own lives, cybersexists endeavor to capture and waste women's time and attention. These forms of harassment often take the form of sea lioning, in which blocking is met with a hyperbolic reaction of supposed hurt feelings and astonishment that women could even be so rude as to not want to converse with them, or with accusations of fear and intellectual weakness. The rules of this game are never fixed but always rigged in favor of the harasser, who is inevitably the one who seeks out a target for the interaction.

This mindset was common within Gamergate, where women who blocked each wave of harassing accounts were called cowardly for refusing to waste their time talking to a crowd of people who were demonstrably unwilling to genuinely converse or who were sending them threats and abuse. One woman recounted a particularly upsetting form of this behavior. "A few weeks ago, a friend caught her 12yr old [*sic*] son harassing women with death/rape threats in the name of #Gamergate," she wrote in one tweet. "'Mom, it's just a game,' he insisted. 'You try to get them to block you. It's kinda funny. I wouldn't really do any of those things.'"[11] During a period of time in which multiple women were sent realistic enough threats that they went to the police and FBI and were told to leave their homes, the people sending them were recruiting children to their cause and teaching young boys that illegally threatening to kill a woman to get her to block you is a method of demonstrating your dominance in online spaces. It should not need to be said that this is not an optimal online experience for anyone but the abusers.

Blocking, which should realistically be considered a reasonable way to end a discussion with someone, especially someone who is deliberately ignoring the online social cues that signal a conversation's end, is regularly positioned as a challenge instead. Harassers who have been blocked attempt to make themselves seem like the victor, rather than someone who has been dismissed, and often accuse women of infringing on their free speech for choosing not to talk to them. Many abusers go on to look for ways to continue harassing the original target, such as leaving anonymous comments on a blog if their original account has been banned.

When that starts happening, women with their own blogs—on Tumblr or otherwise—are forced to choose between allowing people to contact them anonymously (and then having to sort through the abuse) and preventing anonymous contact entirely. A common first reaction, of course, would be to encourage women to deny their audience the ability to ever contact them anonymously; some have even called for all actions on the Internet to be connected to an individual's offline identity, to destroy anonymity for everyone. One article somewhat hyperbolically reports that "by allowing anonymous communication we actually risk an incremental breakdown of the fabric of our society" by removing the possibility of holding people accountable, and it goes on to suggest that anonymity is synonymous with cowardice.[12]

The ability to access the Internet and communicate with one another in anonymous ways, however, is an important part of a free and open Internet. There are numerous valid reasons people may wish to be anonymous—for example, transgender persons who have not yet come out to their family or community may want the ability to ask questions without their being connected to existing online profiles. A woman attempting to escape an abusive relationship may reach out anonymously for help. Political dissent in a number of regions and countries must be expressed anonymously to avoid state repercussions or retribution from other citizens. Sarah Jeong writes about a woman with the pseudonym Del Harvey. She volunteered "with the site Perverted Justice, which would catch predators on the Internet by posing as children," and as a result of her work and for her own safety, the rest of Del Harvey's Internet activity must necessarily involve some level of anonymity.[13] Even something as simple as looking for information about a new job might require some form of anonymous interaction in order to keep a current job while looking for a change in career.

Women, especially those writing or working on issues of feminism and other forms of justice, often find there is a great need for the ability to talk to people honestly and anonymously. Cybersexist abusers, therefore, are forcing women to choose between fully interacting with their communities and cutting off necessary lines of communication. As the U.S. Congress begins to pay more attention to online harassment and abuse, anonymity will probably be a focus of that attention, since so much abuse occurs anonymously. However, it must be frequently asserted that anonymity itself is not the problem: abusers are—as we can see from the amount of abuse committed by people under their offline identities. When we seek solutions to online abuse, the impetus to put anonymous interactions on the chopping block must be fully interrogated to avoid the fallout and ineffectiveness of implementing that solution.

As we have seen, the ability to block and mute cybersexist harassers is an important one for making a woman's online space marginally safer, but it is flawed in a number of ways. Harassers regularly seek and utilize methods that negate the effect of being blocked, and very few methods of blocking prevent an abuser from continuing to send abusive comments to or about their target. In these moments the burden is still placed on women, who are expected to take time out of their day, every day, to cut off the latest avenue of access abusers are using. While blocking and muting remain important tools, their function is still fundamentally a reactive task that requires women to have been exposed to abuse.

Reporting Cybersexists

In a counterpart to blocking, many websites—including Twitter, Facebook, and others—offer their users reporting options. These options may include reporting someone for offensive comments or harassing behavior, filing DMCA claims about stolen content, and more. However, reporting cybersexist abuse is rarely the most effective strategy for women. While the existence of forms and pathways to report abuse is encouraging, they often place a disproportionate burden on the individual who is being abused and rarely offer a satisfactory result. As with blocking, when a website enables an abuser to simply create a new account and carry on with the abuse, filing a report can sometimes feel like more trouble than it's worth.

I have dozens of "report received" notifications and emails from Facebook, Twitter, and YouTube for various threats I have reported across those platforms. Only a fraction of them have ever resulted in an account being removed, despite clear violations of the websites' terms of service or antiharassment policies. Brianna Wu, who has had to hire someone to keep track of the threats she receives and reports, occasionally releases the figures on how many reports have resulted in an account being suspended; in July 2015 she noted that 85 percent of her reports, of which she made fifteen to twenty a day, had been effective. "As sad [as] those numbers are, 85 percent effectiveness is a huge step up in Twitter taking action. They deserve credit for improving things," she wrote.[14] Any woman with a substantial platform has come to expect a similar experience.

The scholar Rena Bivens has written about Facebook's reporting and moderation strategies after gaining access to a leaked moderation manual. As she writes, "the moderation system designed for Facebook places the onus on the user to report offenses that are then assessed to determine whether the content should be removed and/or the offending user reprimanded," and she goes on to note that the actual moderation work is typically outsourced to low-paid workers outside the United States.[15] Bivens's paper notes that typical moderation tactics mimic stereotypical expectations of gender and sexuality, including the expectation that victims should bear the brunt of the work in solving the problem of abuse. While Facebook is certainly not the only site to respond to abuse in that way, it provides a clear example of the often dismissive way in which abuse is treated and the implications such treatment can have for low-wage workers.

Reporting online abuse fails women in a number of ways: it is often time-consuming, fails to address abuses in a clear way, requires women to relive and document the harassment, and generally does not provide efficient or effective results. Sending in an abuse report can require a woman to provide links to or screenshots of the abuse, which may include graphic images, threats, or other content. While providing evidence of

Dealing with Cybersexism

abusive content is necessary, systems could be built that simply allow a woman to enter a link to the profile, which from there can be reviewed by the security team to identify the content. Requiring an individual to access abusive content in order to attempt to have that content taken down is, at best, somewhat counterproductive.

With regard to the website, most reporting functions are either automated to the point of being useless or place a heavy burden on the underpaid human teams assigned to review such content. Finding a solution that allows companies to swiftly review and assess profiles and users who are engaging in abuse without exposing women and workers to abusive content must be a higher priority for websites and social media platform providers.

Privacy Settings

Another method many women use to reduce their exposure to cybersexist harassers and abusers is to enhance their privacy settings. As cyberstalking is now included in one out of every four reported stalking cases, the ability to control who has access to one's social media profiles, email address, and personal websites, and what information they are able to gather, is becoming a matter of vital importance.[16] Women may use multiple privacy settings to protect themselves from infrequent or everyday harassment, as well as to attempt to secure their lives from invasion by a stalker. As is the case for offline stalking, many online stalkers are former husbands or boyfriends, meaning that women may have to contend with mutual friends and other factors when assessing their privacy and vulnerability. Reducing exposure to cybersexist abusers in general may involve using Facebook's various settings to limit who can see and comment on their posts or view their profile as a whole, creating private blogs rather than public ones, and setting their Twitter account to private.

Privacy in the online world is often presumed to be an issue related to government interference or to concerns about the theft of personal data when engaging in online shopping or other forms of commerce, or to fears about social media websites such as Facebook aggregating and selling users' personal information. One meta-analysis of online privacy studies found that "not many empirical studies were recognized in the psychological field. This may be interpreted by the fact that privacy is more of a social and legal issue than a personal psychological issue" and that online privacy as a concept was barely studied at all before 1999.[17] However, as online harassment continues to become a more and more important issue, additional analysis of whether and under what circumstances enhanced privacy settings can mitigate harassment without limiting users' access to communication will be necessary. Research on how privacy affects online interactions and users' psychology has become more popular in recent years, although it is still a drastically understudied area, especially with regard to the intersections of gender, race, and sexuality.

A study on how various users approach Facebook as a tool of self-presentation, and users' attitude toward privacy control, showed that women tend to care more about having a positive representation than men do and are more concerned about the availability of privacy controls to maintain such presentation.[18] The authors of the study suggest that social media networks should avoid relying on one-size-fits-all solutions for privacy settings and controls and should approach solutions based on gender. Different demographic groups, as defined by and intersecting with race, age, disability, sexuality, and other factors, might also have varying desires and needs around privacy settings and what information they wish to make public, highlighting the importance of diversity among development and design teams.

Most social media websites offer two-factor authentication, which is a privacy setting that helps reduce the likelihood of an account being hacked. Two-factor authentication sends an email or text message to a previously identified account each time an individual logs in, requiring them to enter a numerical code or password before being logged in. Having two-factor authentication in place can alert an individual to a compromised password, while also preventing hackers from gaining complete entry to the account. This setting is one of the few that has no obvious drawbacks—aside from the time it takes to get and enter a log-in code. The comfort of knowing it is more difficult for even a dedicated harasser to access an account is a major boon.

The goal of privacy settings is to control who has access to an individual's posts and information, and different websites and networks approach these concerns in different ways. Twitter's privacy functions are perhaps the starkest of all major social networks: either the user's posts are all public or the account is completely private and accessible only to approved followers. Similarly, the newer social network Ello tells its users that all of their posts save private messages will be public and accessible to all; in the early stages of the network's use there was not even a blocking or muting option, and the only privacy setting was whether or not a profile could be viewed by those outside the network.[19] Individual videos on YouTube can be made private and shared with a select audience, or a whole private channel can be created. Facebook allows for a far more nuanced approach to privacy than most social media sites—users can make their entire account public or private, or they can decide on a post-by-post basis which audiences will have access. Tumblr does not allow its users to make their main blog private; while a secondary, private blog can be added later, the original blog must always remain open to the public.

Privacy options regardless of website tend to be opaque, challenging to access, and inconsistently applied. Facebook, for example, regularly comes under fire for changing users' privacy settings without notification or altering what privacy settings are available. Most websites encourage users to keep their content public, since it's easier for advertisers to aggregate that information and send out targeted communications. When faced with cybersexist abuse, however, many women want to increase their sense of privacy.

Every method of increasing privacy settings has both benefits and drawbacks that users must navigate. Twitter, for example, can be said to penalize those with private accounts by limiting their ability to reach a broad audience unless they already have a large number of followers. While harassers lose the ability to see a private account's tweets whether the owner is logged in or out, since content from a private account cannot be seen by anyone except confirmed followers, tweets from that account can impact only those who are already reading them. The inability to have free discussions is a source of frustration for women, and on a website where interaction is largely determined by retweets and shared content the limitations of locking an account are keenly felt. Women are often presented with the choice of not engaging in open conversations or becoming the target of harassment campaigns, and they are blamed for any negative outcomes regardless of which method they choose.

Some women choose to briefly make their accounts private during periods of intense harassment and abuse and then make them public again once the abuse seems to have subsided. Others with consistently private accounts may ask that their followers manually retweet certain things—a follower can copy the content of a tweet into their own, unlocked account and note that it came from a locked account when posting it. Both strategies, however, can reduce the amount of interaction an account gets, and having to assess and approve new follower requests is time-consuming. Additionally, all existing followers remain followers when setting an account to private. If a woman notices that many of her followers are abusive, she must still go through and manually block them. Women who are public figures or running a business have even further disincentives to make an account private, as it can cut them off from an important audience or result in diminished revenue and a smaller customer base.

To solve the issue, women sometimes choose to maintain two separate Twitter accounts—one a public account where they share articles and links but avoid discussing their personal lives or political beliefs (two areas where cybersexist harassment is common) and one a private account for having more in-depth conversations with a smaller audience of approved followers. The drawback to maintaining two accounts is that users must toggle between each account, logging into one and out of the other, and compartmentalize their online presentation and personality, often for the sole purpose of avoiding or minimizing harassment.

Many of the same concerns apply to Facebook, despite the higher level of customization available to Facebook users. On Facebook women can set their profile and posts to be visible to everyone, only to friends and friends of friends, friends alone, or only themselves as the poster and user. This functionality achieves basically the same result as having both a public and a private Twitter account. As a result of Facebook's customized posting

Dealing with Cybersexism

capabilities, a woman can craft public posts for all to see while having different discussions with a select audience of friends. This strategy can help reduce the likelihood of harassment and abuse, while still allowing women to engage a large audience. Women with a large enough audience may also create a public fan page solely for posts and discussions with the public while maintaining a more private Facebook account for friends and family; this strategy is common among bloggers and published authors, musicians, celebrities, and business owners.

These privacy settings on Facebook offer significantly more control to women than other social media sites. In fact, Facebook received the highest grade of three networks studied by Take Back the Tech! for their responsiveness to abuse—a D+ (Twitter and YouTube both received an F for their ongoing failures to protect women from harassment and violence).[20] While Facebook had the best transparency around reporting and redress for abuse, along with simplified and easily accessible mechanisms for those reports, and had taken steps to deal with violence against women, Take Back the Tech! noted a distinct failure to respond quickly to women outside the United States and Europe, along with a poor public commitment to human rights standards.

Cyberstalking also remains a serious problem on Facebook. As mentioned in chapter 2, Anthony Elonis used Facebook to stalk his estranged wife and threaten her, FBI officers, and even local children. One study of the stalking of former romantic partners among college students also found that, among participants who admitted to some form of stalking behaviors, they "did so online, offline, and on Facebook."[21] Some of the most common stalking behaviors on Facebook include writing angry or inappropriate public posts about an ex-partner or an ex's new partner and engaging in public forms of harassment such as setting up fake pages and posting embarrassing or private photographs. Most forms of Facebook stalking are intended to control the behavior of a former partner and maintain some form of access to and communication with that individual. Those who engage in more regular and severe forms of stalking and harassment on Facebook are also more likely to engage in offline abuses as well; stalking is rarely contained to one avenue of access to a target.

Apart from stalking, however, harassment and abuse on Facebook tend to be more generally directed, and public pages reported for hate speech and inciting violence often remain up for days or weeks. Multiple pages maligning women in the public eye can be found, along with pages that encourage rape and interpersonal or domestic violence, outing or encouraging the harassment of transgender women, and racist and white supremacist pages. Pages put up by groups who espouse such views often contain harassment, threats, libelous claims about individual women, and more, yet Facebook is notoriously poor at responding to reports about these groups and removing their pages. Facebook is often lambasted for deleting pictures of breastfeeding parents or breast cancer survivors while allowing hate speech to flourish. Women's privacy settings may protect them from many forms of direct harassment on Facebook, but cybersexism is still permitted.

Privacy settings online are, at a basic level, intended to help people control how much of their information can be easily accessed by an audience. For women, however, privacy settings become a tool for warding off abuse—or attempting to. Such settings act simultaneously as walls to keep out some of the less intrusive abusers and as walls that keep women from fully experiencing online life. The decision to shut oneself in by increasing privacy settings is a trade-off that too many women have to make and one that will never fully prevent harassment from occurring.

Moderating Comments

Moderating interactions is another strategy put in place by existing website functionalities that aim to help women deter cybersexist abuses. Moderation occurs in two main fashions—women can engage in moderation of comments and posts on their own blogs or websites and websites with multiple writers can assign moderators from their team and set rules for leaving comments (or close comments sections entirely), while large websites can outsource moderation or hire moderators to watch for and delete any content that violates site rules.

An individual writer maintaining her own website typically has a variety of options to moderate comments. As mentioned earlier, this monitor-

Dealing with Cybersexism

ing can involve choosing to allow or disallow anonymous commenting and setting specific rules of engagement that will determine whether a comment is approved or deleted. There are content filters for different website hosting platforms, and these filters enable women to flag certain key words that mark a comment for further review before it is approved. Many women choose to shut down the comment sections on certain posts or YouTube videos that they feel will be targeted with harassment. YouTube comments are notoriously odious and filled with overt sexism, racism, and other abuses, with little recourse for the original poster but to delete comments one by one—an impractical solution at best—or close comments entirely, which results in lower engagement with the video. Despite such drawbacks, women can ensure that they have an opportunity to partially control the quality of discussion on the websites they run by exploring their options for comment moderation.

Websites with multiple writers often have defined commenting policies that are visible to viewers before they enter a comment. These rules inform users of what types of comments may be suspended for review, what comments may be deleted, and what comments may result in a ban. *The Mary Sue*, for example, has flags in place for various curses and slurs, for using Disqus (a commenting tool) without a verified email address, and for reader-submitted flags. Comments will be deleted for engaging in personal attacks, making jokes about or attacks on someone's personal appearance, and using hate speech.[22] *The Mary Sue* bans accounts for engaging in those behaviors consistently or with a particularly egregious comment the first time around, for visiting the site for the purpose of starting fights with other readers, and for behaving in a way the editors feel is a detriment to the general atmosphere of the comment section.

Such rules provide a framework for discussion, let viewers to the site know immediately what types of behaviors are unacceptable, and give women a structure to point to for defending their decision to delete a specific comment or ban a user. While these strategies are useful for protecting the site's readers, site moderation still requires an individual or team to view and read all comments that are flagged for review. Prolonged exposure to such content can take a significant toll on moderators. Large websites, often news sites and other major media companies, will hire a team of moderators to sift through their comment sections and delete material that violates their rules.

In one article on the jobs of these moderators, *New Inquiry* reported that moderator roles tend to be disproportionately held by young women and tend to be underpaid and poorly supported. Jason Wilson interviewed a young woman "who combs the threads of an Australian broadcaster's website and social-media pages for the output of users 'who will just post the word cunt 50 times for like three hours.'" Other women described the emotional toll that extensive contact with such comments took on them, with Wilson noting that "not only do women face streams of hate directed at themselves on personal accounts, they also scrub similar threads clean for their employers."[23] Moderating comments is a poorly paid job that relentlessly exposes women to cybersexist abuse, racism, homophobia, transphobia, and all other forms of antisocial and unpleasant statements left in the comment sections of blogs and websites. That young women make up much of the workforce assigned to moderation and that there are so few resources in place to support them and ensure their mental health is not negatively impacted by the work is a serious concern.

In a surprising change in the summer of 2015 Reddit made the decision to change its site policies and remove subreddits that incite harm, post illegal activity, or host the personal information of private individuals.[24] However, while subreddits such as "/r/Beating Cripples" and "/r/raping-women" would be taken down for the incitement to violence made explicit in the name, the implicit violence of "/r/CoonTown" was apparently not enough to get it removed initially.[25] Members of the "CoonTown" subreddit were known for infiltrating and brigading the subreddits of other groups, especially those primarily occupied and moderated by black women, who are among their primary targets for racist harassment. As a result, moderators for other subreddits were still being forced to contend with the racist and sexist harassment originating in "CoonTown," which often does meet Reddit's updated criteria for banning or deletion. Eventually "CoonTown" and other harmful subreddits were removed; however, their removal was more an effort to avoid the bad PR that had become associ-

Dealing with Cybersexism

ated with them, rather than recognition of the toxicity they generated.[26] While a step in the right direction, Reddit's decisions still leave much to be desired, as the site remains a hub of harassment.

Comment moderation, like all forms of defense against cybersexist harassment, is a double-edged sword. While filters may help snag the worst of it, websites with a large audience or an individual writer with an article that quickly becomes popular can be deluged with hatred that is impossible to contain, much less read and approve or delete. Strict comment moderation requires that moderators spend more time reading flagged submissions and less time doing anything else, such as producing content for the site or forum, while not having any moderation in place can result in the site being popular with only the most unpleasant types of harassers and abusers. Not only that, however, but the prevalence of negative or harassing comments can have a serious impact on readers and how they perceive the original information in the article or blog post.

A study by Dominique Brossard, a professor at the University of Wisconsin-Madison, found that, on scientific articles posted online, negative comments, ad hominem attacks, and abuse tend to polarize readers and their response to the research that was presented.[27] While "don't read the comments" is such a common refrain that it is embroidered on samplers, sold in the form of brightly colored statement necklaces, and thriving in memes across the Internet, many people are taking a new approach to dealing with the toxicity represented by too many comment sections and the burden they place on individuals and groups: getting rid of the comment section entirely.

As the ethics writer and culture analyst Tauriq Moosa puts it, "[Comment sections] are, like the internet itself, tools: we don't discard wrenches because of a few accidents. Yet, if people start using wrenches to mostly beat each other with, maybe it's time to radically rethink whether they should be allowed at all."[28] Comment sections, he writes, have gotten out of control—writers avoid engaging in discussion in the comments on their own pieces because the immediate and overwhelming toxicity has a tendency to render such conversation pointless and unpleasant, especially on topics relating to things like gender or race, or even certain areas of science, such as climate change and vaccinations. Moosa's advice is simple: if moderating comments proves to be unfeasible, shut the comment sections down entirely. After all, a comment section is an option for a website, not a requirement; those with opinions about a piece are free to share them elsewhere.

While Moosa's stance might sound extreme, he is certainly not alone in adopting it. Multiple major websites have gone the route of closing down their comments and, in fact, are reaping the benefits of doing so. After the *National Journal*, a political news and analysis website, shut down its comment section, "return visits climbed by more than 20%. Visits of only a single page decreased, while visits of two pages or more increased by almost 20%."[29] *Popular Science* closed its comment section, with the editors stating that they would open comments only on articles that seemed to lend themselves to productive discourse. They exhorted readers to "chime in with your brightest thoughts. Don't do it for us. Do it for science."[30] A site that rarely opens its comments and heavily moderates them when it does is much less likely to have moderators who are regularly and repeatedly exposed to abusive content, and readers coming to the site can comfortably engage with the piece without fearing they will have to read or engage with abusive or hostile voices in the comment section.

The problem of sites without institutional support for writers and moderators made itself clear in the summer of 2014, when Gawker website *Jezebel* released an article calling attention to the fact that the comment sections on their articles were being repeatedly flooded with GIFs of violent pornography and rape. The article highlighted the distress this harassment was causing to readers and "the staff, who are the only ones capable of removing the comments and are thus, by default, now required to view and interact with violent pornography and gore as part of our jobs. None of us are paid enough to deal with this on a daily basis."[31] The staff of *Jezebel* noted Gawker's refusal to implement IP banning, which would have enabled them to fully block the person or people behind the GIF-posting but which would also have made anonymous commenting more challenging—and anonymous commenting is an activity that Gawker relies on to get many of its tips for articles. Gawker eventually implemented a

Dealing with Cybersexism

solution that prevented images and GIFs from being posted in comments, which was seen as a loss for many of those engaged with the site but a workable solution for preventing the original harassment.

In writing about the incident for the *Pacific Standard*—which has itself closed its comment section—Nicholas Jackson, the digital director for the *Pacific Standard*, noted that there seem to be few good solutions to the problems posed by comment sections (abusive comments, stressed-out moderators, and readers fleeing sites known for allowing toxic comments). Even forcing people to use their real names by connecting comment sections to Facebook rarely seems to serve as a deterrent. Instead, Jackson suggests, comments "belong on personal blogs, or on Twitter or Tumblr or Reddit, where individuals build a full, searchable body of work and can be judged accordingly."[32] By removing the ability to comment directly on a piece and instead ensuring that comments must be left elsewhere, in a place that enables subsequent viewers to contextualize the comments with the remainder of the writer's opinions, the worth of the discussion can be more easily determined.

This solution seems like a reasonable one for news sites, major publishers, and larger websites with multiple writers where targeted harassment of female writers is common and where fractious and aggressive comment sections can damage the mission of the publication, especially for science-related writing. Individual writers and bloggers, however, often count on dedicated visitors to their sites and cultivate active comment sections to increase traffic and build a sense of community. In those scenarios, deleting the comment section entirely is not optimal but neither is it affordable for those individuals to hire their own moderators, while moderating comments themselves may be too stressful or time-consuming to manage.

As with all solutions to online harassment and abuse, individual women are left largely to their own devices, to choose between a free and open online experience and constraining access to cut down on some forms of cybersexism. Very little focus is placed on finding strategies that enable women to fully participate in online environments while protecting users from abuse and creating disincentives for people to engage in cybersexist abuse in the first place.

Blocking individuals, increasing privacy settings, and moderating comments are all methods of dealing with cybersexist abuse as it occurs—reacting to and attempting to reduce its presence. However, women have created other methods of responding to abuse that rarely, if ever, see the public eye. Private backchannel discussions between women are an essential part of dealing with the onslaught of cybersexist abuse many women experience. Such discussions, like blocking, are not solutions to abuse but instead function as coping mechanisms that enable women to continue to face an unwelcoming online world. These types of conversations are also far from new.

The cyberfeminist Sadie Plant (who is usually credited with coining the term "cyberfeminism") has characterized the Internet as an "intrinsically" female space, reflecting her vision of explicitly gendered communication styles online, along axes of male and female users.[33] Plant has written that the ones and zeroes of binary code represent, respectively, men and women and that the potential online benefits of the "feminine, distributed, nonlinear" communication at which women already excelled offline would be a source of liberation online.[34] As a result, Plant felt direct feminist intervention in overcoming oppression online was unnecessary; she saw the overthrow of patriarchal domination as an inevitable result of the femaleness she assigned to Internet use.

Plant's characterization of Internet communication as female did not necessarily reflect the dominant user patterns of the Internet at the time of her writing. However, she was able to connect the collaborative form of communication common to online work with women's social roles as collaborators and sharers rather than competitors, a role more typically assigned to men and one that Plant believed would not be conducive to the online world. Plant writes, "Like woman, software systems are used as man's tools, his media and his weapons; all are developed in the interests of man, but all are poised to betray him," because, as she believed, women adjust better and more quickly than men to distributed, egalitarian, and constantly changing communication environments.[35] The role of cyberfeminism, in that framework, was to start the revolution.

One of the initial challenges of cyberfeminism was to show that the presumed link between technology and masculinity was not due to biological sex differences, a stereotype that persists today despite the long history of women creating, and working with, technology.[36] Remember that computer programming was once assumed to be the province of women until it was made profitable, and Ada Lovelace is widely regarded to have been the mother of computer programming. The correlation between technological prowess and hegemonic ideals of masculinity has largely been due to cultural constructions of engineering as the domain of men, along with the disassociation of technological activities from women's activities. And, as the writer and activist Judy Wajcman has noted elsewhere, when cyberfeminism moved away from "asking how women can be more equitably treated within and by science," the question became "how a science apparently so deeply involved in distinctively masculine projects could possibly be used for emancipatory ends."[37] The deliberate association of technology and feminism was intended to undermine stereotypes about technology, and cyberfeminists such as Donna Haraway and Sadie Plant sought to overturn preconceptions and highlight how computers and the Internet might be reshaped to eliminate gendered oppression.

Despite the lofty goals espoused by cyberfeminists, many of them—including Plant—relied on a deeply binary interpretation of online communications. Women and men were theorized as inherently different, and gender was often written about as the core and defining oppression that must be dealt with online; transgender men and women tend to be erased from analysis that sees men and women as ones and zeroes, and race, sexuality, disability, and so forth make little to no appearance at all. A modern cyberfeminism must be an intersectional cyberfeminism, with room to examine how technology and the Internet can be used to combat multiple oppressions, rather than creating easy metaphors that erase variety and disguise problems that have many roots.

Cyberfeminism became less of a buzzword during the mid-to-late 1990s, as access to the Internet increased and online life became a more central aspect of offline life. "Cyber" became an unnecessary appendage as feminist activism was increasingly written about and coordinated through online networks. However, many of the principles espoused by cyberfeminists hold true—women's networks in online spaces are subversive, protective, and nourishing environments. Women use the Internet to connect with one another and to defend one another from the predations of an Internet and a society that often do serious harm.

One study of Twitter, again focused on gender rather than intersections, assessed the reasons that men tend to get more retweets than women do. Allison Shapp, a linguistics doctoral student, found that women "use more 'commentary' hashtags that express emotion, like #soexcited," which are useful for connecting to one's existing followers but do not connect women to broader conversations.[38] As with any broad observation, exceptions certainly exist; women—and black women in particular—can be credited with the creation of multiple popular and long-running hashtags that are more informational than emotive and that resulted in trending discussions (the writer Mikki Kendall, for example, created the world-wide trending hashtag #solidarityisforwhitewomen, among others).[39] However, communication differences between men and women in online spaces tend to make it easier for women to form and maintain deep emotional connections with other women. Social networks, in fact, are dominated by women; with the exception of LinkedIn, the user bases on Facebook, Tumblr, Twitter, Pinterest, and Instagram all have more women than men.[40]

Many studies have explored the relationship between the Internet and self-esteem, social happiness and connection, and even cross-cultural acclimatization. Several of those studies have found that women tend to fare better from a psychological perspective in cross-cultural settings due, in large part, to the way the women studied were using the Internet. In one study the researchers found that "online social support was significantly and positively related to the cross-cultural adaptation of international students in China," enabling women studying or living internationally to more easily adjust to their surroundings.[41] Online social interactions

Dealing with Cybersexism

provided women who had been unhappy and even physically unwell with a place to connect with other people, discuss their emotional experiences and everyday lives, and get information on how to adjust to their international relocation.

Women also use formal and informal networks in online spaces to share their lives with one another and spread information about opportunities, education, activism, and even predators. Many men who are revealed to be serial harassers and abusers had long been identified among women's private networks in their industries; each time such abuse is made public, a flood of women come forward to finally share their stories publicly. Women's private networks in online spaces might consist of email chains, private Facebook groups, or other messages sent outside the public eye. Discussions among women have been used as a form of self-defense both online and off; study after study shows that such networks have immense benefits for women who have been living in shelters after fleeing domestic violence.[42] History reveals the importance of women's social networks back even to ancient Greece, from women's friendships through their contributions to civic life.[43]

In online spaces women have found new ways to construct social networks—both through social media and through the creation of their own spaces. One such space was created by a group of women in the mid-1990s, within Amsterdam's digital city, De Digitale Stad (DDS). Although the designers did not create a space only for women, outside users saw the need for one and worked to create it. The writer and professor Els Rommes has examined the creation of Amsterdam's digital city in 1994 and why it took women from outside the original design group to build a women's section. At the creation of DDS in Amsterdam feminism was considered "old fashioned," and the new wave of feminists "articulated an individualistic approach" that rejected the notion of collective women's spaces as a beneficial method of organizing.[44] As a result, the designers thought that including a women-only section was counterfeminist, as women should expect to have a seat at the table in the new online world.

Women themselves, however, thought that having their own space, to which they controlled access and where they could work collaboratively, was essential. The Women's House in Amsterdam has a physical, offline location where women's groups organize and rent space; it was this group that founded the DDS Women's Square after identifying opportunities for expanding their feminist work online, according to Rommes. The Women's Square offered women the ability to work on a variety of subjects within the website—something that would not have been possible offline. When creating the Women's Square the group had to overcome the gender scripts that define Internet use and access, the designers' gendered expectations of who would utilize DDS and for what purposes, and the design of DDS itself.

Additionally, issues of women's technological skill, access to computers, and protecting users from male harassment had to be addressed. The difficulties faced by the Women's House in creating their online space demonstrate how technology can limit activities focused on women, as well as how the Internet can be a space that prioritizes women's needs and protects them from harassment. Although the Women's Square had an uphill battle in "[creating] a place where women . . . could discuss women's issues without having to defend their space against hostile male contributions," they were eventually successful in developing an online meeting place that met their needs.[45] Women's networks are often self-created and developed in the face both of technological beliefs that run counter to women's needs and of outright hostility to women's desire for such networks.

Women's networks even expand to the professional realm, with groups such as Hire This Woman serving to move beyond the backchannel. "Hire This Woman is a recurring feature on ComicsAlliance that shines a spotlight on female comics creators, whether they're relative newcomers or experienced pros who are ready to break out," according to the site.[46] Comics are notoriously dominated by males, and developing a network that is specifically focused on counteracting the often unconscious prejudices that go into hiring and promoting talent is one area in which women's networks are especially beneficial. Social and professional networks are developed deliberately and emerge naturally from the ways women communicate with one another online.

Women's networks, whether public, private, or both, fill a number of necessary roles in online and offline spaces. Through these discussions,

Dealing with Cybersexism

women learn about one another, connect to other women with similar interests, promote each other's work, engage in activism, and more. In addition to their extensive hopes for the future of the Internet, cyberfeminists planned for their present: they frequently wrote about strategies and tactics for undermining the sexism they encountered during their daily lives, proposing innovative ways to use technology to subvert and overcome the effects of living in a sexist society. Women's ability to form and sustain networks in online spaces remains one of the core strategies.

WHAT CAN MEN DO?

One of the most common questions I am asked by male friends online who understand the gravity of cybersexist abuse is, "What can I do?" Many men want to help alleviate the pressure women feel when dealing with cybersexists and mob abuse but don't know how to help. In this section I briefly cover a few of the things men can do to prevent cybersexism and support women who are dealing with it.

The most obvious and easy way to combat cybersexism is for people not to engage in it. This statement might seem fanciful or even silly, but many otherwise thoughtful people can engage in cybersexism without even realizing it or while supporting other causes. One of the simplest ways men can reduce instances of cybersexism online is by refusing to give in to the temptation of participating in it. While healthy criticism of ideas and serious engagement with statements is an important part of a robust intellectual online community, that criticism is often reduced to mocking a woman or condemning her for the way she speaks or how she looks. For men who want to be part of the solution rather than part of the problem, containing their criticism to the ideas and statements at hand is one way to make an impact.

Many of the cybersexist attitudes described throughout this book rely on implicit biases about women—about how women talk, what women say, and what women's proper role should be. Before responding to a woman they disagree with or telling women they are taking up too much space in online communities, men who examine their responses before sending them might be surprised by how they are coming across. Taking a moment to ensure that criticism is focused on an actual problem or area needing further discussion can help men avoid contributing to some of the low-level types of cybersexism that many women experience.

In casual social conversation, men are often taught that it is acceptable and welcome for them to offer their evaluation of women's work, appearance, and thoughts without being asked to do so. Although not a form of cybersexism on the level of abuse that is discussed throughout this book, casually sexist behaviors like these reinforce gender-based stereotypes and have a tendency to make women feel unwelcome. Before offering an opinion, men who take a moment to ensure that their input is wanted can make significant strides toward breaking down power structures, show respect to their friends, peers, and colleagues, and engage in a conversation on equal footing.

Leigh Alexander, the journalist and author briefly discussed in the previous chapter, has also written on how men can best respond in situations of online harassment and abuse aimed at women. She suggests that men need to stop asking women what to do, stop expecting women to educate them about the abuse they are suffering, stop trying to explain the harassment, and stop telling women how to respond to it. As she notes, "sometimes people simply want to be heard and understood, and you do not need to prove you are a good person," which is what most of these behaviors are an attempt to indicate.[47] However, offering women advice they haven't requested or asking them to give information on abuse while they are experiencing it are both additional stresses that women dealing with cybersexists do not need.

A woman who is dealing with cybersexist harassment, whether from a single individual or a mob, is often flustered, frightened, and overwhelmed. Although many men mean well when they ask for advice on what to do or offer suggestions on how to react, to a woman in the midst of an already-exhausting situation these statements regularly end up being just more unwanted input. At best these behaviors tend to be counterproductive—at worst they can feel like mansplaining or victim-blaming, neither of which is something a woman facing an onslaught of cybersexism should be

Dealing with Cybersexism

expected to deal with. Avoiding these behaviors is one of the simplest things men can do when they know a friend is being targeted.

Alexander makes some suggestions about what men can do in lieu of these burdensome behaviors. She advises that men start expressing support for women on a one-on-one basis, considering how their response will affect the woman they see being harassed, supporting a woman's work rather than simply noting the ways she is being victimized, taking on some of the conversations to distract harassers (without keeping the original target involved), and becoming aware of their relative power in online situations.[48] All of these actions offer opportunities for men to engage in truly supportive behaviors in the face of cybersexist abuse and in ways that do not paint a bigger target on the women they want to support.

Two key strategies Alexander mentions are distracting harassers by drawing their attention away from an original target and supporting women without making their support specifically about victimization. In instances of online harassment many cybersexists will actually converse relatively pleasantly with other men—it is women who receive the brunt of their anger; as a result, men who intervene privately will likely have a greater chance at a real (or at least less abusive) conversation and draw at least a few abusers away from the original target. Helping to distract cybersexists can take an immense amount of pressure off of a woman simply by reducing the number of people who are actively harassing her.

While distracting cybersexists can be beneficial in the short term, supporting women's work outside the context of online abuse and harassment has significant long-term power. By taking a stand alongside women who have been harassed, but not making that harassment the focus of their support, men can help break down the stereotypes that characterize the Internet as a male-only space while also offering concrete support to individual women and women-led organizations. This approach emphasizes the fact that women's presence online is worthwhile because the Internet is a valuable space, helps amplify the voices and work of those who are traditionally marginalized online and off, and does both of those things without making the victimization of women the primary basis of that support.

Men have the ability to help reduce the damage caused by cybersexist abuse in online spaces through the mere act of being aware of how their actions affect the women around them. Privilege is insidious, and unintentionally sexist behaviors are perhaps even more common than the extreme behaviors of deliberate cybersexist abusers. Following even some of the advice in this section will help men to improve their relationships with women online.

This chapter has explored a variety of approaches to cybersexism thus far. One aspect of online harassment and abuse that often lacks critical analysis, however, is the relationship between cybersexism and the police.

CYBERSEXISM AND LAW ENFORCEMENT

Often when women discuss being on the receiving end of cybersexist abuse and harassment they're asked why they don't go to the police. This question is used as a taunt by the abusers themselves ("If what I'm doing is so wrong, why haven't I been arrested?") and as a genuine question ("If this is such a serious problem, shouldn't the police be involved?"). In both cases, a fundamental assumption is being made: that the world is just and that reporting crimes to the police will result in the criminal being caught and punished. Therefore, from a cybersexist's perspective, they have not been punished and have thus done nothing wrong; from another perspective, a conflict with the asker's sense of justice is introduced. Whether the assumption is based on viewing too many formulaic cop shows or simply built on a deeply held belief about the way the world should work, it's an assumption that flies in the face of reality for many women.

While approaching cybersexist abuse as a problem, many people advocate for involving the legal system. Brianna Wu, as quoted earlier in this book, called upon an Ohio prosecutor to address the death threats she had received from a man in Columbus. "Ron O'Brien, this case could not be more clear. The evidence on tape speaks for itself," she wrote, "and you have it in your power to subpoena his name from phone records."[49] Another article references Wu's disappointment with the legal response to the threats she has received—"She said she's in touch with the FBI, Homeland Security and her local law enforcement"—and yet a woman

Dealing with Cybersexism

reporting abuse to the police often encounters "incompetence or apathy."[50] Despite her frustration Wu still recommends that women report their abuse to the relevant law enforcement agency.

The scholar and writer Danielle Citron takes a similar approach in her excellent and thorough book on online harassment and abuse, *Hate Crimes in Cyberspace*, writing that "criminal convictions are powerful deterrents because of their lasting collateral consequences," but she goes on to note that criminal charges will be pursued only "assuming law enforcement and prosecutors take victims' complaints seriously."[51] Here, as Wu has also noted, is one of the key factors in why women don't take reports of cybersexist abuse to the police: law enforcement typically does not take victims' complaints seriously, and their abusers know it.

As Amanda Hess wrote in 2014 about a particularly graphic threat that she reported to the police, "this was not the first time that someone had responded to my work by threatening to rape and kill me. The cop anchored his hands on his belt, looked me in the eye, and said, 'What is Twitter?'"[52] Hess describes multiple attempts to report threats to the police, as well as the responses she received, which ranged from the incredulous to the dismissive. Local law enforcement agencies simply are not trained in how to respond to threats sent online—a threat sent via the mail or even made over the telephone is, at least, a known quantity. To many police officers, however, the Internet is a total mystery, threats are ephemeral, and they are unable or unwilling to do anything about it.

This situation leads one to wonder, then, what good it will do to encourage women to report the threats they receive. While Citron reviews an extensive list of existing laws that can be used to address some of the common abuses aimed at women (libel, which includes, for example, "falsely accusing someone of having a sexually transmitted infection," or criminal activity such as sending credible threats of violence, stalking, and using the Internet to encourage others to stalk or attack another person), there is no discussion of the fact that when women make such reports they are frequently dismissed without their complaints being pursued by the police or any other legal body.[53] In a segment on John Oliver's television show *Last Week Tonight*, Annmarie Chiarini, a professor targeted by a "revenge porn" website, described her experience with reporting the abuse and attempting to get legal representation. The first lawyer she spoke with told her she should "get better boyfriends. I won't take this case." The next lawyer said she would be charged a $5,000 retainer, with possible charges of $10,000 to $15,000 to resolve the issue.[54]

Not only was Chiarini unable to get one lawyer to take her case seriously, but when she found another she could not afford even the retainer, much less the projected costs. She was left entirely on her own to figure out how to respond to an attack that had the potential to ruin her career and had already caused her to attempt suicide. While many states are increasingly making the form of abuse she experienced illegal and while online threats and harassment are often already illegal due to existing libel and criminal laws, police departments and officers range from ignorant to dismissive of women's reports of online harassment, and legal redress tends to be beyond the financial reach of all but the most well-off women.

Calls for women to report their abuse to the police or engage in civil action presume that such reports will be heard and taken seriously and that the women making the reports have the time, energy, and financial resources to see their cases through to the end. Suggestions that women need to take legal action also rest on the assumption that the police can be trusted to listen to victims, pursue the perpetrator, and not harm those who make the reports. Additionally, few police departments currently have a sufficient knowledge base or the appropriate resources to assist women who have been threatened online. Many women have found that the police will say that they are unable to help with instances of severe and illegal online abuse or that they fail to understand why such threats should even be taken seriously.

Even when a threat is taken seriously, the outcome is not necessarily that the police spring into action and track down the perpetrator. In a previous chapter I mentioned that I once reported an online stalker to the police. When I arrived at the police station I was fully prepared for a response similar to the one Hess received—denial, dismissal, or ignorance. I took my laptop with me, which had records of all previous threats from the stalker, and followed a step-by-step guide to using Twitter's law enforcement report page.

The officer I met with understood what Twitter was and agreed that the threats were serious; he asked me to send in the law enforcement report form using his information and told me that he would follow up. He never did. Even when I received another series of threats and called to update the report on file, I heard nothing back. I don't know what information the police department received from Twitter (if any) or if they have any information on the identity of my stalker that might help me protect myself.

In many ways I am a "model" victim of online harassment: I am white, cisgender, thin, able-bodied, educated, working full-time, and was married to a white, cisgender, thin, educated man who worked full-time. Even with my full complement of social privileges, reporting a series of illegal death and rape threats made across a period of more than a year got me absolutely no closer to safety or justice than if I had done nothing at all. Many women with fewer privileges but in the same situation cannot even feel safe reporting their stalkers and abusers to the police. Legal outlets for responding to cybersexist harassment must take into account the safety of the women involved in any legal process, and yet we know that is not always what happens. Take, for example, reports of rape; chapter 5 discussed the myriad reasons a report might be labeled false without actually being untrue. There are also, at any given time, multiple news articles about rape and abuse victims being revictimized by the police after filing a report.

A police chief in Ohio "did nothing when an officer drugged and raped two female police cadets, then threatened the victims."[55] In Oklahoma a cop named Daniel Holtzclaw was charged with raping at least seven black women while on duty, using his authority as a police officer to ensure their silence.[56] Black Lives Matter, an on- and offline protest movement founded by a group of queer black women, tracks and protests the violence aimed at black people by the police and by society in general, which the founders consider essentially white supremacist in nature.[57] Thanks in large part to social media, such stories are being brought into the news cycle, highlighting not only the abuse of power that often comes with a police badge, from assault and rape to the unpunished murders of men, women, and children, but also the reason that many abuses go unreported.

Black women, sex workers, and transgender women in particular have reason to fear such abuses. Death and assault at the hands of police are disproportionately common for all three groups of women, as well as individuals in one or more of those categories. These women are also more likely to be on the receiving end of abuse in offline and online situations and yet be unwilling or unable to report their abuse due to fears of being attacked by the police or incarcerated themselves. We cannot believe that simply getting Congress to pass new laws regarding online abuse will solve the problem when so many people are unable to trust the police forces that should be there to enforce whatever laws are enacted. When and if such laws are implemented, we must also seriously consider adequate responses to online abuses. Is relying on the American prison system the right method for deterring cybersexists? How can a legal approach account for the global nature of the Internet?

A true legal reform solution will not merely take the form of new laws put in place at the national level and more people thrown into an increasingly for-profit prison system. A much larger project is required, and solving online abuse will require a cultural shift that incorporates dealing with offline abuse as a society and that addresses the abuses committed by the police themselves. While laws will be necessary for a framework that enables reports to be made and justice to be sought, we cannot rely on the laws themselves to create a more just society.

Many current theorists have proposed multimodal solutions to dealing with cybersexism that take numerous methods into account, including social changes, education, legal solutions, and alterations to Internet systems that can help curb the rate at which cybersexism occurs. Looking at cybersexism as a social ill that has both social and legal ramifications—and solutions—makes it easier to challenge the attitudes creating and promoting cybersexism, rather than enabling us to respond to only the most extreme examples of online abuse with the often imbalanced force of law. Among the multimodal solutions proposed, education, defense,

Dealing with Cybersexism

self-defense, the law, financial penalties, and the involvement of public and private businesses have all been considered as potential methods of responding to cybersexism and helping protect women's presence online. It is these solutions that are considered in the next chapter as possibilities and as a call to action.

7 | FIGHTING BACK
Remixing Cyberfeminism and Strategizing to Reduce Cybersexism

Ending the epidemic of online abuse aimed at women is of critical importance to a future that includes a functional Internet. The Internet is increasingly intertwined with everyday life, but if cybersexist abuse is allowed to remain a cornerstone of the online experience the whole thing will crumble. Figuring out what strategies to use to combat cybersexism will require analysis of how technology can be used to support the marginalized and make abuse less prevalent, but it will also require a cultural shift. Too often women who describe their experiences of dealing with cybersexist abuse are met with disbelief and dismissal; it is not possible to create a solution when those experiencing the problem are not heard in the first place.

In addition to ensuring that women's stories are heard, however, charting a better course for the future can mean taking a moment to consider the past. While cyberfeminism has largely disappeared from mainstream and online feminist work, the concepts, goals, and ideals the cyberfeminists shared can provide us with guideposts for the future. The present moment must also be taken into consideration: technology changes rapidly, and dealing with cybersexism will require the work not just of activists but of those persons responsible for the websites and platforms from which abuse is dealt.

In this chapter I discuss remixing cyberfeminism—going back to the ideals of theorists and repurposing useful concepts for the present day—as well as the multimodal solutions that we can consider for creating true solutions to online abuse, from education through reformation.

REMIXING CYBERFEMINISM

"I would rather be a cyborg than a goddess." That is Donna Haraway's central statement in the essay "A Cyborg Manifesto" and is perhaps the most well known cyberfeminist motto. It still appears frequently in writing on women and technology, although much of the context and many of the critiques made within the manifesto are left out of current works on women and technology. Cyberfeminism came into being as part of a resistance to the male-dominated and masculine perceptions of technology during the mid-1980s. As we begin to work on solutions for the pervasive issue of cybersexism, looking back at the cyberfeminist theories and theorists who analyzed the early Internet can give us a partial roadmap to a better future. As computers and the Internet became more widely accessible and readily used, early discourses around feminism and technology focused on the possibilities cyberfeminist theorists saw for using that technology to overcome oppression.

Cyberfeminist theory of the 1980s tended to be utopian in nature, with theorists imagining ways technology use could solve many of the world's ills and oppressions but sometimes forgetting to consider the ways technology reinforces and re-creates those same problems. Although the cyberfeminists were heavily engaged in pushing back against oppressive and sexist attitudes within technology spaces and online, they felt sure that the Internet would become a space of liberation for women. Characterizations of computers and the Internet as masculine became a flashpoint for the cyberfeminists, who were determined to explore the ways in which technology could be used to free women from patriarchal domination both online and off.

In considering cyberfeminism it might be more appropriate to think instead of *cyberfeminisms*; one of the key tenets of early online feminist theorizing was a refusal to create or be tied to a specific definition. Feminisms that focused on, theorized about, and were conducted in online and technological environments often had competing beliefs and goals but could all be accurately considered part of cyberfeminism. Many of the theories discussed here as springboards into new ideas, or as ways to challenge stereotypical or unfounded assumptions, come from these various cyberfeminisms.

CHALLENGING GENDER STEREOTYPES

One of the initial challenges cyberfeminism faced was to show that the presumed link between technology and masculinity was not due to biological sex differences—a stereotype that, unfortunately, persists.[1] Despite the work of cyberfeminists and others in showing that women are equally capable of working with, utilizing, and innovating with technology and online platforms, women are still underrepresented in technological fields, and persistent bias against women—along with deeply ingrained racism—remains prevalent throughout the tech industry.

The cultural connection between technological prowess and stereotypical ideals of masculinity is primarily due to deliberate constructions of engineering as the domain of men, along with the equally deliberate disassociation of technological activities from women's activities.[2] Although women were the first computer programmers, and women such as Adm. Grace Hopper created the foundation for much of modern computing, men began to take over the industry for its prestige, power, and pay.[3] Women were driven out of the rapidly growing computer industry and have yet to make truly significant inroads back into the field. Many sources show that, in fact, women's numbers in technology spaces, from college to the tech industry itself, have been declining.[4]

In response to the male-dominated technology environment of the 1980s and 1990s cyberfeminists purposefully linked technology and feminism in an attempt to undermine stereotypes about women, computers, and the Internet. Cyberfeminist theorists such as Haraway and Sadie Plant sought to overturn preconceptions about women and technology and to highlight how computers and the Internet might be used to eliminate gendered oppression. Groups such as the Old Boys Network, formed by a small group of women, led conferences and workshops that included everything from basic to high-level instruction in technology and Internet use to lectures, presentations, and dinner parties.[5] The goal of such online and offline organizing was to connect women with an interest in technology, provide a safe place to learn and explore, and explode the rapidly stabilizing stereotype of the tech wizard as a white male nerd.

If there were one cyberfeminist project that could still be said to exist today—although it might not use that name—it would be the drive to uncouple the tech field from these gender stereotypes. Women at every level in tech call out the problem: a culture that conforms to limiting and stereotypical norms that tend to keep women out, a career pipeline that leaks women almost as fast as they enter it, and the speed with which girls' interest in technology drops as they get older. Outdated stereotypes about who is suited to work in technology—and thus shape the future of tech—continue to affect the field.

Organizations such as Girls Who Code, founded by Reshma Saujani, Black Girls Code, founded by Kimberly Bryant, and Dames Who Game are notable for their intention to continue breaking down those stereotypes. On the Girls Who Code website the nonprofit is described as an "organization working to close the gender gap in the technology and engineering sectors," a goal nearly identical to early cyberfeminist attempts to break down the stereotypes that keep women out of tech.[6] Taking it a step further, Black Girls Code notes that "there's still a dearth of African American women in science, technology, engineering, and math professions, an absence that cannot be explained by, say, a lack of interest in those fields," which is a common response to feminist claims that already marginalized groups are underrepresented in technology spaces.[7] While focused on women in game development spaces, Dames Who Game is explicitly inclusive of "all people of any gender, sex, sexual orientation, gender expression, gender identity, race, religion, disability, nationality, socioeconomic status and immigrant status as members and community participants" and is designed to be welcoming and safe.[8] Each group emphasizes the need for such spaces to enable marginalized groups to work with technology and challenge the oppression and privilege that affect the industry.

All of these organizations are responding to the ongoing issue of race and gender in tech spaces, a project that was first recognized by cyberfeminists. Placing a continued emphasis on breaking down the stereotypes in technology spaces at every level of the technology environment—from childhood through college and into professional spaces, online and offline alike—is critical for reducing the extreme racial and gender imbalance prevalent in tech spaces and organizations.

In turn, such a shift will bring diverse perspectives into the development process. People with experience in dealing with online abuse are more likely to understand how best to combat it in ways that are sensitive to the experience of cybersexist harassment, and they can offer perspectives that are often sorely lacking in current organizations and development teams. Diverse teams will have the ability to offer perspectives not possessed by people who do not experience cybersexist or racist abuse and, as a result, to usher in better solutions.

EXAMINING THE RELATIONSHIP BETWEEN TECHNOLOGY AND OPPRESSION

Cyberfeminism involved not only challenging the gender stereotypes that shaped technological development but also examining the ways technology itself can either contribute to or reduce oppression. A major focus within cyberfeminism was whether access to the Internet and technology would enable women to subvert their online and offline oppression or whether technology would be used to reproduce sexism, racism, and other abuses in online spaces. The answer to both questions was—and still is—yes.

That is, technology and the Internet were created and are used by gendered and raced individuals working in a sociocultural context that shapes our thought patterns, our interactions with one another, our access to technology, and the purposes to which such technological advancements will be put. Technology was not created with oppression in mind, but, by virtue of being cast as the domain of cisgender white men of a certain class and education level, the privileges and oppressions that already exist necessarily shaped the outcome of technology development. Cyberfeminists, therefore, were not seeking to subvert sexism and other ills in technological spaces primed for success but fighting the stereotypes and sexist assumptions that are often built into the code of the Internet itself.

Additionally, it is worth noting that nearly every technological advancement throughout history has been seen as too liberating for women—and therefore dangerous. "From the late 18th century through the middle of the 19th, . . . women 'were considered to be in danger of not being able to differentiate between fiction and life,'" and "'novel reading for women was associated with inflaming of sexual passions; with liberal, radical ideas; with uppityness; with the attempt to overturn the status quo.'"[9] In the late 1880s "skeptics also worried that bicycling would encourage promiscuity by offering women greater mobility away from their homes and that it would prevent them from fulfilling their domestic duties," and such skeptics also speculated about the scandal that could be caused by women straddling a bicycle.[10] Everything from the telephone to the washing machine has been considered a worrying technological advancement that will make women too independent, and it was this independence that the cyberfeminists wished to claim for themselves.

Examining the relationship between technology and oppression meant seeking out ways to use technology for liberation, rather than merely following the prescribed pathways that had been built previously. Sadie Plant, for example, considered it "an alliance of the goods against their masters, an alliance of women and machines."[11] Outside of academic theorizing, cyberfeminists placed great emphasis on the power of art to highlight and then break down sexist stereotypes in technology.

As Jessie Daniels writes, however, "it is exceedingly rare within both cyberfeminist practices and critiques of them to see any reference to the intersection of gender and race" or any examination of the global labor practices that make access to technology possible for cyberfeminism to exist in the first place.[12] Cyberfeminism was primarily focused on gender as the universal binding tie and main source of oppression for women, often disregarding or even erasing factors such as race, sexuality, or disability.

Despite that narrow lens of focus, Daniels and other writers have called attention to and demand a more holistic understanding of oppression when viewed through a cyberfeminist lens. For example, Daniels and others point out that women of color working in developing nations often take on the labor of "technology manufacturing as quintessential cyborgs"—not in

Fighting Back

the liberated, sensual way of an end user that Haraway advocated but in deeply unsafe and unhealthy working conditions, for inadequate pay. Given that cyberfeminism was (and, to the extent that it still exists, remains) dominated by white, well-educated women in Western and developed nations, a failure to seriously consider such issues is a major problem.[13]

However, this issue also represents something that cyberfeminism was—and can be revived to be—ideally suited to address. As the Internet has become increasingly accessible and available on a global scale due to the proliferation of mobile, rather than desktop, devices, it is possible for women in otherwise marginalized areas to stake a claim in the feminist conversation. Although research on this area was not as robust as it should have been, many cyberfeminists did write about the importance of inter- and intracommunity theorizing, activism, and communication between white women and women of color, and women in industrialized and developing nations. In practice, many of these communities already exist; it should be the project of a reinvigorated cyberfeminism to connect them, provide resources, and amplify the voices of women who are otherwise unheard.

In terms of combating abuse, a cyberfeminist commitment to examining, analyzing, and challenging the relationships between technology and oppression is essential. We cannot solve a problem we don't understand, and learning about the ways in which technology and Internet spaces still create, contribute to, and reinforce stereotypes about race, gender, sexuality, and other intersections of oppression is one of the best ways to start a conversation about how we break those stereotypes down. Ensuring that women from traditionally marginalized groups and regions have a prominent, supported, and self-directed space within feminist activism is essential to creating solutions that meet the disparate needs of a global feminist community.

ANDROGYNY, THE CYBORG, AND DISEMBODIMENT

There are a number of other ways in which cyberfeminists believed that the Internet and technology use could become a platform on which to liberate women from the offline effects of sexism and patriarchal oppression. Haraway's cyborg metaphor appeared regularly, along with "identity tourism," androgyny, and disembodiment as ways women could overcome offline stereotypes online.[14] Daniels defines identity tourism as the ability for individuals to present an online persona using different gender or race markers than they possess in offline spaces. Cyberfeminists believed that blurring online identities or presenting an androgynous self was a beneficial activity, since it was seen as a way to reduce the psychological pressures of navigating throughout the world while contending with sexism, racism, homophobia, and other prejudices. The ability to play with perception online was regarded as a positive factor, and the Internet was seen as a place where oppressed identities could be abandoned or alternative ways of being could be explored.

"The chance to escape embodiment" that so many cyberfeminists pursued is deeply connected to identity tourism; it is the ability "to escape race and gender visibility" online, which has been discussed throughout this book.[15] Through assuming existence as someone other than a woman or a person of color online, or not laying claim to any identity at all through being effectively disembodied, cyberfeminists felt that oppressions based on previously visible distinctions would be undermined and ultimately destroyed. As Susan Luckman writes, much cyberfeminist thought is built on technological determinism, "which holds that the political problems of today will be resolved as technology brings the world closer to a cyber-utopia," reflecting a belief that technology is intrinsically progressive.[16] While not all cyberfeminists held utopian beliefs about technology, most early cyberfeminist writing was enthusiastic about the possibilities for a radically altered world through the ability to shed marginalized identities in online spaces.

However, not all feminist theorists saw disembodiment via technology as inevitably leading to gender equality. Susanna Paasonen looks at some of the ways in which utopian cyberfeminist thought was unable to completely account for gender relations in a technologically connected world, as "cyberdiscourse of the 1990s sort was premised on disembodiment," which Paasonen challenges, suggesting that a truly disembodied online life never existed and denying that it could exist now, as the web is increasingly

Fighting Back

integrated with daily life (think Facebook and selfies).[17] Paasonen shares Daniels's rejection of the cyberfeminist ideal of disembodiment, which is regarded as "an assumption of an exclusively text-based online world that belies the reality of digital video and photographic technology."[18] According to Paasonen, "the separation of [body and mind] is increasingly artificial and hardly descriptive of the experiences of internet usage characterized by ubiquitous access and multimodal representations of the self," due to the widespread availability of image, sound, and video used to create a visible online presence as one's actual self, rather than a persona of another race, gender, sex, or age.[19] The shift away from text-only online communication to video or voice chatting, the use of one's actual picture for avatars, the rise of social media, and other changes have made it effectively impossible for most people to fully participate in online life and remain disembodied in the cyberfeminist sense of the word.

Far from the cyberfeminist ideal of an androgynous or genderless cyborg community, most individuals who still attempt to remain disembodied (or at least unidentified) online do so because being other than a straight, cisgender white man is to be at risk for harassment. As Susan Herring has shown through her examination of online harassment, "when women attempt to participate on an equal par with men, they risk being ignored, trivialized, vilified, and—if they persist—accused of censoring or silencing male participants," as male respondents react negatively to women's voices in many online spaces.[20] Women who assume their full identities online are subjected to the same types of sexist oppression experienced offline, and although it was regarded as liberating to shed one's identity in favor of a presumably level playing field, the Internet still privileges straight, cisgender white men.

In addition to that privilege, men are seen as the default users of Internet spaces. As a result, for self-defense "[many] women choose to identify themselves as male online in order to avoid the unwanted attention of men," and while women's presence is challenged, the ability of men to harass and abuse women in online spaces "is unquestioned," since men are seen as the standard users and women, as newcomers, interlopers, or problems.[21] When women, LGBT individuals, and people of color shed their identity markers to either try on privileged identities or disguise themselves to pass as men—white, straight, or cisgender—the act of hiding those markers reifies both the concept of the Internet and technology as a space dominated by straight, cisgender white men.

And, as Daniels writes, "gender-switching online is only acceptable within very narrow boundaries" as "people actively seek out online spaces that affirm and solidify social identities along axes of race, gender, and sexuality," meaning that online interactions have a tendency to follow offline patterns of interaction by privileging those who present as straight, cisgender, white, or male online, regardless of their offline identity.[22] It is safer for most people who wish to be free of a marginalized offline identity to claim a particular type of privileged identity in online spaces wherever possible. However, while it's safer on an individual level, it also reinforces the idea of the default Internet user as white, straight, cisgender, and male. Thus, while cyberfeminists championed the idea of divesting one's online identity as a positive force, existing prejudicial attitudes often go unchallenged out of fear of sexist, racist, and other reprisals, and stereotypes about already marginalized groups are reinforced.

In addition, cyberfeminist writing did little to address the idea of celebrating one's identity as "other" as a form of empowerment, which limited the ability of cyberfeminist theorists to approach the presence of oppressive behaviors online from an intersectional perspective. While some individualist cyberfeminist thinking advocated loudly and proudly claiming space as a woman in online environments, the "cybergrrl," as Faith Wilding describes her, often reproduced stereotyped images of women without much deconstruction or critical analysis.[23] An appreciation of the variable axes of oppression in online spaces, along with firmer predictions about the ways in which online spaces might mimic offline sexism, might have made cyberfeminism less utopian about the possibilities for the Internet and might have encouraged deeper forays into making the Internet safe for people of all races and genders, instead of attempting to erase them in favor of an androgynous cyborg ideal.

The world cyberfeminists sought—an online and offline world free of sexism—has not materialized, and the current state of gender and race

Fighting Back

relations online makes it seem that utopia is perhaps farther away than ever before. While cyberfeminist writers generated complex, interesting, and often joyous methods for re-appropriating technology for the purpose of subverting offline patriarchal dominance, their assessment of the potential of the Internet did not account for the times in which almost all Internet users are so thoroughly connected to their offline bodies. Instead of encouraging the marginalized to shed their identities in pursuit of a genderless world, however, we can interrogate cyberfeminist thinking about gender to reach a greater understanding of the current state of the Internet. Whereas the cyberfeminists might have encouraged the marginalized to look outside their identities for freedom, a revolutionary approach to online life might be to celebrate and create safer spaces for people regardless of identity. Using the cyberfeminist strategies of analyzing, subverting, and rejecting stereotypes can still make the Internet safer for self-expression.

Research often shows that poor representation of marginalized groups enhances stereotypes; increasing representation is met with resistance at first but, eventually, acceptance of parity. For example, an NPR interview with Geena Davis on the representation of women in film revealed that if 17 percent of a group is women, men perceive the ratio as 50-50; if women make up 33 percent of a group, men feel as if they are outnumbered by women. "What we're, in effect, doing is training children to see that women and girls are less important than men and boys," Davis said.[24] To challenge these deeply ingrained attitudes, filmmakers and actresses Alysia Reiner and Sarah Megan Thomas began filming a movie about women on Wall Street, one in which, "in every bar scene and on every street, we will make sure that it is 50% women," to better reflect the reality of the world.[25] Cyberfeminist work online can take a similar tack—not by ensuring that people shed their offline identities but by accurately representing the diversity of online spaces.

Although resistance to better representation is likely to be strong at first, it is only by creating spaces for such representation that the biased impressions of who occupies online space can be challenged. Support for websites, movies, new technologies, creative endeavors, and other projects that have a diverse creator base and demonstrate diversity in their outcomes is a simple but powerful way to help reshape online spaces to reflect the diverse groups that use them.

CONTESTING THE INTERNET AS A "BLANK SLATE"

One of the most enduring myths about the Internet is that it was created as a blank slate—a neutral tool, one to be used for writing a new future for humanity, divorced from offline identities, politics, and histories. While some cyberfeminists thought that the Internet could be approached in this way, many were more interested in complicating the idea of the Internet as a value-neutral arena. As the "Wild West" ethos of the Internet was increasingly championed by early users in ways that would have long-lasting impacts, cyberfeminists sought to situate technology in its historical and cultural settings.

One of the most well known figures in the early years of the Internet was Howard Rheingold, who wrote a book called *The Virtual Community: Homesteading on the Electronic Frontier.* In a rather on-the-nose reference to the Wild West attitude many straight white men had about the Internet (and often still possess today, as we saw in earlier chapters), Rheingold discusses "the air of camaraderie and pioneer spirit" of early Internet users, the "young computer wizards and the grizzled old hands" who made up his community, and the almost entirely male group of early adopters with whom he spent time. In the first two chapters of *The Virtual Community* Rheingold barely mentions women at all—his wife gets a mention as a nagging killjoy early on: she was "concerned, then jealous, then angry" that he spent so much time online.[26] Apart from Rheingold's wife, women seem to have been peripheral to the early years of "homesteading" online.

Although Rheingold effuses about the possibilities of an Internet where, "[because] we cannot see one another in cyberspace, gender, age, national origin, and physical appearance are not apparent unless a person wants to make such characteristics public," his early online community was shaped, run, and controlled almost entirely by a small group of white men like himself.[27] It is this particular unwillingness to examine context that many cyberfeminists wished to challenge—that just because cyberspace could provide a space where race and gender were not determining factors in design and power didn't mean it would. While straight white men, often considered the default Internet user, see the Internet as a neutral tool because it conforms so exactly to their expectations, everyone else had to make adjustments and look for loopholes in order to use the Internet in the way they wanted. Technological tools are not developed in a cultural vacuum, and so the perspectives, biases, and beliefs of those who are in charge of design and dissemination are reflected in the end product. As cyberfeminists pointed out, the dominance of white men in the creation and control of the Internet shaped its outcome in many ways; to other white men the outcome seemed like a blank slate. To marginalized groups the slate was already covered in writing only they seemed to be able to see.

This problem persists today, with design groups lacking in diversity missing the glaring issues that affect end users. For example, the Apple Watch, which was supposed to revolutionize the wearable technology field, suffered a major design issue: it didn't appear to work for people with tattoos on their wrists.[28] Early adopters began remarking that their Apple Watch refused to unlock, as it requires skin contact to function and was not recognizing their tattooed skin as skin at all. That is, the Apple Watch was not programmed using technology capable of recognizing dark skin, which could have an impact on an even larger group of users: black people. One mechanical engineer, Steven LeBoeuf, said that the design of the Apple Watch was likely to be ineffective for anyone with darker skin, due to the type of light used in its sensors. Having a more diverse development team from the beginning could have alerted Apple to this problem long before the product went to market.

Apple, like most major tech companies, has dismal diversity figures—in 2014 only 2 percent of people working for Apple were black, and only 30 percent of their global employees were women.[29] As a result, things like including menstrual tracking in health apps and developing technology that works for users other than white people were unlikely to even cross the design team's mind. It is in these types of design values that cyberfeminist work on challenging the idea of the Internet and technology as value-neutral tools remains critically important.

A core tenet of cyberfeminist analysis is that all technology is developed in non-neutral settings by non-neutral actors. As Wilding has written, "the new media [cyberspace and computers] exist within a social framework that is already established in its practices and embedded in economic, political, and cultural environments that are still deeply sexist and racist." Even when racism and sexism are expressed without deliberate intention, as in the design of technology that unintentionally excludes certain end users, technology "is already socially inscribed with regard to bodies, sex, age, economics, social class, and race."[30] Many early users of the Internet were, like Rheingold, overjoyed at the prospect of an Internet that disguised those differentiating factors but never stopped to analyze how ignoring them could tilt the already uneven playing field.

A lack of diversity in the development stage will have unforeseen but potentially disastrous effects on the end product. As a result, cybersexism flourishes in online spaces in large part because such spaces are designed to be permissive with regard to abusive behaviors—they are seen as part of an environmental norm that formed in online spaces, rather than the extension of offline beliefs and behaviors. Those who designed online spaces were not those who dealt with sexist, racist, or other forms of harassment offline, and so they rarely stopped to consider how such behaviors could be enacted online.

A revisited cyberfeminist analysis of the historical, cultural, and social attitudes that influenced the formation of Internet spaces and established those norms is an essential part of understanding how to look for and create solutions. This analysis shows that having diverse teams at every stage of development, testing, and release is essential. Companies that rely on perceptions of elite users and thinkers, who somehow manage to be overwhelmingly straight, white, and cisgender men, are excluding perspectives, experiences, and expertise that will play a role for everyone who uses their products. Finding ways to combat online abuse requires working with those who experience it if we are to create true solutions.

STRATEGIC SEPARATISM

One of the earliest methods of online feminist activism was strategic separatism—the recognition that liberation, freedom, and subversion required women-only spaces to explore new ways of existing in the world. While some of those spaces, then and now, attempt to exclude transgender women and nonbinary people, I argue that strategic separatism within a robust and revived cyberfeminism must be inclusive. A key factor in online and offline communication is that men tend to dominate discussions and to regard women's participation as secondary and often as undesirable. Forming women-only communities gave cyberfeminists the opportunity to experiment with alternative conversational structures, new forms of leadership, and the possibility of productivity and discussion outside the control of a patriarchal gaze.

The use of strategic separatism is reflected in the women-only spaces discussed in the previous chapter: for example, women's private Facebook groups and email threads, online/offline hybrid groups that connect women across time zones and geography, Amsterdam's digital city for women—all of these forms of strategic separatism are intended to give women safer spaces. Cyberfeminism advocated strategic separatism as an intentional method of disrupting traditional power structures and conversational patterns; many women intuitively desire a "room of one's own" online—or a room to share with a few friends—for the same reason.

While Sadie Plant would have argued that those communities would be inherently liberating due to her belief that women and men were different in fundamental and immutable ways, it is important to remember that women are still raised and socialized in societies that place strict expectations and limitations on expression based on gender. The formation of women-only spaces is no guarantee that the outcome will be egalitarian, and continued oppression along the axes of race, class, sexuality, and more is still present too often in those communities. Although Wilding writes that "cyberfeminists want to avoid the damaging mistakes of exclusion, lesbophobia, . . . and racism, which sometimes were part of past feminist thinking," these issues are still very much present in online and offline feminist communities today, along with transphobia, classism, and other issues that cannot be confronted without discussion and education.[31]

Strategic separatism must therefore be as much about separating women from men as separating women from privileged modes of thinking and acting—creating new spaces in which to revel in the freedom of not being constantly interrupted by men, as well as to unpack our own biases and prejudices in order to more fully liberate ourselves and each other. Cisgender women have a specific set of social privileges around gender and expression, and excluding transgender women and nonbinary people from spaces designed to be outside of narrow patriarchal control is at best counterproductive. As mentioned in previous chapters, women who experience multiple forms of oppression, such as transmisogyny (the misogyny associated with being a transgender woman) are more likely to be in need of safe spaces for discussion, organization, and activism than the predominantly white cisgender women who wish to keep them out. Inclusive spaces offer better opportunities to learn, strategize, and attempt to create pathways to a better future.

Strategic separatism cannot be an effective method for liberating women if it is used as a way to give women who are otherwise privileged (by being white, cisgender, well educated, or middle or upper class) the center stage, access to media and publishing opportunities, and the ability to drown out the voices of women dealing with not only sexism but also transmisogyny, misogynoir, racism, homophobia, ableism, and other intersecting oppressions. This area is one where cyberfeminism can be repurposed to suit a new era, where cross-platform organizing, inclusiveness, and a commitment to resisting dominant norms and methods of limiting women's possibilities can come into play.

Women can, at least temporarily, escape some forms of cybersexist abuse by engaging in strategic separatism and forming safe spaces. This type of separatism, however, can result in liberation only when it is inclusive of all the varying experiences that defy the limitations placed on women by patriarchal expectations. The project of cyberfeminism, to inscribe new ways of being in online and offline spaces, will be right at home here.

Fighting Back

Strategic separatism can also be used to design, test, and refine new forms of online communities. One of the major problems leading to online abuse is that many websites are set up in ways that enable and allow cyber-sexist harassment to flourish. By creating their own communities to search for new ways to exist online, cyberfeminists and other groups have the potential to develop better and more effective solutions to this problem. While dedicated harassers will seek ways into such communities, investing time and energy in spaces where harassment is deterred and controlled can help marginalized groups find ways to implement those solutions in other online communities.

ART AND CRITIQUE

Many of the previous cyberfeminist theories discussed in this chapter have been academic in nature; these are the topics of lived reality, yes, but also of conference papers, academic organizations, and dissertations. Where cyberfeminism really came to life, for many people, was through the creation of art, as well as through the writing and publication of cultural and media criticism. Of all of the cyberfeminist theories discussed in this chapter, art and critique have remained perhaps the most vibrant since early in the twenty-first century. While these newer projects are not neces-sarily labeled as being cyberfeminist, the ethos of "joy and affirmation," of becoming "the virus of the new world disorder," remains present in them.[32]

One of the most well known pieces of cyberfeminist art was *Cyberflesh Girlmonster*, a piece created by Linda Dement in the mid-1990s.[33] The artist created the work using scanned images of various women's bodies, as well as insects, tools, and technological images. The reader/viewer/player could click on various "monsters," causing text to appear, sound to play, or another monster to enter the screen. The work, while interactive, offered no control to its audience beyond clicking. The limited narratives imagined women's bodies through a cyberfeminist lens, deconstructed them, and presented brief, decontextualized stories of sexuality, revenge, desire, and violence.

The messages sent in the piece were closely aligned to many cyber-feminist theories. Gender in *Cyberflesh Girlmonster* is, as the title implies, monstrous—it is something to be feared, explored, loved, and hated. The interaction between technology and the viewer is intended to disturb comfortable ideas about bodies and their presentation. Many pieces of cyberfeminist art relied on hyperlinks and limited interaction to guide viewers through scenarios or images meant to upset stereotypes about technology and about women.

Other works of art and critique blurred the lines between art, theory, and activism, as cyberfeminism often sought to do. The VNS Matrix, an Australian art collective credited with originating the term "cyberfeminism" nearly simultaneously with Sadie Plant, released a manifesto—part declaration, part poem—that took the sensuality of the cyborg concept and wedded it to a declaration of war on the limitations of patriarchal thinking. In part, that "Cyberfeminist Manifesto for the 21st Century" reads,

We are the modern cunt
positive anti reason
unbounded unleashed unforgiving
we see art with our cunt we make art with our cunt
we believe in jouissance madness holiness and poetry
we are the virus of the new world disorder
rupturing the symbolic from within
saboteurs of big daddy mainframe
the clitoris is a direct line to the matrix[34]

While the manifesto connects cyberfeminism to cisgender representations of female sexuality, VNS Matrix also released an interactive video game called *All New Gen* as an art installation, which was described as being "for non-specific genders" and as "a zone where gender is a shufflable six-letter word and power is no longer centered in a specific organization," reflecting the possibility of moving beyond the limitations of binary gender.[35] Such works of art were deliberately provocative, even upsetting, and deliberately blurred the lines between online and offline interaction.

Cyberfeminist art had a strong connection to the do-it-yourself ethos that led to the creation of zines and other offline modes of expression commonly favored by young women in the mid-1990s. Participatory art—art that, in the early days, involved hypertext links to move a story or game forward—was common, and collaborative critical thinking and hacking were seen as essential parts of cyberfeminist artwork. The goal of cyberfeminist art was not only to provide women with a space in which to be creative but also to disseminate messages about technology-based environments: all is not what it seems, and it can be different than what it is.

Today, cyberfeminist art and critique take a variety of forms. Anita Sarkeesian's *Feminist Frequency* is perhaps the most well known source of feminist critique in online spaces, and while her series on gaming gets the most attention, she has also done videos that look at advertising, Lego, TV shows, and more. Similarly, the Invisibility Blues project, run by Dr. Samantha Blackmon and Alisha Karabinus, aims to critically examine race and representation in video games. "For years, the gaming industry has centered on and around white male heroes," they stated in their Kickstarter video. They explained that their goal was "to broaden the spotlight" and, through a series of videos, help viewers think about how race impacts the gaming experience and gamer culture.[36] Twine is an open-source gaming tool that helps anyone create interactive gaming experiences online without having to learn code. It has opened the field up to a variety of diverse and marginalized creators who might otherwise have been kept out of the independent game development space.[37]

Many independent video games have been created to explore specifically feminist and Internet-related feminist topics. These games are often targeted with hatred from cybersexist groups, rather than with reasonable critique. *Freshman Year*, a short game by Nina Freeman, takes the player through an evening as a young woman. Combining limited animation, music, and text, the game gives the player a small number of options that direct the character to go to a bar.[38] The outcome of all choices in the game is the same: a bouncer at the bar attempts to assault her. The game is not "fun" in the traditional sense. Instead, it is a look at the powerlessness many women feel when confronted with these situations. By having all choices lead to the same conclusion, Freeman demonstrates that these attacks are not related to a woman's decisions but to her attacker's choices.

Games like Freeman's use technology and the Internet to share a message with others, in keeping with the cyberfeminist artwork of previous years. Taking control of technology and creating new forms of expression that challenge dominant messages was and could still be seen as a key part of cyberfeminism.

Outside of gaming spaces, feminist art continues to develop along a variety of paths in online spaces. The *gURLs* event in 2013 was an offline celebration of online feminist art, a nine-artist gallery event that "featured art that celebrates girl culture within social media, dissolving the line between digitally rendered performances and online-based poetry," and revealed that "digitally rendered femininity takes on a hyper-self-aware, confessional, and often-humorous tone," which the cyberfeminists would have intimately recognized as part of their own desire for the continuation of women's art online.[39] When Rupi Kaur's image of herself, clad in gray sweatpants and having bled through them onto her sheets, was removed from Instagram not once but twice, feminist artists from around the world responded. "Both women and art have been censored for centuries. But now, because of the internet—and the fact that we have access to multiple channels of communication where we can share our thoughts—we are able to bring attention to who is censoring us and what is being censored," Lessa Millet told the *Huffington Post*.[40] The *Huffington Post* published statements and images from fifteen female artists protesting the censorship of Kaur's photograph, which represented the kind of artistic and theoretical protest that has characterized the cyberfeminist movement.

Both of these examples feature feminists using technology and art as a direct response to sexism. The *gURLs* event showcased a group of women who had continued the cyberfeminist project of blurring the distinctions between online and offline identity, while owning and subverting gender stereotypes. The resistance to Instagram's ongoing policing of women's bodies and expression found its home in the creation of even more art, which was displayed in online spaces.

One artist using her art to respond specifically to online harassment is Lindsay Bottos, who became well known for her photo project *Anony-*

mous. Anonymous superimposed misogynistic comments she had received over a series of selfies.[41] The selfies feature Bottos with her hair pulled back, wearing the same checkered outfit throughout, smiling wryly at the camera or gazing at the viewer from the corner of her eye, each frame showcasing a comment that speculates on her promiscuity, calls her ugly, or otherwise relays the hatred a woman can expect for being a woman and online. Another project, according to her Tumblr page, would use a similar strategy: additional self-portraits overlaid with various comments she received in response to *Anonymous* and her continued work in photography.[42] Responding to cybersexist criticism by showcasing it has become a form of catharsis for many women who are targeted, and Bottos's art provides a relatable canvas for other women to consider.

Art, critiques of art, and criticism through art are part of any vibrant movement, and online activism is no different. Cyberfeminism may not be recognized as the direct inspiration for the videos, photographs, essays, stories, and games produced by today's feminist artists, but the foundations laid by Linda Dement, vns Matrix, Critical Art Ensemble, Shu Lea Cheang, and others provide a useful framework for considering how art can be used to talk back to a still-sexist culture.

Taking control of technology that was not designed with women in mind and finding ways to repurpose it for feminist ends has always been a core part of cyberfeminism. Continuing to use art and critique to build online communities of engaged and informed viewers is one way to build a dialogue about and around the topic of online harassment and abuse. Cybersexism can be shown for what it is through creative arts, and the attitudes that create it can be explored through critique. While cyberfeminism and the arts are not by themselves solutions to cybersexism, having avenues to discuss the problem is an essential outlet for many of the people who experience it.

INDIVIDUALISM VERSUS COLLECTIVE/DISTRIBUTED ACTION

Two main schools of thought emerged during the cyberfeminist heyday regarding the ideal strategy for feminist activism. One school of thought was very much in line with the mainstream feminism of the 1990s: activism should be highly individualistic, with women focused on getting ahead and getting theirs. The other school of thought sought an activism grounded in a thorough understanding of and reckoning with the offline history of feminism and focused on assisting women as an oppressed and intersectional group through collective and distributed actions. These two lines of thinking were rarely in direct conflict, but they can be said to represent something of a missed opportunity for early cyberfeminists.

Wilding describes proponents of the individualist position (who may, by virtue of having that position, not even recognize it as one at all) as cybergrrls, writing that "most cybergrrls don't seem interested in engaging in a political critique of women's position on the Net—instead they adopt the somewhat anti-theory attitude which seems to prevail currently; they'd rather forge ahead to express their ideas directly in their art and interactive practices."[43] That is, the cybergrrls wanted to take the Internet by storm, one at a time or in small groups, declaring their presence in the form of art, hacking, and, in many ways, a rejection of the feminism that existed before the Internet. While not quite adopting the "clean slate" idea, many of these individualist feminists saw the Internet as an opportunity to break with some of the issues that had plagued feminist activism in offline spaces.

The other leading line of thought saw historical feminism and feminist theory as something to learn from and build on. While the need for direct, individual impact was great, cyberfeminists who emphasized learning and sharing theory emphasized the risks of ignoring history. Many of the missteps and divisions within feminism as a whole come from a failure or refusal to examine past mistakes and the current impact of history, privilege, and intersecting forms of oppression. An intentional cyberfeminism driven by an understanding of history and theory is better positioned to create an Internet that benefits all women, rather than reproducing the issues caused by privilege structures that already exist between women.

Each strategy offers different benefits, depending on who is utilizing it and to what end. To use the current state of the Internet as an example, the ability for an individual person to write a Facebook post or series of tweets about an experience of sexism (cyber or otherwise) and receive support or find resources is a positive outcome. Women who can act on their own to

Fighting Back

address their own lives, whether through art, blogging, academic writing, or other means, are well positioned to be at the forefront of their own liberation. Finding individual empowerment in online spaces is a central goal of cyberfeminism. Another central goal, however, is to not leave other women behind. To that end, a thorough understanding of feminist history and theory and a grasp of collective activism in addition to individual empowerment is essential. As Wilding, drawing on Haraway, puts it, "If I'd rather be a cyberfeminist than a goddess, I'd damned well better know why, and be willing to say so."[44] Her critique of strategies that attempt to make a clean break from the historical feminist theories—successes and failures alike—that were necessary to generate cyberfeminism must be taken into account.

Of course, an ideal solution, and one that Wilding also proposes, is a melding of the two strategies—not a rejection of collective action or feminist history but a willing acknowledgment of it and a determination to move forward productively; not an endless discussion of theory but a joyous movement that also celebrates individuality and feminist journeys as worthwhile on their own. As Wilding puts it, "If grrrl energy and invention were to be coupled with engaged political theory and practice . . . Imagine! . . . Imagine cyberfeminist theorists teaming up with brash and cunning grrl net artists to visualize new female representations of bodies, languages and subjectivities in cyberspace!"[45] A remixed and modern cyberfeminism must work to use the energy individual activists bring to the table in combination with the theory and lessons provided by feminisms of the past.

When dealing with things like cybersexist abuse, it cannot be said often enough that there is no way to solve a problem without understanding it. Individual feminist activists can only do so much to draw attention to the issue without finding ways to explore and examine its causes and look for serious solutions. A workable cyberfeminist future must be inclusive of the feminist past but malleable enough to respond to the constantly changing environment that is the Internet, and for that we need everyone.

Too much high-profile online feminism at present relies on the individualist line of thinking. While analysis of sexism is common, much mainstream feminism fails at assessing the basic intersections of identity beyond solely considering gender. The concerns of thin, white, straight, and cisgender women tend to take the forefront of online feminist conversations, while drawing on the work of black feminists and other groups without attribution or pay. Dealing with the issue of online abuse must account for intragroup issues as well, and feminism cannot be separated from these problems without addressing them.

A reinvigorated cyberfeminist outlook can help provide new methods for online organizing and interaction that take a plurality of voices and perspectives into account. By creating inclusive communities and methodologies, feminism in online spaces will be better positioned to respond to incidents of cybersexist abuse and to everyone who experiences it.

THE PERSONAL COMPUTER IS THE POLITICAL COMPUTER

One of the key messages of cyberfeminism that can be used in thinking about how we deal with the problem of cybersexism is that the personal computer is the political computer. Whether a person is acting as an individual or as part of a group, gaining access to technology and computers is always a political act, one that is bound up in questions of gender, race, class, sexuality, age, ability, and more. Cyberfeminism understood that the mere presence of women in online spaces was, in many ways, a radical act—and it remains one today, especially in the face of so many attempts to keep women silent or invisible.

The theories discussed to this point in the chapter are wide-ranging, taking in everything from challenging gender stereotypes to creating new art to asking whether or not it's possible to be disembodied in online spaces. While the goal of cyberfeminism was not explicitly to combat the online harassment women deal with, understanding what their various projects looked like then and how they can be repurposed to fit a new online world can keep us from reinventing the wheel as we seek methods for making the Internet safe. The remainder of this chapter addresses that goal by discussing possible strategies for dealing with cybersexism as we go forward and by profiling a handful of organizations and individuals who embody these cyberfeminist principles in their work to prevent cybersexism or alleviate its impact.

DEVELOPING SOLUTIONS FOR CYBERSEXISM

The nature of the Internet allows sexist harassment and abuse of women to take place on an unprecedented scale. However, as cyberfeminism predicted, the Internet can also be used as a tool to undermine and fight back against harassment and abuse, both online and offline. There are a number of groups, individuals, and organizations working to combat the harms caused by online abuse and to find ways of making the Internet more inclusive and safer for everyone to use. Additionally, while much cybersexist behavior falls outside the scope of law, there are potential legal avenues for responding to abuse that can and should be considered.

While cyberfeminist activism has been discussed throughout this chapter, basic web design principles are also at play when cybersexist abuse occurs. There are a number of methods that can be used to deter, limit, or prevent patterns of abuse from escalating. As discussed previously, moderating or even closing comment sections can be a useful strategy for reducing the amount of harassment that occurs on a certain website. While difficult to scale and still reliant on human interaction when comments are permissible, many websites and online communities should consider stronger moderation policies, clear codes of conduct, and escalating consequences for repeat abusers.

Another important aspect of the Internet that has been discussed is anonymity. While protecting the ability of individuals to be anonymous is an important part of maintaining a free and open Internet, it must also be possible for communities and individuals to restrict the amount of anonymous online abuse that occurs. In situations such as Gamergate and other large-scale harassment initiatives, finding ways to prevent anonymous abuse while still enabling legitimate anonymous users to exist is an important balancing act. Fortunately, there are methods site owners can adopt that will not only protect the anonymity of their users but also protect their users from those who want to use anonymity to cause harm.

In *Hate Crimes in Cyberspace* Danielle Citron suggests that websites and online communities "could adopt anonymity as their default setting" but make it a privilege contingent upon users' behavior. Furthermore, "users who violate terms-of-service agreements could be required to authenticate their identities in order to continue their site privileges."[46] In this way, websites and communities can allow users to maintain an anonymous presence, while still being empowered to enforce terms of service and enact consequences on those who refuse to abide by community standards. The knowledge that losing site access or the ability to participate anonymously may act as a deterrent for many abusers. I would add that websites should also give themselves the option to terminate accounts and engage in IP banning or blocking for repeat offenders; as we have seen with too many instances of harassment to count, sometimes one barrier is not enough. IP banning is a process by which traffic from a specific IP address is prevented from accessing a website. It is in essence a digital blacklist.

In *The Internet of Garbage* Sarah Jeong recommends making architectural changes to websites and social media platforms. These changes can be used to create safer online spaces, because "code . . . can inhibit and enhance certain kinds of speech over others," enabling communities to explicitly and implicitly send messages to users about acceptable conduct while, when necessary, removing abusive content. Tools such as Block Together "are a [user interface] tweak that takes away the low, angry buzz that comes with being a target on the internet," she writes, suggesting that similar platform-based tools should be created by websites, with the input of site moderators and those who are familiar with how online abuse functions in that particular environment.[47] The ability of websites and social media platforms to subtly influence content creation in ways that protect users without requiring the expense and inefficiency of contracted moderators should not be ignored.

Citron and Jeong both discuss the success of the online video game *League of Legends* in dealing with a harassment problem associated with it. The *League of Legends* chat function had developed a reputation for toxicity, as many online gaming spaces have. Instead of entirely banning the chat function or instituting hired moderators, however, "developer

Riot Games announced a new instant feedback system that would punish players" for speech deemed offensive or abusive by reviewing chat logs and sending what amounts to a report card. Each report to the offending player "includes details of their harassment," along with their penalty for the abusive speech.[48] Penalties vary in intensity, including suspensions of varying lengths depending on the harassment and permanent bans immediately following a game in instances of severe harassment.

A player-based jury system called the Tribunal reviews reports, metes out punishment, and enables players to vote on the harassment reports, allowing people with investment in the game and its community to make decisions about how it should run. The most encouraging sign is that, by and large, it works. According to Citron, "Those who had been suspended for three days had 13 percent fewer reports going forward; those who had been suspended for fourteen days had 11 percent fewer reports," a fact that the developers attributed to the punishment including detailed explanations of why the player was being suspended and what they could do to avoid penalties in the future.[49] People who understand that there are consequences for their actions and what actions are generating those consequences may be less likely to repeat the behavior that landed them in trouble in the first place.

Additionally, players who went through the Tribunal review system found value in the experience. Some players "have actually asked to be placed in a Restricted Chat Mode, which limits the number of messages they can send in games," and making the chat feature opt-in instead of opt-out resulted in a marked decrease in harassment during gaming sessions.[50] All of these solutions together created an environment on *League of Legends* that was much more pleasant for those who chose to participate in it, and those who violated community norms saw consequences in proportion to their actions.

While these solutions cannot be transplanted in their entirety to other websites or online communities, the basic principles provide success stories and guidelines for potentially reducing the incidence of online harassment and abuse. Allowing community members to participate in the enforcement of established norms, implementing penalties for those who violate stated rules and terms of service, explaining why those penalties have been issued, and creating small but simple measures to fight abuse (like making various communication features opt-in rather than opt-out) can all be extremely effective ways of limiting cybersexist harassment. Empowering users to be involved in the setting and resetting of expectations for engagement in a particular community or forum can result in a repeat of the anything-goes philosophy that so often permits abuse, but as *League of Legends* demonstrates, it is entirely possible to create buy-in to norms that discourage abusive behavior from occurring in the first place and reduce repetitive abuse by the same individuals.

One other method of reducing online harassment deals with how abuse is reported and handled. While, as discussed previously, user-submitted reports are often an after-the-fact burden on targets of harassment, sites cannot know that abuse has occurred unless there is a way for users to tell them. As Citron notes, "user-friendly reporting mechanisms help facilitate the process" of identifying abusers or policy violators and dealing with their transgression, whether by removing their access to the target, temporarily suspending the account, revoking their account on the site entirely, or some other solution as defined by the community's standards.[51] Automating reports as much as possible is one way to reduce the burden on potential targets, although ensuring that any manual reports that must be submitted are user-friendly is also critical; people who are being targeted for online abuse, especially by mobs, often are not willing or able to spend time filling out complex reports that require them to go back through the abuse to direct a reviewer to the abusive accounts or content.

While review of abuse is labor-intensive work, especially for large websites like those of news organizations and for social media sites such as Facebook, there are ways to reduce the likelihood that other users will be exposed to potentially abusive content during the review process. For example, websites that allow upvoting or downvoting on comments also often hide comments that are downvoted too many times. On Reddit, for example, "negative-rated comments are grayed-out and automatically minimized," which places a barrier between new viewers and comments that the community has decided are outside its accepted norms.[52] Such a

Fighting Back

strategy could be adopted for comments, tweets, Facebook posts, and other interactions once an abuse report is submitted; until the report is reviewed, that content could remain invisible unless other users choose to view it.

The obvious downside to this, of course, is that much legitimate content could be mass reported by harassment mobs in order to hide it from its intended audience. Anita Sarkeesian's Tropes vs. Women in Video Games Kickstarter project and YouTube videos are regularly falsely reported in just this way, and individuals with smaller platforms could quickly find themselves overwhelmed by false reports. However, a balance between protecting users from abusive content and protecting users from abuses of the reporting system is something that service providers and websites should be able to achieve.

In addition to these solutions, Internet service providers (ISPs) and individual websites themselves have a role to play in dealing with cyber-sexist harassment. As Citron puts it, "digital gatekeepers have substantial freedom to decide whether and when to tackle cyber stalking and harassment"—and the fact that so few have done so is a testament to the lack of importance many companies place on the safety of their end users.[53] Many ISPs see themselves as neutral actors in online situations, providing access to all and passing judgment on none. In many ways this stance is important for protecting valuable speech, but, as we have seen, ISPs and "search engines . . . may block speech to comply with foreign laws," thus demonstrating that neutrality is not necessarily the deciding factor in their decision about what speech to permit.[54] Cyberfeminists would challenge any site's claim to be neutral on the issue of allowing or disallowing speech, as well. Choosing to allow all speech (and choosing to restrict certain forms of speech based on various governmental wishes) is an inherently political decision and one that will have unseen ramifications for users of the service. When cybersexist content and other abusive speech is permitted to flourish, free speech for the targeted groups actually suffers; simply permitting all speech under the guise of remaining neutral is far from a neutral choice. However, ISPs and many websites are companies—they are reliant on and beholden to their advertisers and shareholders, not their end users. With this knowledge, some companies have been pressured to make significant changes to their harassment and content policies to avoid losing money.

For example, "in 2011 Facebook users began an online campaign protesting pro-rape pages," which Facebook had refused to remove on the basis that "they could be seen as humor."[55] Although the protest campaign pointed out that the pages violated Facebook's own stated terms of service, it was the threat of major advertisers pulling out after learning their ads were being placed on pages explicitly condoning violence against women that spurred Facebook to action. Placing pressure on advertisers and companies to take responsibility for abusive content and users is one area where online feminist activism continues to play an important role. Similarly, pressuring companies to develop policies and structures that prevent abuse or make it more difficult to engage in abusive tactics will be more important for long-term victories against cybersexist abusers than simply protesting harmful messages or sites after the fact.

While IP banning is not always effective, it is one way for websites to track abusive users and stop individuals from posting comments or content from that address. IP banning is relatively easy for abusers to get around, but as Laura Hudson has observed with the *League of Legends* success, "creating a simple hurdle to abusive behavior makes it much less prevalent," and knowing that an IP ban is a possible outcome of cybersexist abuse and other forms of harassment may be enough to deter some of the cybersexist nastiness that characterizes many online spaces.[56] Websites that permit anonymous commenting and interaction can take steps to protect the anonymity of their users while still ensuring that it is possible to implement penalties for abusers and to provide a review or remediation process for those who feel their accounts have been banned in error or who wish to be reinstated.

Many of the situations that lead to mobbing behaviors and the extreme examples of cybersexist abuse result from the ease of messaging one person constantly from the same account or of signing up for a number of new sockpuppet and burner accounts for the purposes of harassment and evading blocks. Creating what Jeong calls "technical friction in orchestrating a sustained campaign" is one way websites and companies can step between harassers and their intended targets by reminding them that their behavior is crossing a line. "What if," Jeong asks, "after your fifth unanswered tweet within the hour to someone who didn't follow you, a pop-up asked if you really wanted to send that message?"[57] While there may be legitimate reasons for that volume of unsolicited tweeting at a stranger, having a simple reminder sent by the system that the account you're talking to is actually a person can act as a deterrent. This reminder would also free the target from having to do the work of finding a way to disengage from the harasser without the fear of escalating the harassment into abuse or threats.

With Twitter again as an example, the site could go further and implement a system so that accounts continually tweeting at those who don't follow them, and that don't respond to the automated message by backing off, are muted automatically after a certain period of time. The targets could undo this function if they choose, which the harasser will not see, but doing so also removes the burden of having to engage with the account at all. When the account is doing something like tweeting unsolicited nude photographs at young women (which, as mentioned previously, is an extremely common predatory behavior in online spaces such as Twitter), not having to interact with that person can increase the target's feeling of safety. Having an email go out to the harassers letting them know that they are repeatedly violating the community standards by excessive unwanted communication may also take on the role of the punishment report card used by *League of Legends*. It would not require individual women to report harassers but would be generated by the system's observation of people and the number of times an account was automatically muted.

That example, inspired by Jeong's hypothetical, is obviously specific to Twitter, where muting is a common function. All websites have their own functionalities, purposes, and design quirks that either facilitate harassment or make it more difficult. It is up to each individual site to examine current policies, understand how much harassment users face and how they are trying to deal with it, and determine what architectural changes can be made that place barriers between harassers and users and that implement reasonable consequences for those engaging in harassment.

Two key areas for websites to focus on are preemptively making it more difficult for cybersexist abuse to occur in the first place and, if it does occur, ensuring that users have clear and effective paths to resolution and safety.

One aspect of reporting abuse that is frightening, frustrating, and exhausting for many targets of abuse is having to provide evidence of the abuse itself. This evidence gathering often means going to a website page, a link, a tweet, or a comment and getting the URL or taking a screenshot of the abuse to include in the report. Doing so forces the target to re-see and reread what could very well be a graphic threat or other upsetting material. As we saw in the summer of 2014 when *Jezebel* was targeted with GIFs of violent pornography, this process quickly becomes overwhelming. Instead of forcing users to reread the abuse they were already subjected to, websites could react to an abuse report by freezing all of an account's previous content or content from a past period of time (such as a week). This way, the abuser cannot leave a cybersexist comment or threat and then delete it once they think it has been seen, thus preventing an effective report from being sent. Additionally, it allows the review team to see the reported content in context and does not force the person being abused to sift through the account to make the report. On Twitter this method also removes the possibility of cybersexist abusers simply deleting their accounts to prevent detection.

Other aspects of making abuse prevention and reporting more effective should include better blocking strategies and functions. For example, Twitter's dismal blocking ineffectiveness remains a serious problem for its users. Everything from using an incognito browser to simply searching for a target's name or key words can bring up the target's entire tweet history to those who want to find it for abusive purposes. Many of my dedicated harassers use exactly this tactic and pass around screenshots of and links to months- or year-old tweets in order to encourage new abusers, who appear and begin harassing me. In a recent example I received more than two hundred mentions in the space of half an hour, many of which were referring to me as a bitch and a cunt for something I had said a year prior to that round of harassment; the perpetrators were using a screenshot of a tweet that had been taken out of its explanatory context and presented

Fighting Back

as merely an inflammatory statement about men. Preventing people who have been blocked from seeing the account that blocked them and saving their content for abusive purposes is the entire point of having the block function available; as it does not work, Twitter is failing in this most basic safety measure for its users.

The blocking function on Twitter, as on Facebook, should prevent the blocked user from seeing the account entirely when they are logged in. While this type of blocking does not prevent the harasser from creating an alternate account or logging out, that is often not even necessary due to the ease with which blocked content can still be accessed on Twitter. Creating those small hurdles to harassment remains important. Additionally, Twitter should provide the option for accounts to be hidden from public view—not simply locking their account from access by all accounts that don't follow them, which is the current privacy option, but the ability to not show up for people who are logged out or not yet using Twitter. As an opt-in function, this feature would give users a measure of privacy from harassers who like to log out and scroll through their account, without forcing targets of harassment to close off their profile entirely.

Most websites have demonstrated an inability to provide a simple path to reporting abuse (especially when it takes the form of mob abuse), and this failure reflects the refusal of most websites to respond to abuse after the fact. Even Facebook, which claims it responds to all abuse reports quickly, can take up to a week to respond—and the result is often that pages with content condoning violence, homophobia, racism, and misogyny are left up.

Websites and online communities are poorly designed in that their focus on freeing up communication placed no emphasis on what types of communication users might want to avoid; from that stance, they are unprepared to deal with the fallout of the abuse and harassment that develop. While a total redesign is impractical and likely cost-prohibitive for major websites, simple tweaks to comment mechanisms and moderation policies and penalties for violating the rules of the community can go a long way toward helping reduce instances of online abuse and harassment. Giving community members the ability to invest in decision-making around community standards is also a way to create and enforce norms more easily, and doing so allows for the possibility of abusers being dealt with by a group of their peers in a way that they can understand.

All of these ideas are still merely ideas as of this writing, and many of them need elaboration, revision, and development by those with the technical know-how to implement them. However, central to that process will be incorporating the people who are specifically targeted by abuse. A solution to online harassment cannot be a top-down initiative developed by a heavily male or all-white team; such a team will never be able to fully understand the impact of abuse and will miss important factors of that abuse while working on solution design. Including people from every demographic that deals with serious online harassment—teens, women and men of color, black women and men, white women, disabled women and men, LGBT women and men, women and men from religious minorities, and so on—and learning about the intersections of abuse they face is the only way sites will be able to develop harassment policies that are proactive enough to actually prevent the abuse people are dealing with and strong enough to handle the reports when they do come in.

Even as websites continue to develop their own architectural solutions, however, there are times when women will want or need to consider legal action for the abuse they are receiving. Criminal law and civil law both have a role in the regulation of what activities are acceptable online. Although largely country-based and challenging to implement for a variety of reasons, laws do exist that are intended to curb the worst forms of online behavior. There are a number of common cybersexist behaviors that actually cross the line into criminal behavior and defamation or libel, particularly in the United States, the region on which this section focuses. Leaving aside the very real challenge of finding perpetrators of online abuse and positively identifying them, there are various difficulties associated with responding to cybersexism through legal channels that must also be discussed.

Sending direct threats of rape and other physical violence is against the law in all U.S. states and can be punished in civil or even criminal court. "Using the internet to solicit strangers to physically stalk or attack another person is a crime" as well, and thus doxxing people and encouraging a cyber mob like Gamergate to SWAT targets, mail things to their home or office, or engage in other forms of harassment and violence could be punishable by law.[58] Along with impersonation for the purpose of causing harm, many of the other common tactics engaged in by cyber mobs and cybersexist harassers not only fall well outside online community norms but also are within the boundaries of criminal law. Hacking into a woman's computer or email, to obtain compromising photographs, for example, which was the strategy of Hunter Moore's online "revenge porn" operation, is a crime that can lead to jail time. Publishing information obtained by doxxing, such as a home address, Social Security number, or driver's license, is also illegal. While many people rely on anonymity or sockpuppet accounts to get away with these criminal acts, some of the solutions outlined previously in this chapter would make such activities slightly more challenging.

Even some forms of sexual harassment common to cybersexists are actually illegal. Falsely accusing women of having inappropriate affairs or having a sexually transmitted infection are both incredibly common sexist attacks on women, and both are a form of "libel that does not require proof of special damages" for an everyday person (although the standard of proof in defamation cases is different for those considered to be public figures).[59] While tracking down the individual posting defamatory things may be difficult, if harassers know there is a possibility that they could be facing a case in civil court, they may become less likely to engage in that form of abuse. The mere knowledge of their targets' ability to respond with a lawsuit is enough to keep some cybersexists from engaging in more overt types of harassment.

However, as with any approach to using the law to deal with social problems, there are pros and cons. The U.S. justice system, as discussed in chapter 1, is unequally implemented to a significant degree; thus, any steps taken toward criminalizing online behavior will be more likely to have an impact on men of color and black men, regardless of which demographic groups engage in the most harassment. Further, placing people in jail for online behavior is not necessarily a proportionate response, especially given that many prisons in the United States are for-profit institutions with no intention of rehabilitating inmates. The specter of jailing people for harsh Internet comments is also likely to haunt any serious discussion of legal penalties for the dangerous and illegal behavior of people who engage in sustained harassment campaigns, regardless of the effect on their targets. A full reform of the justice system and incarceration processes is required to make jailing people for the most serious breaches of law online a realistic or just possibility.

That does not, however, mean that containing all online legal action to civil courts will necessarily be effective either. While the government is responsible for the cost of a criminal prosecution when a victim cannot afford it themselves, "victims bear the costs of bringing tort and copyright claims" to court, which can be prohibitively expensive for all but the wealthiest of women.[60] As Danielle Citron points out, if harassment has already cost a woman a job or other source of income, the financial burden of initiating a lawsuit and seeing it through to the end—with no guarantee of success—is likely to be a major stumbling block. Even when the cost is manageable, finding an attorney who will take on the case is not easily done either, as few lawyers specialize in the type of law that governs online harassment, and many are unwilling to take on what they regard as challenging cases or cases that will not result in an easy victory.

However, it is important for women on the receiving end of cybersexist abuse and harassment to know what legal recourse may be available to them. Some women have been able to make use of the laws around online abuse in an attempt to make a point about what women experience in online spaces. The actress Ashley Judd pursued a lawsuit against a number of men who sent her threatening and cybersexist tweets, and the MLB player Curt Schilling tracked down and sued men who made degrading and threatening online comments about his daughter.[61] While high-profile cases of harassment that result in legal action may not reflect the most effective long-term strategies for dealing with cybersexist abuse, they are valuable for reminding people that actions online can still have serious consequences.

Fighting Back

Although it remains challenging to take legal action against online harassment, evidence exists that the law is beginning to expand its definitions to better deal with such abuse. One of the main limitations of current legal solutions to cybersexism is the fact that "sexual harassment doctrine has developed around a restrictive list of single, protected settings"—mainly school and the workplace—where harassment is legally actionable.[62] The law in many cases does not address sexual harassment that takes place in one location but has effects in another; thus, cybersexism historically falls outside the scope of most legal remedies. Due to this single-setting view of harassment, few women have recourse to the law when dealing with cybersexism, although behaviors such as cyberbullying have been legally pursued, opening the path to further redefinitions of harassment.

Citron has proposed applying a civil rights perspective to legal attempts to control cybersexism on multiple occasions. Her article "Cyber Civil Rights" deals specifically with this idea. She notes that "online, bigots can aggregate their efforts even when they have insufficient numbers in any one location to form a conventional hate group," which is "crucial to the growth of anonymous online mobs."[63] In the article she outlines six major roadblocks to successfully applying civil rights law to online harassment. They include filling "the gap left when . . . the Internet allows individuals to escape social stigma for abusive acts," along with addressing "inequalities of power," convincing "a legal community still firmly rooted in an analog world that online harassment and discrimination profoundly harm victims," dealing with the "free speech argument asserted by online abusers," highlighting "the harms inflicted on traditionally subjugated groups," and overcoming "the challenges that law faces in coping with any sweeping social change."[64] These areas have all been addressed repeatedly throughout this book and should not be a surprise. Citron's goal in applying civil rights law to online harassment is to attempt to use its legal framework to shape social thinking about how the Internet affects our everyday life and what responses to abuse are appropriate.

In her book *Hate Crimes in Cyberspace* Citron spends additional time examining the current state of the law as it applies to online harassment and abuse and how civil rights laws can be effectively applied to the extremes of online behavior. "Civil rights law not only could repair and deter harms that civil and criminal law cannot, but it has the potential to transform our social attitudes about cyber harassment and cyber stalking," she writes. She also reminds readers that the same laws were brought to bear on workplace sexual harassment just a few decades ago. Citron hopes that civil rights law, when applied to cybersexist abuse, "would signal that online abuse produces corrosive harm to individuals, groups, and society" and that it will provide a framework for developing better solutions.[65] The possibility of updated civil rights approaches to the Internet is one area that legal scholars should explore further.

The law professor Jacqueline Lipton, however, notes that "while Citron's suggested civil rights agenda is well reasoned, it remains untried."[66] Like others who have written on the topic, Lipton raises the problem of "identifying often anonymous defendants," but she concedes that stronger enforcement around civil rights and cyber harassment could be beneficial for those targeted by online abuse and suggests that extralegal approaches such as education and activism are more likely to be an effective long-term solution. Lipton outlines a number of potentially beneficial "multi-modal regulatory [approaches]" that can be taken to combat cybersexism.[67] The suggestions she makes have the advantage of being more broadly applicable to cybersexist activity in general, rather than just seeking to fight illegal activities. Dealing with cybersexism from the perspective of a social ill that has both social and legal solutions makes it easier to challenge the attitudes creating and promoting cybersexism, rather than responding only to extreme examples of it.

The ideas Lipton presents are a multimodal set of responses to cybersexism that "include social norms, system architecture, market forces, public education, and the use of private institutions."[68] Lipton sees opportunities for combining all aspects of online life to challenge and overcome cybersexism, which is an attitude that has been adopted by many individuals currently working to fight online abuse. The outlined concepts of education and changing social norms focus on teaching potential victims how to better protect themselves online through reduced information sharing. However, Lipton's proposed solutions often end up being self-defense rather than prevention: self-limiting their use of public online profiles is not a viable option for women who want to participate in most Internet activities, for example. Changing social norms, which is a major focus of Lipton's, should be aimed less at the behavior of potential targets and more at the behavior and beliefs of potential perpetrators.

One of the key methods for overcoming sexism starts, as Lipton maintains, with education—not, however, by educating people on how to protect themselves from becoming targets for cybersexism and offline sexist harassment but by educating the people most likely to be engaging in sexist activities. Simply directing women to protect themselves from cybersexist harassment puts a burden on women while doing nothing to address the true problem. As with the "commonsense" advice women receive on the subject of rape and self-defense, telling women they must be responsible for avoiding harassers online has the same limiting effects as telling women they must spend their evenings out focused on watching their drinks and their backs. Meanwhile, if they do those things, the harasser or abuser will merely choose another target. To avoid a situation in which targets or survivors of cybersexism are blamed for the harassment they receive, it is critical to develop a group of proactive strategies focused on individuals who are committing the abuses. By using the Internet and other technological tools to challenge the mindset and thought patterns that lead to online and offline sexism, rather than responding to sexism after the fact, it is possible to reduce cybersexist activities.

Lipton also encourages "labeling, naming, and shaming websites that provide a platform for cyber-wrongs" like cybersexist abuse.[69] While it is important to know what websites or ISPs do not respond to complaints about abuses committed through their services, simply "shaming" such a website or company is unlikely to have much of an effect. In the United States ISPs are protected from most liability under "section 230 of the Communications Decency Act (CDA) and the Safe Harbor Policy based upon section 512C of the DMCA."[70] As a result of the limited circumstances in which ISPs and websites can be held accountable for the material published on them, a list of companies that do not protect targets of cybersexism is only useful for those interested in the subject. Unless legal or financial penalties can be applied to companies or websites hosting illegal communications, the benefits of such a list seem limited.

With the narrow window of application for legal solutions and the issues with other proposed ideas, many feminists turn to direct online activism as a solution. While cyberfeminism may not have been able to predict the ways in which the Internet would embody users and become a platform for reenacting offline behaviors, cyberfeminist theories offer avenues for appropriating technology and the Internet for feminist purposes. In this sense cyberfeminism is not only relevant and active but essential for realizing the progressive goals imagined during the early years of Internet access.

Solutions to cybersexist harassment and abuse are not going to be plug-and-play answers. The attitudes that lead to cybersexism are rooted in offline sexist beliefs, and as long as sexism exists offline, it will also exist online. The best we can work toward right now is changing sexist attitudes and developing methods of existing online that make engaging in abuse more trouble than it is worth. Although the solutions outlined in this chapter are limited and incomplete, many of them represent more effort than some major websites and social media platforms have made to address the issue of harassment.

Online abuse and cybersexism will remain a problem while issues of persistent inequality and injustice continue to exist in all facets of our lives. While it is important to take steps to protect people from abuse online, it is equally important to continue educating people about the problems caused by sexist beliefs and the effects of engaging in harassment. Although changes to social attitudes often occur at what feels like a glacially slow pace, and while the Internet is regularly used to engage in cybersexism, it is possible to uproot sexist beliefs and use technology to forge a better future. Many organizations are working on just that.

ORGANIZATIONS COMBATING SEXISM AND CYBERSEXISM

Responding to sexism is stressful, whether it's dealing with the aftermath of an incident of street harassment or figuring out how to handle a sexist attack online. It is often difficult for people who don't experience sexism to understand how common it is or how it affects those who do experience it. Further, many people feel a sense of helplessness when confronted with the scope of and damage caused by cybersexist abuse and harassment. The last section of this chapter is dedicated to discussing a few organizations that are attempting to educate people about sexism and to make strides in the fight against cybersexist harassment and abuse.

One such effort is the Everyday Sexism Project, which consists of online and offline activism and discussion, as well as training sessions held in schools, governments, workplaces, and more. It started as a Twitter account and a website where women could send in stories about the sexism they had experienced in their day-to-day lives. The existence of sexist microaggressions is often denied outright, and accounts of such experiences are trivialized as jokes, unintentional and therefore not a problem, or not serious enough to "count" as sexism. Laura Bates, who began Everyday Sexism, records instances of microaggressions (along with tales of offline sexual harassment and assault, as well as cybersexist activities such as stalking and threats) "to catalogue women's experiences of gender imbalance at every level."[71] With more than thirty thousand collected examples of sexism experienced, the Everyday Sexism Project uses the Internet as a platform for amplifying the voices of individual women.[72] While cybersexist harassers often use the Internet to ramp up the speed and intensity of their abuse, women are able to use the same strategies to ensure that their voices are heard. The volume of women's experiences with microaggressions, sexism, and cybersexism recorded by Everyday Sexism makes it much more challenging for people to deny the reality of the problem.

Using the Internet to create a space for women to share their stories blends online and offline experiences of gender-based prejudice, making the Internet not only a tool of oppression but also a way for women to speak out and fight back. Everyday Sexism does not cite cyberfeminism as an inspiration for using technology to subvert sexist behaviors; however, the group's very existence employs technology and the Internet in a nonlinear, distributed fashion that promotes the communication of women, among women—something a cyberfeminist like Sadie Plant would celebrate. While organizations like Everyday Sexism provide strong, woman-focused outlets for challenging and subverting cybersexism and offline sexist behaviors, they are fundamentally reactive outlets: Everyday Sexism collects stories that have already occurred, sometimes years in the past. To truly create change, the Internet must become more than a tool for reacting to or reporting on cybersexism and offline sexism. While drawing attention to the prevalence of such behaviors is valuable from the perspective of giving women a space in which to discuss the problem and a way for men to understand its scope, it provides no preventive strategies for reducing sexist actions and behaviors.

The existence of offline training sessions and other forms of activism are important steps toward preventing cybersexist abuse. Organizations that, like Everyday Sexism, wish to create an even broader impact could consider having online educational sessions available or promoting antiharassment campaigns and messages through the platforms they develop. Providing women who are targeted for cybersexist abuse with tools to respond and regroup (beyond merely sharing the story and commiserating with other women) is a simple way to decrease the impact of cybersexist harassment.

One example of an organization using the Internet to take a proactive stance against online and offline abuse is Men Can Stop Rape. The non-profit runs a program called Men of Strength on high school and college campuses, provides online resources for educators and individuals on how to prevent abuse, offers links to assistance for male survivors of sexual assault, contains information on the training sessions the organization offers, and showcases examples of campaigns that target street and sexual harassment, as well as rape.[73] The organization works with men in their teen and college years to uncover and challenge stereotypical ideas about gender and rape and also helps young men develop healthy avenues for sexual expression.

Although Men Can Stop Rape primarily functions offline in terms of its activism, its campaigns include online and offline components, thus enabling wider distribution of facts, resources, and information. The technological aspect of the organization allows the group to promote its message by connecting to individuals on multiple social media sites and online platforms. The multimodal nature of Men Can Stop Rape, as well as its proactive stance on rape and sexual assault prevention, makes it an ideal model for other campaigns or organizations.

The same principles used by Men Can Stop Rape can be applied to cybersexism generally. While creating a classroom setting to teach people not to harass women online may seem farcical, there are elements of the multimodalities used by Men Can Stop Rape that can be circulated by motivated individuals across the Internet. Discussion groups, social media accounts, YouTube videos, and other hybrid online/offline educational methods could inform people of all demographics about the problems with and effects of cybersexism. These online tools are already used by multiple organizations for other purposes, and turning the lens on Internet communications is also a way to quickly and easily spread a message.

Working to Halt Online Abuse (WHOA) is an organization that has been referred to at a few points throughout this book. It is a volunteer organization that was founded in 1997 "to fight online harassment through education of the general public, education of law enforcement personnel, and empowerment of victims."[74] WHOA provides a number of resources for victims of online harassment and abuse, with a particular emphasis on cyberstalking, which is a growing problem. The organization has also produced multiple reports on the abuse that occurs online, having tracked everything from who experiences abuse to who commits it, what form it takes, and more. WHOA tracked abuse and produced reports from 2000 to 2013 based on its research, which is an invaluable resource for anyone who wants to gain a better understanding of what online abuse looks like.

WHOA does not stop at research, however; the organization also provides resources for victims of online abuse, as well as referrals to lawyers "who are willing to work with online victims on a contingency basis" in the hope that people targeted by abusers will be able to explore all possible options for finding safety.[75] Although the organization has been less active since 2012–13 than it was previously, individuals involved with WHOA have spoken at a variety of conferences, and the resources provided on the website offer a wealth of information about online abuse and how those who are being targeted can proceed.

Activism around the issue of cybersexism and online abuse can also take the form of learning to understand it better. Like WHOA, the advocacy organization Women, Action, & the Media (WAM!) has conducted research on cybersexist harassment. Specifically, WAM! got permission from Twitter to act as an authorized reporting agent, which allowed it to create a separate reporting form that people undergoing harassment could use. As a result, WAM! was able to study the types of abuse people were experiencing on the platform and how the social media network responded. "'There are a lot of different ways that women are getting harassed and Twitter's current reporting system isn't catching all of them,'" Jaclyn Friedman, strategic advisor for WAM!, told the *Guardian*.[76] The goal of the reporting function and research was to better advocate for women dealing with online abuse, to develop a deeper understanding of the harassment women were enduring, and to propose changes Twitter could make that would support its users more effectively.

After 811 reports were submitted through WAM! to Twitter across the three-week research period, only 70 accounts were suspended for abusive behavior and only a single account was completely deleted—that is, more than 40 percent of reports escalated by WAM! prompted no further action by Twitter.[77] Among the reports received, nearly a third mentioned a concern with ongoing harassment, and WAM! ended up opening a total of more than 160 tickets. WAM!'s findings indicated that Twitter was less likely to take action when reports were submitted regarding doxxing versus violent threats and that there is significant room for improvement in how abuse is reported and handled once reports are received. Additionally, WAM! noted that a number of reports it received were clearly falsified by what the researchers called "report trolls," who were "pretending to have been harassed," which was determined by "reductive narratives and stereotype expressions," as well as "internal indicators such as word play."[78] During the research period nearly half of the reports received by WAM! were determined to be fake; most of them arrived during a single day and were sent by a bot. The fact that WAM! had been given the opportunity to investigate gendered online harassment at all prompted abuse of the researchers themselves during the process of collecting information, which indicates not that the research is useless but that harassment remains a serious problem.

Some of the recommendations made by WAM! included offering information to viewers as to why suspended accounts had been suspended, making it easier for users to report harassment, and encouraging further research into the problem of online abuse. Although WAM! looked specifically at abuse reports on Twitter, the behaviors witnessed during the research period reflect research conducted by other groups and indicate serious issues with cybersexist harassment in online spaces. Enabling organizations and social media platforms to better understand their issues with online abuse is key to encouraging them to take steps to fight it. WAM!'s research is an important part of developing a thorough understanding of the current state of online abuse and is necessary for creating responses to it.

Like WAM!, *Feminist Frequency* put out a focused but important report on progress and harassment regarding online abuse as part of an update to its ongoing Kickstarter project. *Feminist Frequency*, the video web series developed by Anita Sarkeesian, has taken on 501(c)(3) nonprofit tax status, and it produced a 2014 backer report that highlighted some of the year's successes, as well as the challenge posed by ongoing abuse. As Sarkeesian put it, "the extreme harassment that I experience has become an intrinsic and inseparable part of this project," noting that gendered harassment, hate mobs, and cybersexism have been increasing in intensity around certain issues and people.[79] By creating a nonprofit organization, Sarkeesian hopes to continue raising awareness of the issues of cybersexist online harassment, as well as engaging in the media criticism for which she first became famous.

Organizations like Sarkeesian's represent an important part of a reinvigorated cyberfeminism. Women who are able to combine incisive analysis of media and pop culture, as well as use the Internet to disseminate their messages, are taking advantage of the framework initially seized upon by cyberfeminists. A robust online discussion of pop culture, media, and representation needs more videos and discussions to add nuance to these topics as well; having a variety of viewpoints on the same topics is an easy way to avoid making one woman into a representation (and a scapegoat) for all of feminism. Additionally, while the abuse Sarkeesian faces takes a toll on her, her ongoing presence in the face of cybersexist backlash provides a valuable role model and resource for other women who wish to pursue similar career paths. Creating *Feminist Frequency* as both a nonprofit resource and a media criticism project allows Sarkeesian to stand against the tide of cybersexist abuse.

Other organizations are taking a direct approach to attempting to fight cybersexism and other forms of online harassment and violence. The Online Abuse Prevention Initiative (OAPI), founded by Randi Harper (creator of the Good Game Autoblocker), lists goals that include "reducing and mitigating online abuse through the study and analysis of abuse patterns, the creation of anti-harassment tools and resources, and collaboration with key tech companies seeking to better support their communities."[80] The OAPI's founding members have been involved in a number of high-profile attempts to combat online harassment and abuse, including their voicing of strong opposition to regulatory policies that could negatively affect those already most harmed by cybersexism and other forms of online abuse.

Cofounded by Zoe Quinn and Alex Lifschitz, who are also involved with the OAPI, the Crash Override Network was developed in the wake of Gamergate to help victims of online abuse deal with the fallout such harassment often causes. Crash Override Network is "staffed by a number of online abuse survivors," who remain anonymous to keep from being targeted further. The goal of the network is to work directly with people who are being targeted by online harassment mobs or individual abusers in order to find the best possible solution and ensure that they are able to maintain a normal and safe online presence. According to the Crash Override Network website, "We understand that every case of online harassment is unique in terms of its targets, aggressors, and circumstances, and that no one plan of survival is suitable for everyone. We instead work with clients to tailor a unique [plan] of action," which would support the individual during and after the harassment.[81] Additionally, Crash Override Network worked to create proactive solutions to online harassment and abuse.

Although the organization was developed out of the ugliness of Gamergate, it represents the resilience of women in the face of cybersexist abuse. Despite being the original target of the hate mob that Gamergate became, Quinn was able to take the experience she had and reshape it to help make the Internet a safer place for other people. As Quinn described it to *Engadget*, "What we try to offer people is some best practices, advice and just lending an ear if they'd like to talk because very few people understand what it means to go through this kind of harassment."[82] Resources such as Crash Override Network were not available to Quinn when Gamergate erupted; the ability to take that damaging experience and turn it into a resource for people who are targeted in similar ways would make cyberfeminists proud.

Crash Override Network does not just provide after-the-fact support to victims of cybersexist abuse, however. It also engages in education and community outreach, and it maintains a Tumblr account that offers advice on cybersecurity and steps people can take to reduce their likelihood of being seriously affected by online harassment and abuse. Such advice often requires some work on the part of potential targets, but the organization is also working to "push for more effective policies on the internet at large to better combat online hate, and to minimize the ability for abusers to target and hurt people."[83] Crash Override Network, being staffed by experts in cybersecurity and people who have personally experienced the effects of online abuse, is perhaps uniquely poised to make a significant impact in the effort to create better strategies for dealing with online abuse and harassment.

HeartMob is another organization attempting to directly combat cybersexist harassment, online abuse, and their negative effects. Founded by some of the same people who started Hollaback!, a movement to combat street harassment, HeartMob is an organization devoted to ending sexist abuse in online spaces. Women who are being targeted by cybersexists can go to HeartMob, where a team of volunteers "will be able to use the platform to send her a supportive message, report abuse to platforms like

Twitter and Facebook, or document harassment on her behalf"—responses that were developed in collaboration with and on the advice of people who have experienced online harassment.[84] Unlike many organizational responses to online abuse, which are typically designed and implemented by those who don't experience it, those of Crash Override Network and HeartMob take into account the perspectives of those most likely to have been affected.

HeartMob also "wants to develop a framework for addressing harassers directly," much like the strategy employed by *League of Legends*. The goal of this effort is to explain to harassers why their activities are harmful and attempt to persuade them to stop. Although many harassers respond only to consequences and see appeals to reason as encouragement to escalate their abuse, and while HeartMob itself has no ability to enforce consequences, the fact that external actors are paying attention to online behavior is one way to create better Internet norms that can contribute to lower rates of harassment. However, HeartMob has taken steps to create features that will save copies of harassing behavior on behalf of targets, in the case of any escalation, and hopes to "change . . . the feeling that targets of online harassment are alone."[85] Through including the people most likely to be affected by cybersexist harassment in each stage of development and design, HeartMob, like Crash Override Network, has significantly improved the chances of achieving its goals.

All of the groups, organizations, and individuals discussed in this section are working toward a common goal: a truly free Internet where marginalized groups have as much access to online spaces as the people who currently use the Internet as a tool of oppression and abuse. Reducing cybersexist harassment cannot rely solely on top-down strategies from individual websites or government interference. Change will instead be multimodal, will take place with the effort of grassroots organizations, and will require extensive research.

Cybersexism affects the women who seek to share their lives, opinions, voices, and experiences in online spaces, and its impact differs depending on the sexuality, race, ability, and other intersecting factors of the target's identity. Such a complex scenario will not be dealt with overnight but neither can it be ignored. Each day that ISPs, websites, moderators, and individuals ignore the cybersexist abuse in their midst is a day women are told the Internet is not for them—and this message is not one that can be allowed to come true. The immediate future can represent a turning point in the fight against sexism online, and we have the opportunity and tools to find real methods of creating an Internet that is safe, free, and welcoming.

CONCLUSION
A Call to Action

Cybersexism is one of the most serious problems facing the Internet today. A pervasive culture of online abuse, websites and social media architectures that enable it, and enduring sexist attitudes have created online spaces where cybersexism is rampant. The end result of this situation is that women feel alienated and unsafe in an environment that increasingly shapes media, politics, business, and everyday life. If the Internet is to remain an essential tool on a global scale, making it usable for women must be a higher priority for websites, ISPs, and web developers. However, it will be just as important for educators, researchers, and academics to develop an understanding of what cybersexism is and how it functions and to find the best methods of combating it.

In doing research for this book I repeatedly ran up against a wall: the shocking lack of data on the issue of cybersexist online abuse. Report after report produced by academic journals dealt with hacking and abuse in terms of business and finance, but they placed little emphasis on the human toll exacted by the grind of dealing with harassment day in and day out. It is past time for a serious reckoning with the scope of the problem represented by cybersexism, and this book has been but one small foray into the issue. In-depth research is necessary for us to fully understand the motivations that lead to cybersexist abuse, the impact it has on people who deal with it, and what strategies will be most effective in reducing its prevalence.

Further, most research that does exist relies on gender as its sole variable. While that factor is important for demonstrating that much online harassment is cybersexist in nature, the refusal to consider other variables leads to the erasure and elision of many issues that cannot be addressed by looking at gender alone. The intersections of identity often provide a focal point for harassment, with racism, sexism, and other forms of hatred so deeply intertwined as to be indistinguishable. Research that is sensitive to these nuances of abuse must be conducted in order for us to see the full picture of online harassment and develop solutions that will actually work.

While high-profile hate mobs such as Gamergate and the consistent harassment aimed at women in tech spaces are capable of briefly drawing media attention to the problem of misogyny online, these flare-ups are only the tip of the iceberg. The potential solutions that often emerge from the resulting discussions are aimed at a narrow portion of the actual population of women online. Solving online abuse will require giving voice to the women who are often ignored by those who have the opportunity to report on Internet harassment, as well as relying on their experiences and expertise as guideposts to a better and safer online environment.

The Internet has the potential to be more than a playground where hateful misogynists vent their anger on women and face no consequences, but it will improve only if we make a serious effort to alter the status quo. Those of us with the power to do research, educate others, enforce consequences, and build safer spaces have a responsibility to do so. The Internet is our home, but it was not built with women in mind. It's time for some serious remodeling.

Notes

1. THE MANY FACES OF CYBERSEXISM

1. The Supreme Court case was *Elonis v. United States.*
2. The word *misogynoir*, coined by the black queer feminist scholar Moya Bailey, refers to antiblack misogyny—the common and deeply intertwined sexist and racist hatred targeting black women.
3. Tufekci, "It's a Man's Phone"; Eveleth, "How Self-Tracking Apps Exclude Women"; Turk, "Technology Isn't Designed to Fit Women."
4. "New Congress Includes More Women, Minorities."
5. "Women in National Parliaments."
6. Fairchild, "Women CEOs in the Fortune 1000"; Covert, "Working Single Mothers Are Disproportionately Likely to Be Poor."
7. Hill, "Simple Truth about the Gender Pay Gap."
8. Eisenberg, "29 States Can Fire You for Being Gay."
9. "Issue of Fair Wages for Workers with Disabilities."
10. S. Smith, "Gender Disparity On-Screen and behind the Camera in Family Films."
11. Pérez, "Framing of Dove's 'Choose Beautiful' Campaign Is a Farce."
12. Macintosh, "Negative Stereotypes Stick with You."
13. "What Is Stereotype Threat?"
14. Dean, "Persuasion."
15. Reiss and Dombeck, "Suicide Statistics."
16. "Get the Facts on Eating Disorders."
17. Kerby, "Top 10 Most Startling Facts about People of Color and Criminal Justice in the United States."

18. Kerby, "Top 10 Most Startling Facts about People of Color and Criminal Justice in the United States."

19. Ajinkya, "Top 5 Facts about Women in Our Criminal Justice System."

20. "FBI Releases 2012 Hate Crime Statistics."

21. "Domestic Violence Statistics."

22. Study by Patricia Tjaden cited in "Domestic Violence Statistics."

23. "Domestic Violence Statistics."

24. Starr, "STUDY."

25. *Oliphant v. Squamish* (1978).

26. "Homophobia, HIV and AIDS."

27. Giovanniello, "NCAVP Report."

28. Lee and Kwan, "Trans Panic Defense."

29. Talusan, "Failed Logic of 'Trans Panic' Criminal Defenses."

30. Molloy, "California Becomes First State to Ban Gay, Trans 'Panic' Defenses."

31. McDonough, "CeCe McDonald on Her Time in Prison."

32. Goudreau, "13 Subtle Ways Women Are Treated Differently at Work."

33. Hammond, "Prattle of the Sexes."

34. Kunsmann, "Gender, Status and Power in Discourse Behavior of Men and Women."

35. "Language as Prejudice."

36. "Language as Prejudice."

37. Dahl, "People Who Say 'Like' All the Time Are Surprisingly Thoughtful."

38. Quenqua, "They're, Like, Way Ahead of the Linguistic Currrrve."

39. Daniels, *Cyber Racism*, 3.

40. "WMC's Research Shines Light on Gender Bias in Major U.S. Broadcast, Print, Online, & Wire Outlets."

41. Herring, "Rhetorical Dynamics of Gender Harassment On-Line," 152.

42. Herring, "Rhetorical Dynamics of Gender Harassment On-Line," 152.

43. Herring, "Rhetorical Dynamics of Gender Harassment On-Line," 156.

44. Herring, "Rhetorical Dynamics of Gender Harassment On-Line," 156.

45. Jeong, *Internet of Garbage*, chap. 2.

46. Ritter, "Deviant Behavior in Computer-Mediated Communication," 198.

47. Ritter, "Deviant Behavior in Computer-Mediated Communication," 198.

48. Shifman and Lemish, "'Mars and Venus' in Virtual Space," 257.

49. Pilkington, "Justine Sacco, PR Executive Fired over Racist Tweet, 'Ashamed.'"

50. Lipton, "Combating Cyber-Victimization," 1114.

51. Jeong, *Internet of Garbage*, chap. 2 (original emphasis).

52. Quoted in Eördögh, "Interview with a Troll Whisperer."

53. Citron, "Law's Expressive Value in Combating Cyber Gender Harassment."

54. Staude-Müller, Hansen, and Voss, "How Stressful Is Online Victimization?"

55. Leyden, "AT&T iPad 'Hacker' Breaks Gag Order to Rant at Cops."

56. "*United States v. Andrew Auernheimer.*"

57. Sandoval, "End of Kindness."

58. Schwartz, "Trolls among Us."

59. Biddle, "iPad Hacker and 'Troll' Weev Is Now a Straight-Up White Supremacist."

60. Schwartz, "Trolls among Us."

61. "Weev on Why He Trolls." Subsequent quotes are from this source.

62. The insult displayed on the screen was weev's response in a conversation (the rest of which is not included); it was a tweet that read, "You're fat and your kid has autism."

63. Klepek, "Trolls Are People, Too."

64. Quoted in Klepek, "Trolls Are People, Too."

65. Penny, *Cybersexism*, chap. 1.

66. Citron, "Law's Expressive Value in Combating Cyber Gender Harassment," 397–98.

67. Shifman and Lemish, "'Mars and Venus' in Virtual Space," 254.

2. TYPES OF CYBERSEXISM

1. Mary Spears and Tugce Albayrak were murdered by street harassers, and an unnamed woman had her throat cut when refusing to give a man her phone number; she survived. Roy, "On the Tragic Murder of Mary 'Unique' Spears"; HKearl, "German Woman Killed for Challenging Harassers"; Culp-Ressler, "This Week, Two Incidents of Street Harassment Escalated into Violent Attacks against Women."

2. Mansplaining is Rebecca Solnit's term to describe the act of a man explaining something to a woman, often condescendingly, when she very likely has better knowledge of the subject than the man. It also refers to a situation in which the man presumes he is correct on the basis of his opinion, despite evidence to the contrary. See Solnit, "Archipelago of Arrogance."

3. S. Hudson (@sassycrass), Twitter post.

4. It's also important to note that Hudson has subsequently been erased from the creation of the "not all men" meme in multiple large publications, despite her tweet and subsequent discussions of it being readily accessible—an ongoing pattern in the erasure of black women from their contributions to online discourse.
5. Herring, "Rhetorical Dynamics of Gender Harassment On-Line," 155.
6. Herring, "Rhetorical Dynamics of Gender Harassment On-Line," 156.
7. Solnit, "Archipelago of Arrogance."
8. Solnit, "Archipelago of Arrogance."
9. Vernasco, "Seven Studies That Prove Mansplaining Exists."
10. Herring, "Rhetorical Dynamics of Gender Harassment On-Line," 157.
11. Herring, "Rhetorical Dynamics of Gender Harassment On-Line," 159.
12. Herring, "Rhetorical Dynamics of Gender Harassment On-Line," 160.
13. Herring, "Rhetorical Dynamics of Gender Harassment On-Line," 160.
14. Franks, "Sexual Harassment 2.0," 658.
15. Herring, "Rhetorical Dynamics of Gender Harassment On-Line," 159.
16. Herring, "Rhetorical Dynamics of Gender Harassment On-Line," 160.
17. Camille Paglia is an academic and could be described as an antifeminist's feminist; she supports many of the basic desires of feminist activism while regularly using antifeminist rhetoric.
18. Herring, "Rhetorical Dynamics of Gender Harassment On-Line," 155.
19. Herring, "Rhetorical Dynamics of Gender Harassment On-Line," 155.
20. Herring, "Rhetorical Dynamics of Gender Harassment On-Line," 159.
21. Herring, "Rhetorical Dynamics of Gender Harassment On-Line," 159.
22. Herring, "Rhetorical Dynamics of Gender Harassment On-Line," 160.
23. Tone policing is a phrase commonly used online, being featured in articles on websites such as geek- and feminist-oriented wikis, *Urban Dictionary*, and more.
24. Herring, "Rhetorical Dynamics of Gender Harassment On-Line," 160.
25. Herring, "Rhetorical Dynamics of Gender Harassment On-Line," 151.
26. Jimmydeanskills, Twitter post.
27. Quoted in Valenti, "Free Speech Is a Bad Excuse for Online Creeps to Threaten Rape and Murder."
28. Lithwick, "Schooling the Supreme Court on Rap Music."
29. Quoted in Johnston, "Why Today's Elonis Decision Is a Victory in the Fight against Online Harassment."

30. Johnston, "Why Today's Elonis Decision Is a Victory in the Fight against Online Harassment."

31. A quick search in one university library system reveals nearly three times as many articles about online threats and business as about online threats and women.

32. Stoleru and Costecu, "(Re)Producing Violence against Women in Online Spaces," 98.

33. Duggan, "Online Harassment."

34. Sarkeesian, "One Week of Harassment on Twitter."

35. Gaslighting is typically studied as part of abuse within heterosexual married relationships, but the effects of abusers insisting their targets imagined abuse, made it up, or otherwise imagined the harassment can be devastating. While many women who have been abused online take and maintain screenshots of the harassment, gaslighting can take the form of accusing the women of creating false accounts and sending themselves the abusive content. Why women would do so and which women have time to engage in these nefarious acts remains unexplained.

36. Honan, "What Is Doxing?"

37. "Crime of 'Swatting.'"

38. Robertson, "'About 20' Police Officers Sent to Gamergate Critic's Former Home after Fake Hostage Threat."

39. Sinders, "That Time the Internet Sent a SWAT Team to My Mom's House."

40. Sinders, "That Time the Internet Sent a SWAT Team to My Mom's House."

41. Gagne, "Doxxing Defense."

42. #EndFathersDay was aimed primarily at black women and intended to reinforce stereotypes about black family life. Fake Twitter accounts using pictures of black women were created and used to promote the hashtag and direct harassment at the accounts of actual women. #Freebleeding was created to promote a supposed feminist campaign encouraging cisgender women to refuse to wear pads, tampons, or other products while menstruating and instead "bleed freely." #Bikinibridge was a body-shaming movement referencing the "bridge" a bikini makes between a thin woman's hipbones if she is lying on her back. As with most 4chan and other coordinated hoax movements, the only people fooled by these hashtags were those looking for an excuse to attack women.

43. Ableist language references physical or mental disabilities or illnesses in a mocking or derogatory fashion or presumes such disabilities represent a personal or moral weakness.

44. Valenti, "Elliot Rodger's California Shooting Spree."

45. According to the Treatment Advocacy Center, roughly 1 percent of people with an untreated severe mental illness go on to commit acts of violence; 25 percent or more of people with a mental illness are likely to experience violence in any given year.

46. See, for example, the discussions about this phenomenon in the book *White Women, Rape, and the Power of Race in Virginia* (2004), by Lisa Linquist Dorr.

3. DON'T FEED THE TROLLS

1. "Don't Feed the Trolls!"

2. Phillips, "Don't Feed the Trolls?"

3. Citron, *Hate Crimes in Cyberspace.*

4. The ineffectiveness of police where online abuse is concerned is discussed later in this volume, as are the difficulties encountered in attempting to incarcerate people for such online abuse.

5. That study is Duggan, "Online Harassment."

6. Duggan, "Online Harassment."

7. Citron, "Law's Expressive Value in Combating Cyber Gender Harassment," 379.

8. Citron, "Law's Expressive Value in Combating Cyber Gender Harassment," 379.

9. Citron, *Hate Crimes in Cyberspace*, 14.

10. Golden, "Why I'm Masquerading as a White Bearded Hipster Guy on Twitter (Despite Being a Black Woman)."

11. Houreld, "Online Abuse of Women in Pakistan Turns into Real-World Violence."

12. Gregorie, "Cyberstalking."

13. Gandy, "#TwitterFail."

14. Penny, *Cybersexism*, chap. 1.

15. Jeong, *Internet of Garbage*, chap. 3.

16. Quoted in Tiku and Newton, "Twitter CEO."

17. Hern, "Reddit Finally Bans Its White-Supremacist Subreddits."

18. Jeong, *Internet of Garbage*, chap. 4.

19. Citron, *Hate Crimes in Cyberspace*, 194–95.
20. Citron, *Hate Crimes in Cyberspace*, 196.
21. Jeong, *Internet of Garbage*, chap. 4.
22. Join the Coffee Party Movement, Facebook post.
23. "Prevention for Teens."
24. "2015 Hiring Trends."

4. THE EFFECTS OF CYBERSEXISM

1. Staude-Müller, Hansen, and Voss, "How Stressful Is Online Victimization?"
2. Cited in Citron, "Law's Expressive Value in Combating Cyber Gender Harassment," 379.
3. Citron, "Law's Expressive Value in Combating Cyber Gender Harassment."
4. Citron, "Law's Expressive Value in Combating Cyber Gender Harassment," 388.
5. Stephens, "Ipswich Woman Charged over Muslim Hate Attacks Online."
6. Meyer and Cukier, "Assessing the Attack Threat Due to IRC Channels," cited in Citron, "Law's Expressive Value in Combating Cyber Gender Harassment," 379.
7. Citron, "Law's Expressive Value in Combating Cyber Gender Harassment," 380.
8. Kuznekoff and Rose, "Communication in Multiplayer Gaming," cited/reviewed in Tang, "Reactions to a Woman's Voice in an FPS Game."
9. One aspect often used as an example of "female privilege" is that male players sometimes shower female players with extra ammo, weapons, or other gifts. Such favoritism, however, is often contingent upon the female players putting up with sexist comments and propositions, and it will be quickly withdrawn if female gamers are seen as insufficiently "grateful."
10. Jayanth, "52% of Gamers Are Women—but the Industry Doesn't Know It."
11. Haniver, "Lots of Words."
12. Haniver, "Lots of Words."
13. Franks, "Sexual Harassment 2.0," 658.
14. Citron, "Law's Expressive Value in Combating Cyber Gender Harassment."
15. "2015 Hiring Trends."
16. While most online reputation management products are aimed at businesses, Reputation.com offers personal assistance, with the price of its services starting at $3,000.

17. Crecente, "Plague of Game Dev Harassment Erodes Industry, Spurs Support Groups."

18. Quoted in Crecente, "Plague of Game Dev Harassment Erodes Industry, Spurs Support Groups."

19. "Techie Adria Richards Fired after Tweeting about Men's Comments."

20. Holt, "Adria Richards Publicly Fired amid Violent #Donglegate Backlash."

21. Brush et al., "Diana Report—Women Entrepreneurs 2014."

22. Citron, *Hate Crimes in Cyberspace*, 121.

23. Laws differ by country and state. I am referring most often to U.S.-based laws, as I am most familiar with them. However, sending threats with a stated intent to carry them out can be generally assumed to be illegal. Additionally, the only requirement for a threat to be considered a "true" threat, as described in chapter 3, is that it causes and is intended to cause its target to feel fear of violence.

24. Citron, *Hate Crimes in Cyberspace*, 63.

25. Biber et al., "Sexual Harassment in Online Communications," 33.

26. Swim et al., "Everyday Sexism," 33.

27. Swim et al., "Everyday Sexism," 31.

28. Franks, "Sexual Harassment 2.0," 673.

29. While there is a large-scale and important discussion about the use of trigger warnings in academic spaces and in offline environments, it is not the intention of this book to address that issue at length. It is my belief that trigger warnings can easily be incorporated into academic curricula without "coddling" students or destroying freedom of speech, as is so often direly predicted. Trigger warnings in feminist spaces, however, are a common practice and tend to be widely accepted.

30. Staude-Müller, Hansen, and Voss, "How Stressful Is Online Victimization?"

31. Citron, "Law's Expressive Value in Combating Cyber Gender Harassment."

32. Dickson, "'Casting Couch' Porn Actress Commits Suicide after Being Harassed on Social Media."

33. Staude-Müller, Hansen, and Voss, "How Stressful Is Online Victimization?," 267.

34. "Online Harassment/Cyberstalking Statistics."

35. "Totally in Control."

36. "Eating Disorders Statistics."

37. Citron, "Law's Expressive Value in Combating Cyber Gender Harassment," 392.

38. Citron, *Hate Crimes in Cyberspace*, 216.

39. Futrelle, "Leading MRA Site A Voice for Men Continues to Publish a Holocaust Denier and Marital Rape Apologist."

40. Rainie et al., "Anonymity, Privacy, and Security Online."

41. Cited in Citron, "Law's Expressive Value in Combating Cyber Gender Harassment," 385.

42. Rainie et al., "Anonymity, Privacy, and Security Online."

43. Nigatu, "10 Ridiculously Offensive Things People Tell Asian Women on OkCupid."

44. Tweten, "Bye Felipe."

45. The term "revenge porn" is contested, as the term encompasses a wide variety of nonconsensual uses of photographs or the complete fabrication of compromising images.

46. Stebner, "Audrie Pott Suicide."

47. Woolley, "Time to Make 'Revenge-Porn' Sharing a Criminal Act in Canada."

48. Laws, "I've Been Called the 'Erin Brockovich' of Revenge Porn."

49. Laws, "I've Been Called the 'Erin Brockovich' of Revenge Porn."

50. Kreps, "Revenge-Porn Site Owner Hunter Moore Pleads Guilty, Faces Prison Time."

51. Almasy, "'Revenge Porn' Operator Gets 18 Years in Prison."

52. According to the Digital Millennium Copyright Act of 1998 (DMCA) anyone who posts photos online for which they are not the copyright holder is violating copyright law. Filing a DMCA notice requires proof of copyright, such as providing evidence of who originally took the picture that is being reported.

53. Sterne, "'Fappening' Is Dead."

54. I do not consider telling women to stop taking nude photos of themselves or sharing them with partners to be a solution to the problem of revenge porn; consensually shared photographs are and will likely continue to be a feature of modern relationships. A "solution" to abusive behaviors that relies on women having to restrict participation in activities that men can safely engage in is no solution at all.

55. Oltermann, "'Revenge Porn' Victims Receive Boost from German Court Ruling."

56. Citron, "Law's Expressive Value in Combating Cyber Gender Harassment," 387.

57. Citron, "Law's Expressive Value in Combating Cyber Gender Harassment," 388.

58. Ritter, "Deviant Behavior in Computer-Mediated Communication," 199.

59. Stoleru and Costecu, "(Re)Producing Violence against Women in Online Spaces," 108 (original emphasis).

60. Citron, "Law's Expressive Value in Combating Cyber Gender Harassment," 375.

5. MISOGYNIST MOVEMENTS

1. Broderick, "Activists Are Outing Hundreds of Twitter Users Believed to Be 4chan Trolls Posing as Feminists."

2. Kabay, "Anonymity and Pseudonymity in Cyberspace."

3. Kabay, "Anonymity and Pseudonymity in Cyberspace," 8 (original emphasis). The term "flaming" in this context was used in the late 1990s in much the same way "trolling" would be in 2015.

4. Kabay, "Anonymity and Pseudonymity in Cyberspace," 10.

5. Kabay, "Anonymity and Pseudonymity in Cyberspace," 9.

6. "Misandry" is a counterpart term to "misogyny"; it means "hatred of men and boys." Anyone who publicly self-identifies as a feminist can expect to be labeled a misandrist regardless of actual beliefs and statements. While no evidence exists for systemic, institutional, political, social, professional, or financial biases against men as a group, misandry has become a popular term in certain circles. Feminists often joke about being misandrists as a response to persistently being labeled man-haters.

7. Farrell's oft-cited *The Myth of Male Power*, first published in 1993, contains this telling quote about date rape: "We don't put other salespersons in jail for buying clients drinks and successfully transforming a 'no' into a 'maybe' into a 'yes.' If the client makes a choice to drink too much and the 'yes' turns out to be a bad decision, it is the client who gets fired, not the salesperson. We expect adults to take responsibility" (321). This argument perpetuates the myth that women accuse men of raping them after having had "regrettable" drunk sex, when research consistently shows that rapists use alcohol to incapacitate their targets and make a report or testimony less believable.

8. MRAS who claim to care about male victims of rape frequently make jokes about the rape of men in prison, call male victims of rape "pussies" and "beta" males (thus positioning themselves as "alphas"), and otherwise mock the male survivors they claim to care so much about.

9. Bruch, "Parental Alienation Syndrome and Parental Alienation," 530.

10. Shrek6, comment; Jimmy Wilhelmssohn, comment; Shrek6, comment, respectively, on Kruk, "Parental Alienation."

11. Suzy McCarley, moderator, comment on Kruk, "Parental Alienation."

12. Elam, "Family Courts Have Got to GO and I Mean Right Fucking Now."

13. Belkin, "More Fathers Are Getting Custody in Divorce."

14. "Statistics."

15. McArdle, "How Many Rape Reports Are False?"

16. Quoted in Robbins, "Woman Raped in LES Bar Says Cop Asked If She's 'a Party Girl.'"

17. Fanflik, "Victim Responses to Sexual Assault."

18. Bowcott, "Rape Investigations 'Undermined by Belief That False Accusations Are Rife.'"

19. Elam, "If You See Jezebel in the Road, Run the Bitch Down."

20. Elam, "Fembots Are Already Bent Out of Shape."

21. Futrelle, "Paul Elam, You're No MLK."

22. Elam, "Interdisciplinary Shaming Dept. Part V—Robbie Lieberman."

23. Futrelle, "Paul Elam, You're No MLK."

24. Futrelle, "7 Tactics of Highly Effective Harassers."

25. Barnes, Twitter post.

26. Futrelle, "Men's Rights Website Falsely Accuses Ohio University Student of Being a False Rape Accuser."

27. Gettys, "Ohio University Student Attacked by Internet Trolls after She's Misidentified as Alleged Rape Victim in Online Video."

28. In a blog post about his Pick-Up Artist skills, Valizadeh wrote, "While walking to my place, I realized how drunk she was. In America, having sex with her would have been rape, since she legally couldn't give her consent. It didn't help matters that I was relatively sober, but I can't say I cared or even hesitated." Quoted in Futrelle, "Pickup Guru Roosh V."

29. Naso, "Quitting the Manosphere."

30. Forney, "5 Reasons Why Girls with Tattoos and Piercings Are Broken."

31. Anonymous, "It Happened to Me."

32. Anonymous, "It Happened to Me."

33. Matak, "Student Assaulted."

34. Quoted in Futrelle, "Fidelbogen."

35. Goldwag, "Leader's Suicide Brings Attention to Men's Rights Movement."

36. Jason, "Game of Fear."

37. Malki !, "#1062; The Terrible Sea Lion."

38. Quoted in Wu, "Gamergate Death Threat Is a Slam Dunk for Prosecutors."

39. McDonald, "'Gamergate.'"

40. Quoted in Totilo, "Another Woman in Gaming Flees Home Following Death Threats."

41. The stripes on Vivian James's outfit are a reference to the 4chan "daily dose" meme in which a GIF of one Dragon Ball Z character raping another was posted so often that users who did so were banned. To continue the meme, the colors green and purple are included as often as possible in other posts. Random Man and Smarzeek, "Daily Dose/Piccolo Dick."

42. "Based" in this construction is slang for doing what you want and not caring what other people think. Those notable figures who are "based" in Gamergate lingo are, appropriately enough, those who do what Gamergate wants and care what Gamergate thinks.

43. Arthur, "Kernel Sued by Former Contributors for Nonpayment"; Arthur, "Kernel Could Face £11,000 Payout Order."

44. Alexander, "'Gamers' Don't Have to Be Your Audience."

45. Yiannopoulos, Twitter post, 7:22 p.m.

46. Yiannopoulos, Twitter post, 8:15 p.m.

47. Yiannopoulos, "Feminist Bullies Tearing the Video Game Industry Apart, Breitbart."

48. Cernovich, Twitter post, 2014.

49. Cernovich, "New? Start Here."

50. Cernovich, Twitter post, 8:52 p.m.

51. Cernovich, Twitter post, 6:30 p.m.

52. von Karma, "Mike Cernovich."

53. Robertson, "'About 20' Police Officers Sent to Gamergate Critic's Former Home after Fake Hostage Threat."

54. Olson, "Mods Are Always Asleep."

55. Matias et al., "Reporting, Reviewing, and Responding to Harassment on Twitter."

56. Balo, "72 Hours of #Gamergate."

57. "About," Twitter.

58. Spil Games, "State of Online Gaming Report."

59. Jusino, "When Trolls Attack."

60. Smith-Pearson, "Feminist Deck."

61. Reed, "Hugo Awards"; Reed, "Calgary Expo."

6. DEALING WITH CYBERSEXISM

1. Parti and Marin, "Ensuring Freedoms and Protecting Rights in the Governance of the Internet," 139.

2. Parti and Marin, "Ensuring Freedoms and Protecting Rights in the Governance of the Internet," 147–48.

3. Ho, Lui, and Ma, "Acceptance of Internet Content Filters."

4. It is important to note that, like many studies of online behaviors and preferences, this study (Ho, Lui, and Ma, "Acceptance of Internet Content Filters) ignores race, disability, religion, sexuality, and other factors and provides no opportunity to assess the intersections of identity when considering the desire or need for filtering and blocking.

5. Parti and Marin, "Ensuring Freedoms and Protecting Rights in the Governance of the Internet," 156.

6. Zhang, "Sharing Block Lists to Help Make Twitter Safer."

7. Plante, "You're Not Using Twitter's Best Feature Enough."

8. Hoffman-Andrews, "Block Together (beta)."

9. Harper, "Good Game Autoblocker," *Randi.10*.

10. Harper, "Good Game Autoblocker," Block Together.

11. Carolyn G., Twitter posts.

12. Davenport, "Anonymity on the Internet," 33.

13. Jeong, *Internet of Garbage*, chap. 2.

14. Wu, Twitter posts.

15. Bivens, "Rape 'Jokes,' Social Media Software, and the Politics of Moderation."

16. Dreßing et al., "Cyberstalking in a Large Sample of Social Network Users."

17. Li, "Empirical Studies on Online Information Privacy Concerns," 458.

18. Kuo et al., "Study of Social Information Control Affordances and Gender Difference in Facebook Self-Presentation."

19. J. Smith, "Ello Finally Rolls Out Privacy Features, Races to Finish Beta and Secure the Site."

20. "Take Back the Tech!'s Report Card on Social Media and Violence against Women."
21. Lyndon, Bonds-Raacke, and Cratty, "College Students' Facebook Stalking of Ex-Partners."
22. "The Mary Sue's Comment Policy."
23. Wilson, "Hate Sinks."
24. Chang and Solomon, "Reddit Moves to Revamp Site to Deal with Offensive Posts."
25. Moyer, "'Coontown.'"
26. Matney, "Reddit Finally Bans Racist r/CoonTown and Other Hateful Communities, Updates User Policies."
27. Brossard and Scheufele, "This Story Stinks."
28. Moosa, "Comment Sections Are Poison."
29. Quoted in Moosa, "Comment Sections Are Poison."
30. LaBarre, "Why We're Shutting Off Our Comments."
31. "We Have a Rape Gif Problem and Gawker Media Won't Do Anything About It."
32. Jackson, "Just Kill All of the Comments Already."
33. Referenced in Luckman, "(En)Gendering the Digital Body."
34. Referenced in Daniels, "Rethinking Cyberfeminism(s)," 104.
35. Plant, "Future Looms," 58.
36. Wajcman, "Feminist Theories of Technology."
37. Wacjman, *TechnoFeminism*, chap 1.
38. Brown, "Twitter's Battle of the Sexes."
39. "#SolidarityIsForWhiteWomen Creator, Mikki Kendal [*sic*], Speaks about Women of Color, Feminism (VIDEO)."
40. Clifford, "Women Dominate Every Social Network—Except One."
41. Wang, Hong, and Pi, "Cross-Cultural Adaptation," 117.
42. Krenkel, Moré, and Lima da Motta, "Significant Social Networks of Women."
43. Taylor, "Women's Social Networks and Female Friendship in the Ancient Greek City."
44. Rommes, "Creating Places for Women on the Internet," 403, 404.
45. Rommes, "Creating Places for Women on the Internet," 419.
46. Asselin, "Character Focused."
47. Alexander, "But WHAT CAN BE DONE."
48. Alexander, "But WHAT CAN BE DONE."

49. Wu, "Gamergate Death Threat Is a Slam Dunk for Prosecutors."

50. O'Brien, "'This Is the Year Technology Hit Rock Bottom.'"

51. Citron, *Hate Crimes in Cyberspace*, 123.

52. Hess, "Why Women Aren't Welcome on the Internet."

53. Citron, *Hate Crimes in Cyberspace*, 121.

54. Oliver, *"Last Week Tonight with John Oliver."*

55. LAKANA, "Suit."

56. Flatow, "Cop Charged with Sexually Assaulting 7 Black Women Released from Jail."

57. Garza, Tometi, and Cullors, "About Us."

7. FIGHTING BACK

1. Wajcman, "Feminist Theories of Technology."

2. Wajcman, "Feminist Theories of Technology."

3. "Grace Hopper."

4. "About Us."

5. Wilding, "Where Is the Feminism in Cyberfeminism?"

6. "Who We Are."

7. Bryant, "About Our Founder."

8. "About," Dames Who Game.

9. North, "When Novels Were Bad for You."

10. Hallenbeck, "User Agency, Technical Communication, and the 19th-Century Woman Bicyclist," 291.

11. Caroline Bassett, "With a Little Help from Our (New) Friends?," *mute*, August 1997, citing Plant, per Wilding, "Where Is the Feminism in Cyberfeminism?," 6.

12. Daniels, "Rethinking Cyberfeminism(s)," 103.

13. The irony that I fit the personal description and am writing primarily on the end use of technology is not lost on me.

14. Daniels, "Rethinking Cyberfeminism(s)."

15. Wyer et al., *Women, Science, and Technology*, 360; Grzanka, *Intersectionality*, 282.

16. Luckman, "(En)Gendering the Digital Body," 43.

17. Paasonen, "Revisiting Cyberfeminism," 348.

18. Daniels, "Rethinking Cyberfeminism(s)," 111.

19. Paasonen, "Revisiting Cyberfeminism," 348.

20. Herring, "Rhetorical Dynamics of Gender Harassment On-Line."

21. Luckman, "(En)Gendering the Digital Body," 41.

22. Wyer et al., *Women, Science, and Technology*, 359.

23. Wilding, "Where Is the Feminism in Cyberfeminism?," 8.

24. Quoted in Lyden, "Casting Call."

25. Quoted in Murphy, "How Two Badass Actresses Are Making Hollywood Better for Women."

26. Rheingold, *Virtual Community*, chap. 2.

27. Rheingold, *Virtual Community*, chap. 1.

28. M. Murphy, "People with Tattoos Report the Apple Watch Is Having Trouble Determining They Are Alive."

29. Chowdhry, "Apple CEO Tim Cook Is 'Not Satisfied' with Employee Diversity."

30. Wilding, "Where Is the Feminism in Cyberfeminism?," 9.

31. Wilding, "Where Is the Feminism in Cyberfeminism?," 10.

32. Wilding, "Where Is the Feminism in Cyberfeminism?," 6 (virus), 7 (joy and affirmation).

33. Dement, *Cyberflesh Girlmonster*.

34. "Cyberfeminist Manifesto for the 21st Century" (VNS Matrix).

35. *All New Gen*.

36. Blackmon and Karabinus, "Invisibility Blues."

37. Home page, Twine.

38. Cohen, "This Video Game Shows What Sexual Harassment Can Feel Like."

39. Alvarez, "Artists of gURLS [*sic*]."

40. Frank, "15 Feminist Artists Respond to the Censorship of Women's Bodies Online."

41. Sonenshein, "Powerful Selfies Project Reveals Just How Much Tumblr Hates Women."

42. Bottos, "Screen Shot from a New Series of Web Pieces."

43. Wilding, "Where Is the Feminism in Cyberfeminism?," 8.

44. Wilding, "Where Is the Feminism in Cyberfeminism?," 11.

45. Wilding, "Where Is the Feminism in Cyberfeminism?," 9.

46. Citron, *Hate Crimes in Cyberspace*, 239.

47. Jeong, *Internet of Garbage*, chap. 2.

48. Keating, "'League of Legends' Battles Harassment with Automated System That Could Ban Gamers."

49. Citron, *Hate Crimes in Cyberspace*, 237.

50. L. Hudson, "Curbing Online Abuse Isn't Impossible."

51. Citron, *Hate Crimes in Cyberspace*, 232.

52. Jeong, *Internet of Garbage*, chap. 2.

53. Citron, *Hate Crimes in Cyberspace*, 227.

54. Citron, *Hate Crimes in Cyberspace*, 228.

55. Citron, *Hate Crimes in Cyberspace*, 229.

56. L. Hudson, "Curbing Online Abuse Isn't Impossible."

57. Jeong, *Internet of Garbage*, chap. 2.

58. Citron, *Hate Crimes in Cyberspace*, 125.

59. Citron, *Hate Crimes in Cyberspace*, 121.

60. Citron, *Hate Crimes in Cyberspace*, 122.

61. Bonk, "Ashley Judd Is Not Putting Up with Sexist Tweets Anymore."

62. Franks, "Sexual Harassment 2.0," 659.

63. Citron, "Cyber Civil Rights," 63.

64. Citron, "Cyber Civil Rights," 66, 67.

65. Citron, *Hate Crimes in Cyberspace*, 127, 128.

66. Lipton, "Combating Cyber-Victimization," 1138.

67. Lipton, "Combating Cyber-Victimization," 1139, 1140.

68. Lipton, "Combating Cyber-Victimization," 1140.

69. Lipton, "Combating Cyber-Victimization," 1153.

70. Halder and Jaishankar, "Cyber Gender Harassment and Secondary Victimization," 390.

71. Bates, "Everyday Sexism."

72. Bates, "Everyday Sexism."

73. Home page, Men Can Stop Rape.

74. Home page, Working to Halt Online Abuse.

75. "Lawyers."

76. Epstein, "Twitter Teams Up with Advocacy Group to Fight Online Harassment of Women."

77. Matias et al., "Reporting, Reviewing, and Responding to Harassment on Twitter."

78. Matias et al., "Reporting, Reviewing, and Responding to Harassment on Twitter."

79. Sarkeesian, "How Our Tropes vs. Women Project Has Expanded and Transformed."

80. Home page, Online Abuse Prevention Initiative.

81. "About," Crash Override Network.

82. Khaw, "How a Gamergate Target Is Fighting Online Harassment."

83. "About," Crash Override Network.

84. Kessler, "Meet HeartMob."

85. Kessler, "Meet HeartMob."

Bibliography

"About." Crash Override Network, August 1, 2015. http://www.crashoverride network.com/.

"About." Dames Making Games, November 7, 2015. https://dmg.to/about.

"About." Twitter, accessed January 14, 2015. http://about.twitter.com/.

"About Us." Women in Technology Education Foundation, July 7, 2015. http:// www.womenintechnology.org/witef/about-us.

Ajinkya, Julie. "The Top 5 Facts about Women in Our Criminal Justice System." Center for American Progress, March 7, 2012. https://www.americanprogress.org /issues/women/news/2012/03/07/11219/the-top-5-facts-about-women-in-our -criminal-justice-system/.

Alexander, Leigh. "But WHAT CAN BE DONE: Dos and Don'ts to Combat Online Sexism." LeighAlexander.net, July 5, 2014. http://leighalexander.net/but-what -can-be-done-dos-and-donts-to-combat-online-sexism/.

———. "'Gamers' Don't Have to Be Your Audience: 'Gamers' Are Over." *Gama-sutra*, August 28, 2014. http://www.gamasutra.com/view/news/224400/Gamers _dont_have_to_be_your_audience_Gamers_are_over.php.

All New Gen. Multimedia installation by VNS Matrix at the Experimental Art Foundation, Adelaide, South Australia, 1993.

Almasy, Steve. "'Revenge Porn Operator Gets 18 Years in Prison." *CNN.com*, April 4, 2015. http://www.cnn.com/2015/04/03/us/califomia-revenge-porn-sentence/.

Alvarez, Ana Cecilia. "The Artists of GURLS [*sic*]." *Daily Beast*, September 22, 2013. http://www.thedailybeast.com/witw/articles/2013/09/22/feminist-online-art -and-the-women-of-gurls.html.

Anonymous. "It Happened to Me: I Went on a Date with an MRA, and He Assaulted Me When I Wouldn't Have Sex with Him." *xoJane*, June 26, 2014. http://www.xojane.com/it-happened-to-me/my-date-with-an-mra.

Arthur, Charles. "The Kernel Could Face £11,000 Payout Order." *Guardian*, January 8, 2013. http://www.theguardian.com/media/2013/jan/08/kernel-face-payout-order-contributor.

———. "The Kernel Sued by Former Contributors for Nonpayment." *Guardian*, September 12, 2012. http://www.theguardian.com/media/2012/sep/12/the-kernel-sued-former-contributors.

Asselin, Janelle. "Character Focused: An Interview with Cartoonist Natalie Nourigat [Hire This Woman]." *ComicsAlliance*, May 26, 2015. http://comicsalliance.com/natalie-nourigat-hire-this-woman/.

Balo, Andy. "72 Hours of #Gamergate." Medium, October 27, 2014. https://medium.com/message/72-hours-of-gamergate-e00513f7cf5d.

Barnes, Jack. Twitter post, January 26, 2015. https://twitter.com/jackbarnesmra/status/559761561028669440.

Bates, Laura. "Everyday Sexism." The Everyday Sexism Project, May 3, 2015. http://usa.everydaysexism.com/.

———. "The Everyday Sexism Project." Catapult, June 3, 2014. http://catapult.org/fighting-everyday-sexism/.

Belkin, Lisa. "More Fathers Are Getting Custody in Divorce" (blog post). *The Motherlode*, NYTimes.com, November 17, 2009. http://parenting.blogs.nytimes.com/2009/11/17/more-fathers-getting-custody-in-divorce/?_r=0.

Biber, J. K., D. Doverspike, D. Baznik, A. Cober, and B. A. Ritter. "Sexual Harassment in Online Communications: Effects of Gender and Discourse Medium." *Cyberpsychology and Behavior* 5, no. 1 (2002): 33–42.

Biddle, Sam. "iPad Hacker and 'Troll' Weev Is Now a Straight-Up White Supremacist." *Gawker*, October 2, 2014. http://gawker.com/ipad-hacker-and-troll-weev-is-now-a-straight-up-white-1641763761.

Bivens, Rena. "Rape 'Jokes,' Social Media Software, and the Politics of Moderation." RenaBivens.com, June 12, 2015. http://renabivens.com/category/uncategorized/#console-ing-passions-2015.

Blackmon, Samantha, and Alisha Karabinus. "Invisibility Blues." Kickstarter, July 20, 2015. https://www.kickstarter.com/projects/113093954/invisibility-blues-exploring-race-in-video-games?ref=nav_search.

Bonk, Lawrence. "Ashley Judd Is Not Putting Up with Sexist Tweets Anymore: So She's Going to Go After Them . . . in Court." *IJ Review*, March 2015. http://www.ijreview.com/2015/03/273874-ashley-judd-pressing-charges-bullies/.

Bottos, Lindsay. "Screen Shot from a New Series of Web Pieces." Tumblr, July 26, 2015. http://lindsaybottos.tumblr.com/post/125127539827/screen-shot-from-a-new-series-of-web-pieces-im.

Bowcott, Owen. "Rape Investigations 'Undermined by Belief That False Accusations Are Rife.'" *Guardian*, March 13, 2013. http://www.theguardian.com/society/2013/mar/13/rape-investigations-belief-false-accusations.

Broderick, Ryan. "Activists Are Outing Hundreds of Twitter Users Believed to Be 4chan Trolls Posing as Feminists." *Buzzfeed*, June 17, 2014. http://www.buzzfeed.com/ryanhatesthis/your-slip-is-showing-4chan-trolls-operation-lollipop#.gtwm4Qm6o.

Brossard, Dominique, and Dietram A. Scheufele. "This Story Stinks." *New York Times*, March 3, 2013. http://www.nytimes.com/2013/03/03/opinion/sunday/this-story-stinks.html?_r=0.

Brown, Molly. "Twitter's Battle of the Sexes: Why Men Get More Retweets Than Women." *Geekwire*, May 20, 2015. http://www.geekwire.com/2015/twitters-battle-of-the-sexes-why-men-get-more-retweets-than-women/.

Bruch, Carol S. "Parental Alienation Syndrome and Parental Alienation: Getting It Wrong in Child Custody Cases." *Family Law Quarterly* 35, no. 3 (2001): 527–52.

Brush, Candida, Patricia Greene, Lakshmi Balachandra, and Amy Davis. "Diana Report—Women Entrepreneurs 2014: Bridging the Gender Gap in Venture Capital." Arthur M. Blank Center for Entrepreneurship, Babson College, September 2014. http://www.babson.edu/Academics/centers/blank-center/global-research/diana/Documents/diana-project-executive-summary-2014.pdf.

Bryant, Kimberly. "About Our Founder." Black Girls Code, 2014. http://www.blackgirlscode.com/about-bgc.html.

Cernovich, Mike. "New? Start Here." *Danger and Play*, December 4, 2014. http://www.dangerandplay.com/new-start-here/.

———. Twitter post, 6:30 p.m., January 22, 2012. https://twitter.com/cernovich/status/161591733086466048.

———. Twitter post, 8:52 p.m., August 11, 2012. https://twitter.com/Cernovich/status/234452349790322690.

———. Twitter post, 2:57 p.m., August 28, 2014. https://twitter.com/Cernovich/status/505066536873521152.

Chang, Andrea, and Daina Beth Solomon. "Reddit Moves to Revamp Site to Deal with Offensive Posts." *Los Angeles Times*, July 17, 2015. http://www.latimes.com/business/la-fi-reddit-content-policy-20150718-story.html.

Chowdhry, Amit. "Apple CEO Tim Cook Is 'Not Satisfied' with Employee Diversity." *Forbes*, August 13, 2014. http://www.forbes.com/sites/amitchowdhry/2014/08/13/apple-ceo-tim-cook-is-not-satisfied-with-employee-diversity/.

Citron, Danielle. "Cyber Civil Rights." *Boston University Law Review* 89 (2009): 61–125.

———. *Hate Crimes in Cyberspace*. Cambridge MA: Harvard University Press, 2014.

———. "Law's Expressive Value in Combating Cyber Gender Harassment." *Michigan Law Review* 108, no. 3 (2009): 373–415.

Clifford, Catherine. "Women Dominate Every Social Network—Except One." *Entrepreneur*, March 4, 2014. http://www.entrepreneur.com/article/231970.

Cohen, Rebecca. "This Video Game Shows What Sexual Harassment Can Feel Like." *Mother Jones*, April 11, 2015. http://www.motherjones.com/media/2015/04/video-game-shows-what-sexual-harassment-feels.

Covert, Bryce. "Working Single Mothers Are Disproportionately Likely to Be Poor." *Think Progress*, February 19, 2014. http://thinkprogress.org/economy/2014/02/19/3305931/income-single-mothers/.

Crecente, Brian. "Plague of Game Dev Harassment Erodes Industry, Spurs Support Groups." *Polygon*, August 15, 2013. http://www.polygon.com/2013/8/15/4622252/plague-of-game-dev-harassment-erodes-industry-spurs-support-groups.

"The Crime of 'Swatting.'" FBI, September 3, 2013. https://www.fbi.gov/news/stories/2013/september/the-crime-of-swatting-fake-9-1-1-calls-have-real-consequences/the-crime-of-swatting-fake-9-1-1-calls-have-real-consequences.

Culp-Ressler, Tara. "This Week, Two Incidents of Street Harassment Escalated into Violent Attacks against Women." *Think Progress*, October 9, 2014. http://thinkprogress.org/health/2014/10/09/3578215/street-harassment-escalates/.

"Cyberfeminist Manifesto for the 21st Century" (VNS Matrix). *Sterneck*, 1991. http://www.sterneck.net/cyber/vns-matrix/index.php.

Dahl, Melissa. "People Who Say 'Like' All the Time Are Surprisingly Thoughtful. *New York Magazine*, June 10, 2014. http://nymag.com/scienceofus/2014/06/i-mean-its-just-thoughtful-you-know.html.

Daniels, Jessie. *Cyber Racism: White Supremacy Online and the New Attack on Civil Rights*. Lanham MD: Rowman & Littlefield, 2009.

———. "Rethinking Cyberfeminism(s): Race, Gender, and Embodiment." *Women's Studies Quarterly* 37, nos. 1–2 (2009): 101–24.

Davenport, David. "Anonymity on the Internet: Why the Price May Be Too High." *Communications of the ACM* 45, no. 4 (2002): 33–35. http://www.csl.mtu.edu /cs6461/www/Reading/Davenport02.pdf.

Dean, Jeremy. "Persuasion: The Third-Person Effect." *PsyBlog*, August 3, 2010. http://www.spring.org.uk/2010/08/persuasion-the-third-person-effect.php.

Dement, Linda. *Cyberflesh Girlmonster*. LindaDement.com, accessed July 9, 2015. http://www.lindadement.com/cyberflesh-girlmonster.htm.

Dickson, E. J. "'Casting Couch' Porn Actress Commits Suicide after Being Harassed on Social Media." *Daily Dot*, May 21, 2014. http://www.dailydot.com/lifestyle /alyssa-funke-casting-couch-porn-suicide/.

"Domestic Violence Statistics." American Bar Association (ABA) Commission on Domestic Violence, December 3, 2014. http://www.americanbar.org/groups /domestic_violence/resources/statistics.html.

"Don't Feed the Trolls!" Skepchick, February 3, 2015. http://skepchick.org/dont-feed -the-trolls-2/.

Dreßing, Harald, Josef Bailer, Anne Anders, Henriette Wagner, and Christine Gallas. "Cyberstalking in a Large Sample of Social Network Users: Prevalence, Characteristics, and Impact upon Victims." *Cyberpsychology, Behavior, and Social Networking* 17, no. 2 (2014): 61–67.

Duggan, Maeve. "Online Harassment." Pew Research Center: Internet, Science & Tech, October 22, 2014. http://www.pewinternet.org/2014/10/22/online -harassment/.

"Eating Disorders Statistics." National Association of Anorexia Nervosa and Associated Disorders (ANAD), January 1, 2015. http://www.anad.org/get-information /about-eating-disorders/eating-disorders-statistics/.

Eisenberg, Rebecca. "29 States Can Fire You for Being Gay: Is Your State One of Them?" *Upworthy*, 2012. http://www.upworthy.com/29-states-can-fire-you-for -being-gay-is-your-state-one-of-them.

Elam, Paul. "The Family Courts Have Got to GO and I Mean Right Fucking Now." A Voice for Men, June 16, 2011. http://www.avoiceformen.com/men/fathers /the-family-courts-have-to-go-and-i-mean-right-fucking-now/.

———. "The Fembots Are Already Bent Out of Shape." A Voice for Men, June 28, 2011. http://www.avoiceformen.com/mens-rights/activism/the-fembots -are-already-bent-out-of-shape/.

———. "If You See Jezebel in the Road, Run the Bitch Down." A Voice for Men, October 22, 2010. Archived at WayBack Machine. http://web.archive.org/web /20110702180031/http://www.avoiceformen.com/2010/10/22/if-you-see-jezebel -in-the-road-run-the-bitch-down/.

———. "Interdisciplinary Shaming Dept. Part V—Robbie Lieberman." A Voice for Men, February 25, 2015. http://www.avoiceformen.com/education/interdisciplinary -shaming-dept-part-v-robbie-lieberman/.

Eördögh, Fruzsina. "Interview with a Troll Whisperer." *Motherboard*, May 19, 2015. http://motherboard.vice.com/read/interview-with-a-troll-whisperer.

Epstein, Kayla. "Twitter Teams Up with Advocacy Group to Fight Online Harassment of Women." *Guardian*, November 8, 2014. http://www.theguardian.com /technology/2014/nov/08/twitter-harassment-women-wam.

Eveleth, Rose. "How Self-Tracking Apps Exclude Women." *The Atlantic*, December 15, 2014. http://www.theatlantic.com/technology/archive/2014/12/how-self -tracking-apps-exclude-women/383673/.

Fairchild, Caroline. "Women CEOs in the Fortune 1000: By the Numbers." *Fortune*, July 8, 2014. http://fortune.com/2014/07/08/women-ceos-fortune-500-1000/.

Fanflik, Patricia L. "Victim Responses to Sexual Assault: Counterintuitive or Simply Adaptive?" National District Attorneys Association, 2007. Accessed June 3, 2015. http://www.ndaa.org/pdf/pub_victim_responses_sexual_assault.pdf.

"FBI Releases 2012 Hate Crime Statistics." FBI National Press Office, November 25, 2013. https://www.fbi.gov/news/pressrel/press-releases/fbi-releases-2012 -hate-crime-statistics.

Flatow, Nicole. "Cop Charged with Sexually Assaulting 7 Black Women Released from Jail." *Think Progress*, September 6, 2014. http://thinkprogress.org/justice /2014/09/06/3564082/cop-who-allegedly-assaulted-7-black-women-released -from-jail/.

Forney, Matt. "5 Reasons Why Girls with Tattoos and Piercings Are Broken." Return of Kings, October 14, 2014. http://www.returnofkings.com/81129/5 -reasons-why-girls-with-tattoos-and-piercings-are-broken.

Frank, Priscilla. "15 Feminist Artists Respond to the Censorship of Women's Bodies Online." *Huffington Post*, April 13, 2015. http://www.huffingtonpost .com/2015/04/13/artists-respond-female-body-censorship-online_n_7042926 .html.

Franks, Mary Anne. "Sexual Harassment 2.0." *Maryland Law Review* 71, no. 3 (2012): 655–904.

Futrelle, David. "Fidelbogen: Men's Rights Activists! Forget about DV Shelters for Men. Focus on the Important Issue: Yelling at Feminists." *We Hunted the Mammoth*, August 29, 2013. http://wehuntedthemammoth.com/2013/08/29 /fidelbogen-mens-rights-activists-forget-about-dv-shelters-for-men-focus -on-the-important-issue-yelling-at-feminists/.

———. "Leading MRA Site A Voice for Men Continues to Publish a Holocaust Denier and Marital Rape Apologist." *We Hunted the Mammoth*, June 24, 2014. http://wehuntedthemammoth.com/2015/06/24/leading-mra-site-a-voice-for -men-continues-to-publish-a-holocaust-denier-and-marital-rape-apologist/.

———. "Men's Rights Website Falsely Accuses Ohio University Student of Being a False Rape Accuser." *We Hunted the Mammoth*, October 22, 2013. http:// wehuntedthemammoth.com/2013/10/22/mens-rights-website-falsely-accuses -ohio-university-student-of-being-a-false-rape-accuser/.

———. "Paul Elam, You're No MLK: A Voice for Men Offers a $100 Bounty for a Clear Photo of Its Latest Feminist Foe." *We Hunted the Mammoth*, January 19, 2015. http://wehuntedthemammoth.com/2015/01/19/paul-elam-youre-no-mlk -a-voice-for-men-offers-a-100-bounty-for-a-clear-photo-of-its-latest-feminist -foe/.

———. "Pickup Guru Roosh V: End Rape by Making It Legal." *We Hunted the Mammoth*, February 17, 2015. http://wehuntedthemammoth.com/2015/02/17 /pickup-guru-roosh-v-end-rape-by-making-it-legal/.

———. "7 Tactics of Highly Effective Harassers: How A Voice for Men's Internet Hate Machine Works." *We Hunted the Mammoth*, January 27, 2015. http:// wehuntedthemammoth.com/2015/01/27/7-tactics-of-highly-effective-harassers -how-a-voice-for-mens-internet-hate-machine-works/.

G., Carolyn. Twitter post, 8:44 p.m., March 30, 2015. https://twitter.com/Arumi_kai /status/582705113715855360.

———. Twitter post, 8:46 p.m., March 30, 2015. https://twitter.com/Arumi_kai /status/582705394314813440.

Gagne, Ken. "Doxxing Defense: Remove Your Personal Info from Data Brokers." *Computerworld*, November 20, 2014. http://www.computerworld.com/article /2849263/doxxing-defense-remove-your-personal-info-from-data-brokers .html.

Gandy, Imani. "#TwitterFail: Twitter's Refusal to Handle Online Stalkers, Abus-ers, and Haters." *RH Reality Check*, August 12, 2014. http://rhrealitycheck.org

/article/2014/08/12/twitterfail-twitters-refusal-handle-online-stalkers-abusers
-haters/.

Garza, Alicia, Opal Tometi, and Patrisse Cullors. "About Us." Black Lives Matter,
July 30, 2015. http://blacklivesmatter.com/about/.

"Get the Facts on Eating Disorders." National Eating Disorder Association
(NEDA), May 14, 2015. http://www.nationaleatingdisorders.org/get-facts-eating
-disorders.

Gettys, Travis. "Ohio University Student Attacked by Internet Trolls after She's
Misidentified as Alleged Rape Victim in Online Video." *Raw Story*, October 22,
2013. http://www.rawstory.com/2013/10/ohio-university-student-attacked-by
-internet-trolls-after-shes-misidentified-as-alleged-rape-victim-in-online
-video/.

Giovanniello, Sarah. "NCAVP Report: 2012 Hate Violence Disproportionately Target
[*sic*] Transgender Women of Color." GLAAD, June 4, 2013. http://www.glaad.org
/blog/ncavp-report-2012-hate-violence-disproportionately-target-transgender
-women-color.

Golden, Jamie Nesbitt. "Why I'm Masquerading as a White Bearded Hipster
Guy on Twitter (Despite Being a Black Woman)." *xoJane*, April 4, 2014. http://
www.xojane.com/issues/why-im-masquerading-as-a-bearded-white-hipster
-guy-on-twitter.

Goldwag, Arthur. "Leader's Suicide Brings Attention to Men's Rights Movement."
Southern Poverty Law Center, March 1, 2012. https://www.splcenter.org/fighting
-hate/intelligence-report/2012/leader%E2%80%99s-suicide-brings-attention
-men%E2%80%99s-rights-movement.

Goudreau, Jenna. "13 Subtle Ways Women Are Treated Differently at Work." *Business Insider*, June 27, 2014. http://www.businessinsider.com/subtle-ways-women
-treated-differently-work-2014-6.

"Grace Hopper." Biography.com, July 7, 2015. http://www.biography.com/people
/grace-hopper-21406809.

Gregorie, Trudy. "Cyberstalking: Dangers on the Information Superhighway."
National Center for Victims of Crime, 2001. https://www.victimsofcrime.org
/docs/src/cyberstalking—-dangers-on-the-information-superhighway.pdf
?sfvrsn=2.

Grzanka, Patrick R. *Intersectionality: A Foundations and Frontiers Reader*. Boulder
CO: Westview Press, 2014.

Halder, Debarati, and K. Jaishankar. "Cyber Gender Harassment and Secondary Victimization: A Comparative Analysis of the United States, the UK, and India." *Victims and Offenders* 6, no. 4 (2011): 386–98.

Hallenbeck, Sarah. "User Agency, Technical Communication, and the 19th-Century Woman Bicyclist." *Technical Communication Quarterly* 21, no. 4 (2012): 290–306.

Hammond, Claudia. "Prattle of the Sexes: Do Women Really Talk More Than Men?" *BBC: Future*, November 12, 2013. http://www.bbc.com/future/story /20131112-do-women-talk-more-than-men.

Haniver, Jenny. "Lots of Words" (blog entry). *Not in the Kitchen Anymore*, August 12, 2013. http://www.notinthekitchenanymore.com/lots-of-words/.

Harper, Randi. "Good Game Autoblocker." Block Together, July 3, 2015. https:// blocktogether.org/show-blocks/5867111278318bd542293272f75147f8fc5931bea 431e7ca16e9242964965d66494a6fb68f3518b82f171bcf0e419ccc.

———. "Good Game Autoblocker." *Randi.10*, April 17, 2015. http://blog.randi.io /good-game-auto-blocker/.

Hern, Alex. "Reddit Finally Bans Its White-Supremacist Subreddits." *Guardian*, August 6, 2015. http://www.theguardian.com/technology/2015/aug/06/reddit -bans-white-supremacist-subreddits.

Herring, Susan. "The Rhetorical Dynamics of Gender Harassment On-Line." *Information Society* 15, no. 3 (2002): 151–67.

Hess, Amanda. "Why Women Aren't Welcome on the Internet." *Pacific Standard*, January 6, 2014. http://www.psmag.com/health-and-behavior/women-arent -welcome-internet-72170.

Hill, Catherine. "The Simple Truth about the Gender Pay Gap (Spring 2015)." AAUW, April 4, 2015. http://www.aauw.org/resource/the-simple-truth-about-the -gender-pay-gap/.

HKearl. "German Woman Killed for Challenging Harassers." Stop Street Harassment, October 1, 2014. http://www.stopstreetharassment.org/2014/12/german womankilled/.

Ho, Susanna S. Y., S. M. Lui, and Will W. K. Ma. "Acceptance of Internet Content Filters: An Empirical Study." *International Journal of Technology & Decision Making* 2, no. 3 (2013): 477–96.

Hoffman-Andrews, Jacob. "Block Together (beta)." Block Together, July 1, 2015. https://blocktogether.org/.

Holt, Kris. "Adria Richards Publicly Fired amid Violent #Donglegate Backlash."
Daily Dot, March 21, 2013. http://www.dailydot.com/news/adria-richards
-fired-sendgrid-violent-backlash/.

Home page. Men Can Stop Rape, May 15, 2015. http://www.mencanstoprape.org/.

Home page. Online Abuse Prevention Initiative (OAPI), August 1, 2015. http://
onlineabuseprevention.org/.

Home page. Twine, accessed July 1, 2015. http://twinery.org/.

Home page. Working to Halt Online Abuse (WHOA), 2014. Accessed July 1, 2015.
http://www.haltabuse.org/.

"Homophobia, HIV and AIDS." AVERT, April 11, 2014. http://www.avert.org
/homophobia-hiv-and-aids.htm.

Honan, Mat. "What Is Doxing?" *Wired*, March 6, 2014. http://www.wired
.com/2014/03/doxing/.

Houreld, Katharine. "Online Abuse of Women in Pakistan Turns into Real-
World Violence." *Reuters.com*, September 30, 2014. http://www.reuters.com
/article/2014/09/30/us-pakistan-women-internet-idUSKCN0HP0Q620140930.

Hudson, Laura. "Curbing Online Abuse Isn't Impossible: Here's Where We
Start." *Wired*, May 15, 2014. http://www.wired.com/2014/05/fighting-online
-harassment/.

Hudson, Shafiqah (@sassycrass). Twitter post, 10:27 p.m., February 20, 2013.
https://twitter.com/sassycrass/status/304432121223716864.

"The Issue of Fair Wages for Workers with Disabilities." National Federation of
the Blind, August 1, 2015. https://nfb.org/fair-wages.

Jackson, Nicholas. "Just Kill All of the Comments Already." *Pacific Standard*,
August 12, 2014. http://www.psmag.com/nature-and-technology/just-kill
-comments-already-88188.

Jason, Zachary. "Game of Fear." *Boston Magazine*, April 28, 2015. http://www
.bostonmagazine.com/news/article/2015/04/28/gamergate/.

Jayanth, Meg. "52% of Gamers Are Women—but the Industry Doesn't Know It."
Guardian, September 18, 2014. http://www.theguardian.com/commentisfree
/2014/sep/18/52-percent-people-playing-games-women-industry-doesnt
-know.

Jeong, Sarah. *The Internet of Garbage*. New York: Forbes Media, 2015. Kindle
edition.

Johnston, Angus. "Why Today's Elonis Decision Is a Victory in the Fight against
Online Harassment." *StudentActivism*, June 1, 2015. http://studentactivism

.net/2015/06/01/why-todays-elonis-decision-is-a-victory-in-the-fight-against
-online-harassment/.

Join the Coffee Party Movement. Facebook post, March 14, 2015. https://www
.facebook.com/coffeeparty/posts/10153712273138327.

Jusino, Teresa. "When Trolls Attack: Feminist Deck's Kiva Bay and Kickstarter
Battle the Dark Forces of Internet Bullshittery." *The Mary Sue*, May 8, 2015.
http://www.themarysue.com/feminist-deck-kiva-bay-kickstarter/.

Kabay, M. E. "Anonymity and Pseudonymity in Cyberspace: Deindividuation,
Incivility and Lawlessness versus Freedom and Privacy." Paper presented at
the Annual Conference of the European Institute for Computer Anti-virus
Research (EICAR), Munich, Germany, March 16–18, 1998. http://www.mekabay
.com/overviews/anonpseudo.pdf.

Keating, Lauren. "'League of Legends' Battles Harassment with Automated System
That Could Ban Gamers." *Tech Times*, May 26, 2015. http://www.techtimes.com
/articles/55629/20150526/league-legends-battles-harassment-automated-system
-ban-gamers.htm.

Kerby, Sophia. "The Top 10 Most Startling Facts about People of Color and
Criminal Justice in the United States." *American Progress*, March 3, 2012.
https://www.americanprogress.org/issues/race/news/2012/03/13/11351/the-top
-10-most-startling-facts-about-people-of-color-and-criminal-justice-in-the
-united-states/.

Kessler, Sarah. "Meet HeartMob: A Tool for Fighting Online Harassment Designed
by People Who Have Been Harassed." *Fast Company*, May 14, 2015. http://www
.fastcompany.com/3046181/tech-forecast/meet-heartmob-a-tool-for-fighting
-online-harassment-designed-by-people-who-hav.

Khaw, Cassandra. "How a Gamergate Target Is Fighting Online Harassment." *Engadget*,
February 23, 2015. http://www.engadget.com/2015/02/23/crash-override
-interview/.

Klepek, Patrick. "Trolls Are People, Too." *Patrick Klepek Will Now Take Your
Calls*, March 6, 2014. http://patrickklepek.tumblr.com/post/78765268646
/trolls-are-people-too.

Krenkel, Scheila, Carmen Leontina Ojeda Moré, and Cibele Cunha Lima da
Motta. "The Significant Social Networks of Women Who Have Resided in
Shelters / Las Redes Sociales Significativas de Mujeres Encaminadas Para
Casa de Acogida / As Redes Sociais Significativas de Mulheres Acolhidas em
Casa-Abrigo." *Paidéia (Ribeirão Preto)* 25, no. 60 (2015): 125–33.

Kreps, Daniel. "Revenge-Porn Site Owner Hunter Moore Pleads Guilty, Faces Prison Time." *Rolling Stone*, February 20, 2015. http://www.rollingstone.com /culture/news/revenge-porn-site-owner-hunter-moore-pleads-guilty-faces -prison-time-20150220.

Kruk, Edward. "Parental Alienation: Parent-Child Reunification after Alienation." A Voice for Men, December 16, 2014. http://www.avoiceformen.com/men/fathers /parental-alienation-parent-child-reunification-after-alienation/.

Kunsmann, Peter. "Gender, Status and Power in Discourse Behavior of Men and Women." *Linguistik online* 5, no. 1 (2000). http://www.linguistik-online .com/1_00/KUNSMANN.HTM.

Kuo, Feng-Yang, Chih-Yi Tsend, Fan-Chaun Tseng, and Cathy S. Lin. "Study of Social Information Control Affordances and Gender Difference in Facebook Self-Presentation." *Cyberpsychology, Behavior, and Social Networking* 16, no. 9 (2013): 635–44.

Kuznekoff, J. H., and L. M. Rose. "Communication in Multiplayer Gaming: Examining Player Responses to Gender Cues." *New Media & Society* (in press). DOI:10.1177/1461444812458271.

LaBarre, Suzanne. "Why We're Shutting Off Our Comments." *Popular Science*, September 24, 2013. http://www.popsci.com/science/article/2013-09/why-were -shutting-our-comments.

LAKANA. "Suit: Police Chief Threatened Rape Victims, Called Them 'Whores.'" *Click on Detroit*, July 21, 2015. http://www.clickondetroit.com/news/suit-police-chief -threatened-rape-victims-called-them-whores/34273660.

"Language as Prejudice: Language Myth #6." *Do You Speak American?*, PBS.org, 2005. http://www.pbs.org/speak/speech/prejudice/women/.

Laws, Charlotte. "I've Been Called the 'Erin Brockovich' of Revenge Porn, and for the First Time Ever, Here Is My Entire Uncensored Story of Death Threats, Anonymous and the FBI." *xoJane*, November 21, 2013. http://www.xojane.com /it-happened-to-me/charlotte-laws-hunter-moore-erin-brockovich-revenge -porn.

"Lawyers." Working to Halt Online Abuse (WHOA), 2014. http://www.haltabuse .org/resources/lawyers.shtml.

Lee, Cynthia, and Peter Kar Yu Kwan. "The Trans Panic Defense: Heteronormativity, and the Murder of Transgender Women." 66 *Hastings Law Journal* 77 (2014). Archived at Social Science Research Network. http://papers.ssrn.com /sol3/papers.cfm?abstract_id=2430390.

Leyden, John. "AT&T iPad 'Hacker' Breaks Gag Order to Rant at Cops." *Register*, July 7, 2010. http://www.theregister.co.uk/2010/07/07/ipad_hack_follow_up/.

Li, Yuan. "Empirical Studies on Online Information Privacy Concerns: Literature Review and an Integrative Framework." *Communications of the Association for Information Systems*, no. 28 (2011): 453–96.

Lipton, Jacqueline. "Combating Cyber-Victimization." *Berkeley Technological Law Journal* 26, no. 2 (2011): 1103–55.

Lithwick, Dahlia. "Schooling the Supreme Court on Rap Music." *Slate*, September 18, 2014. http://www.slate.com/articles/health_and_science/jurisprudence/2014/09/elonis_v_united_states_facebook_free_speech_case_supreme_court_justices.html.

Luckman, Susan. "(En)Gendering the Digital Body: Feminism and the Internet." *Hecate* 25, no. 2 (1999): 36–47.

Lyden, Jacki. "Casting Call: Hollywood Needs More Women." *Weekends on All Things Considered*, NPR News, June 30, 2013. http://www.npr.org/templates/transcript/transcript.php?storyId=197390707.

Lyndon, Amy, Jennifer Bonds-Raacke, and Alyssa D. Cratty. "College Students' Facebook Stalking of Ex-Partners." *Cyberpsychology, Behavior, and Social Networking* 14, no. 2 (2011): 711–16.

Macintosh, Zoë. "Negative Stereotypes Stick with You." *Live Science*, August 11, 2010. http://www.livescience.com/8480-negative-stereotypes-stick.html.

Malki !, David. "#1062; The Terrible Sea Lion." *Wondermark*, September 19, 2014. http://wondermark.com/1k62/.

"The Mary Sue's Comment Policy." *The Mary Sue*, July 3, 2015. http://www.themarysue.com/comment-policy/.

Matak, Vincent Ben. "Student Assaulted." *Queen's Journal*, March 27, 2014. http://www.queensjournal.ca/story/2014-03-27/news/student-assaulted/.

Matias, J. N., A. Johnson, W. E. Boesel, B. Keegan, J. Friedman, and C. DeTar. "Reporting, Reviewing, and Responding to Harassment on Twitter." Women, Action, & the Media, May 13, 2015. http://womenactionmedia.org/twitter-report.

Matney, Lucas. "Reddit Finally Bans Racist r/CoonTown and Other Hateful Communities, Updates User Policies." *Tech Crunch*, August 5, 2015. http://techcrunch.com/2015/08/05/reddit-finally-bans-rcoontown-and-other-hateful-subreddits-updates-user-policies/?ncid=rss.

McArdle, Megan. "How Many Rape Reports Are False?" *Bloomberg View*, September 19, 2014. http://www.bloombergview.com/articles/2014-09-19/how -many-rape-reports-are-false.

McDonald, Soraya Nadia. "'Gamergate': Feminist Video Game Critic Anita Sarkeesian Cancels Utah Lecture after Threat." *Washington Post*, October 15, 2014. http://www.washingtonpost.com/news/morning-mix/wp/2014/10/15/gamergate -feminist-video-game-critic-anita-sarkeesian-cancels-utah-lecture-after-threat -citing-police-inability-to-prevent-concealed-weapons-at-event/.

McDonough, Katie. "CeCe McDonald on Her Time in Prison: 'I Felt Like They Wanted Me to Hate Myself as a Trans Woman.'" *Salon*, January 19, 2014. http:// www.salon.com/2014/01/19/cece_mcdonald_on_her_time_in_prison_i_felt _like_they_wanted_me_to_hate_myself_as_a_trans_woman/.

Meyer, Robert, and Michael Cukier. "Assessing the Attack Threat Due to IRC Channels." *Proceedings of the International Conference on Dependable Systems and Networks*. Los Alamitos CA: IEEE Computer Society, 2006. http://www .enre.umd.edu/content/rmeyer-assessing.pdf.

Molloy, Parker Marie. "California Becomes First State to Ban Gay, Trans 'Panic' Defenses." *Advocate*, September 29, 2014. http://www.advocate.com/crime /2014/09/29/california-becomes-first-state-ban-gay-trans-panic-defenses.

Moosa, Tauriq. "Comment Sections Are Poison: Handle with Care or Remove Them." *Guardian*, September 12, 2014. http://www.theguardian.com/science /brain-flapping/2014/sep/12/comment-sections-toxic-moderation.

Moyer, Justin Wm. "'Coontown': A Noxious, Racist Corner of Reddit Survives Recent Purge." *Washington Post*, July 17, 2015. http://www.washingtonpost .com/news/morning-mix/wp/2015/07/17/coontown-a-noxious-racist-corner -of-reddit-survives-recent-purge/.

Murphy, Mike. "People with Tattoos Report the Apple Watch Is Having Trouble Determining They Are Alive." *QZ*, April 30, 2015. http://qz.com/394694/people -with-dark-skin-and-tattoos-report-the-apple-watch-is-having-trouble -determining-they-are-alive/.

Murphy, Shaunna. "How Two Badass Actresses Are Making Hollywood Better for Women." *MTV News*, July 14, 2015. http://www.mtv.com/news/2213001 /alysia-reiner-orange-is-the-new-black-production-company/.

Naso, Blair. "Quitting the Manosphere" (blog entry). *The BN Blog*, April 22, 2015. https://blairnaso.wordpress.com/2015/04/22/quitting-the-manosphere/.

"New Congress Includes More Women, Minorities." *New York Times*, January 1, 2015. http://www.nytimes.com/aponline/2015/01/04/us/politics/ap-us-congress -by-the-numbers.html?_r=0 (page discontinued).

Nigatu, Heben. "10 Ridiculously Offensive Things People Tell Asian Women on OkCupid." *Buzzfeed*, April 8, 2013. http://www.buzzfeed.com/hnigatu/10-ridiculously -offensive-things-people-tell-asian-women-on#.ljPGvDGKW.

North, Anna. "When Novels Were Bad for You" (blog entry). *Op-Talk: The New York Times*, September 14, 2014. http://op-talk.blogs.nytimes.com/2014/09/14 /when-novels-were-bad-for-you/?_r=0.

O'Brien, Sarah Ashley. "'This Is the Year Technology Hit Rock Bottom.'" *Click 2 Houston*, KPRC, 2015. http://www.click2houston.com/news/money/this-is-the -year-technology-hit-rock-bottom/34243898 (no longer available).

Oliver, John. "*Last Week Tonight with John Oliver*: Online Harassment (HBO)." *Last Week Tonight*, June 21, 2015. Archived on YouTube. https://www.youtube .com/watch?v=PuNIwYsz7PI.

Olson, Dan. "The Mods Are Always Asleep." Medium, December 23, 2014. https://medium.com/@FoldableHuman/the-mods-are-always-asleep-7f750f 879fc.

Oltermann, Philip. "'Revenge Porn' Victims Receive Boost from German Court Ruling." *Guardian*, May 22, 2014. http://www.theguardian.com/technology /2014/may/22/revenge-porn-victims-boost-german-court-ruling.

"Online Harassment/Cyberstalking Statistics." Working to Halt Online Abuse (WHOA), September 3, 2015. http://www.haltabuse.org/resources/stats/index .shtml.

Paasonen, Susanna. "Revisiting Cyberfeminism." *Communications* 36, no. 3 (2011): 335–52.

Parti, K., and L. Marin. "Ensuring Freedoms and Protecting Rights in the Governance of the Internet: A Comparative Analysis on Blocking Measures and Internet Providers' Removal of Illegal Internet Content." *Journal of Contemporary European Research* 9, no. 1 (2013): 138–59.

Penny, Laurie. *Cybersexism: Sex, Gender and Power on the Internet*. London: Bloomsbury, 2013. Kindle edition.

Pérez, Miriam Zoila. "Framing of Dove's 'Choose Beautiful' Campaign Is a Farce." *Color Lines*, April 15, 2014. http://www.colorlines.com/articles/framing-doves -choose-beautiful-campaign-farce.

Phillips, Whitney. "Don't Feed the Trolls? It's Not That Simple." *Daily Dot*, June 10, 2013. http://www.dailydot.com/opinion/phillips-dont-feed-trolls-antisocial -web/.

Pilkington, Ed. "Justine Sacco, PR Executive Fired over Racist Tweet, 'Ashamed.'" *Guardian*, December 22, 2013. http://www.theguardian.com/world/2013/dec/22 /pr-exec-fired-racist-tweet-aids-africa-apology.

Plant, Sadie. "The Future Looms: Weaving Women and Cybernetics." In *Cyberspace/Cyberbodies/Cyberpunk: Cultures of Technological Embodiment*, edited by Mike Featherstone and Roger Burrows, 45–64. Thousand Oaks CA: SAGE, 1995.

Plante, Chris. "You're Not Using Twitter's Best Feature Enough: Block People." *The Verge*, October 9, 2014. http://www.theverge.com/2014/10/9/6951165/twitter -block-people.

"Prevention for Teens: What to Do If You Are a Cyber Bullying Victim." End to Cyber Bullying, March 21, 2014. http://www.endcyberbullying.org/cyberbullying -prevention/cyberbullying-prevention-for-teens/prevention-for-teens-what -to-do-if-you-are-a-cyber-bullying-victim/.

Quenqua, Douglas. "They're, Like, Way Ahead of the Linguistic Currrrve." *New York Times*, February 28, 2012. http://www.nytimes.com/2012/02/28/science /young-women-often-trendsetters-in-vocal-patterns.html?_r=0.

Rainie, Lee, Sara Kiesler, Ruogu Kang, and Mary Madden. "Anonymity, Privacy, and Security Online." Pew Research Center: Internet, Science & Tech, September 5, 2013. http://www.pewinternet.org/2013/09/05/anonymity-privacy-and-security -online/.

Random Man and Smarzeek (pseudonyms). "Daily Dose/Piccolo Dick." *Know Your Meme*, December 14, 2014. http://knowyourmeme.com/memes/daily -dose-piccolo-dick.

Reed, Nora. "Calgary Expo" (blog post). *What Has Gamergate Ruined*, April 19, 2015. http://whatisgamergatecurrentlyruining.barrl.net/blog/.

――――. "The Hugo Awards" (blog post). *What Has Gamergate Ruined*, April 18, 2015. http://whatisgamergatecurrentlyruining.barrl.net/blog/.

Reiss, Natalie Staats, and Mark Dombeck. "Suicide Statistics." Community Counseling Services, May 14, 2015. http://www.hsccs.org/poc/view_doc.php ?type=doc&id=13737.

Rheingold, Howard. *The Virtual Community: Homesteading on the Electronic Frontier*. Reading MA: Addison-Wesley, 1993; online Rheingold ed., 1998. http:// www.rheingold.com/vc/book/.

Ritter, Barbara. "Deviant Behavior in Computer-Mediated Communication: Development and Validation of a Measure of Cybersexual Harassment." *Journal of Computer-Mediated Communication* 19, no. 2 (2014): 197–214.

Robbins, Christopher. "Woman Raped in les Bar Says Cop Asked If She's 'a Party Girl.'" *Gothamist*, August 3, 2015. http://gothamist.com/2015/08/03/happy_ending _rape_nypd.php.

Robertson, Adi. "'About 20' Police Officers Sent to Gamergate Critic's Former Home after Fake Hostage Threat." *The Verge*, January 4, 2015. http://www.theverge .com/2015/1/4/7490539/fake-hostage-threat-sends-police-to-gamergate-critic -home.

Rommes, Els. "Creating Places for Women on the Internet: The Design of a 'Women's Square' in a Digital City." *European Journal of Women's Studies* 9, no. 4 (2002): 400–429.

Roy, Debjani. "On the Tragic Murder of Mary 'Unique' Spears, Street Harassment and the Very Real Fear of Escalation." *xoJane*, October 13, 2014. http://www .xojane.com/issues/mary-unique-spears-murder-street-harassment.

Sandoval, Greg. "The End of Kindness: Weev and the Cult of the Angry Young Man." *The Verge*, September 12, 2013. http://www.theverge.com/2013/9/12 /4693710/the-end-of-kindness-weev-and-the-cult-of-the-angry-young -man.

Sarkeesian, Anita. "How Our Tropes vs. Women Project Has Expanded and Transformed." Kickstarter, January 23, 2015. https://www.kickstarter.com /projects/566429325/tropes-vs-women-in-video-games/posts/1115560.

———. "One Week of Harassment on Twitter." *Feminist Frequency*, January 20, 2015. http://femfreq.tumblr.com/post/109319269825/one-week-of-harassment -on-twitter.

Schwartz, Mattathias. "The Trolls among Us." *New York Times*, August 3, 2008. http://www.nytimes.com/2008/08/03/magazine/03trolls-t.html?pagewanted =all&_r=0.

Shifman, Limor, and Dafna Lemish. "'Mars and Venus' in Virtual Space: Post-Feminist Humor and the Internet." *Studies in Media Communication* 28, no. 3 (2010): 253–73.

Sinders, Caroline. "That Time the Internet Sent a swat Team to My Mom's House." *Narratively*, August 3, 2015. http://narrative.ly/stories/that-time-the-internet-sent -a-swat-team-to-my-moms-house/.

Smith, Jack, IV. "Ello Finally Rolls Out Privacy Features, Races to Finish Beta and Secure the Site." *Observer*, October 3, 2014. http://observer.com/2014/10/ello-finally -rolls-out-privacy-features-races-to-finish-beta-and-secure-the-site/.

Smith, Stacy. "Gender Disparity On-Screen and behind the Camera in Family Films." Geena Davis Institute on Gender in Media, 2013. Accessed June 3, 2015. http://seejane.org/wp-content/uploads/key-findings-gender-disparity-family -films-2013.pdf.

Smith-Pearson, Kiva. "A Feminist Deck." Kickstarter, June 1, 2015. https://www .kickstarter.com/projects/322895958/a-feminist-deck/.

"#SolidarityIsForWhiteWomen Creator, Mikki Kendal [*sic*], Speaks about Women of Color, Feminism (VIDEO)." *Huffington Post*, August 13, 2013. http://www.huffington post.com/2013/08/13/solidarityisforwhitewomen-creator-mikki-kendal-women -of-color-feminism-_n_3749589.html.

Solnit, Rebecca. "The Archipelago of Arrogance." Reprinted in *TomDispatch*, August 19, 2012. http://www.tomdispatch.com/blog/175584/.

Sonenshein, Julia. "Powerful Selfies Project Reveals Just How Much Tumblr Hates Women." *The Gloss*, January 31, 2014. http://www.thegloss.com/2014/01/31/culture /selfies-project-shows-tumblr-misogyny-lindsay-bottos-anonymous/.

Starr, Terrell Jermaine. "STUDY: More Than Half of Black Girls Are Sexually Assaulted." *News One*, December 2, 2011. http://newsone.com/1680915/half-of -black-girls-sexually-assaulted/.

"State of Online Gaming Report." Spil Games, 2013. Accessed June 3, 2015. http://auth-83051f68-ec6c-44e0-afe5-bd8902acff57.cdn.spilcloud.com/v1 /archives/1384952861.25_State_of_Gaming_2013_US_FINAL.pdf.

"Statistics." Rape, Abuse, and Incest National Network (RAINN), 2009. https:// rainn.org/statistics.

Staude-Müller, Frithjof, Britta Hansen, and Melanie Voss. "How Stressful Is Online Victimization? Effects of Victim's Personality and Properties of the Incident." *European Journal of Developmental Psychology* 9, no. 2 (2012): 260–74.

Stebner, Beth. "Audrie Pott Suicide: Details of Online Chats Emerge a Year after Teen Killed Herself Following Alleged Assault and Cyberbullying." *New York Daily News*, September 18, 2013. http://www.nydailynews.com/news/national /new-details-revealed-audrie-pott-cyber-bullying-suicide-article-1.145 9904.

Stephens, Kim. "Ipswich Woman Charged over Muslim Hate Attacks Online." *Brisbane Times*, February 18, 2015. http://www.brisbanetimes.com.au/queensland /ipswich-woman-charged-over-muslim-hate-attacks-online-20150217-13hamf .html.

Sterne, Marlow. "'The Fappening' Is Dead: From A-List Hacking Victims to D-Listers Accused of Leaking Nudes for PR." *Daily Beast*, October 8, 2014. http:// www.thedailybeast.com/articles/2014/10/18/the-fappening-is-dead-from-a -list-hacking-victims-to-d-listers-accused-of-leaking-nudes-for-pr.html.

Stoleru, Maria, and Elena-Alis Costecu. "(Re)Producing Violence against Women in Online Spaces." *Philobiblon: Transylvanian Journal of Multidisciplinary Research in Humanities* 19, no. 1 (2014): 95–114.

Swim, Janet, Lauri L. Hyers, Laurie L. Cohen, and Melissa J. Ferguson. "Everyday Sexism: Evidence for Its Incidence, Nature, and Psychological Impact from Three Daily Diary Studies." *Journal of Social Issues* 57, no. 1 (2001): 31–53.

"Take Back the Tech!'s Report Card on Social Media and Violence against Women." Take Back the Tech!, 2014. Accessed November 1, 2014. https://www.takebackthe tech.net/sites/default/files/2014-reportcard-en.pdf.

Talusan, Meredith. "The Failed Logic of 'Trans Panic' Criminal Defenses." *Buzzfeed*, August 25, 2015. http://www.buzzfeed.com/meredithtalusan/trans-panic-criminal -defense#.ncgoLEoJP.

Tang, Wai Yen. "Reactions to a Woman's Voice in an FPS Game." *Gamasutra*, February 8, 2013. http://www.gamasutra.com/blogs/WaiYenTang/20130208/186335 /Reactions_to_a_womans_voice_in_an_FPS_game.php.

Taylor, Claire. "Women's Social Networks and Female Friendship in the Ancient Greek City." *Gender & History* 23, no. 3 (2011): 703–20.

"Techie Adria Richards Fired after Tweeting about Men's Comments." *CBS News.com*, March 22, 2013. http://www.cbsnews.com/news/techie-adria-richards -fired-after-tweeting-about-mens-comments/.

Tiku, Natasha, and Casey Newton. "Twitter CEO: 'We Suck at Dealing with Abuse.'" *The Verge*, February 4, 2015. http://www.theverge.com/2015/2/4/7982099/twitter -ceo-sent-memo-taking-personal-responsibility-for-the.

"Totally in Control." Social Issues Research Center (SIRC), 2014. Accessed July 1, 2014. http://www.sirc.org/articles/totally_in_control2.shtml.

Totilo, Stephen. "Another Woman in Gaming Flees Home Following Death Threats." *Kotaku*, October 11, 2014. http://kotaku.com/another-woman-in-gaming -flees-home-following-death-thre-1645280338.

Tufekci, Zeynep. "It's a Man's Phone." Medium, November 4, 2013. https://medium .com/technology-and-society/its-a-mans-phone-a26c6bee1b69.

Turk, Victoria. "Technology Isn't Designed to Fit Women." *Motherboard*, September 12, 2014. http://motherboard.vice.com/read/technology-isnt-designed-to-fit -women.

"2015 Hiring Trends: An Infographic Snapshot." Jobvite Resources, March 25, 2015. http://web.jobvite.com/Q315_Website_InfographiceBook_LP.html?utm_source =website&utm_medium=resources&utm_campaign=infographic-ebook.

Tweten, Alexandra. "Bye Felipe." Instagram, August 1, 2015. https://instagram .com/byefelipe/.

"*United States v. Andrew Auernheimer.*" Electronic Frontier Foundation (EFF), October 17, 2015. https://www.eff.org/cases/us-v-auernheimer.

Valenti, Jessica. "Elliot Rodger's California Shooting Spree: Further Proof That Misogyny Kills; Attributing the Rampage in Isla Vista to a 'Madman' Ignores a Stark Truth about Our Society." *Guardian*, May 24, 2014. http://www.theguardian .com/commentisfree/2014/may/24/elliot-rodgers-california-shooting-mental -health-misogyny/.

———. "Free Speech Is a Bad Excuse for Online Creeps to Threaten Rape and Murder." *Guardian*, June 18, 2014. http://www.theguardian.com/commentisfree /2014/jun/18/free-speech-online-creeps-cyberbullying-laws.

Vernasco, Lucy. "Seven Studies That Prove Mansplaining Exists." *Bitch Magazine*, July 14, 2014. http://bitchmagazine.org/post/seven-studies-proving-mansplaining -exists.

von Karma, Manfred (pseudonym). "Mike Cernovich: Based Lawyer of Gamergate." Medium, January 5, 2015. https://medium.com/@ManfredVonKarma/mike -cernovich-based-lawyer-of-gamergate-419d0617f259.

Wajcman, Judy. "Feminist Theories of Technology." *Cambridge Journal of Economics* 24, no. 1 (2010): 143–52.

———. *TechnoFeminism*. Cambridge: Polity Press, 2004. Google Books online preview.

Wang, Jian, Jian-Zhong Hong, and Zhong-Ling Pi. "Cross-Cultural Adaptation: The Impact of Online Social Support and the Role of Gender." *Social Behavior & Personality* 43, no. 1 (2015): 111–21.

"Weev on Why He Trolls." *Insight SBS*, 2012. https://www.youtube.com/watch?v=hlN_Yq2qcK0.

"We Have a Rape Gif Problem and Gawker Media Won't Do Anything about It." *Jezebel*, August 11, 2014. http://jezebel.com/we-have-a-rape-gif-problem-and-gawker-media-wont-do-any-1619384265/all.

"What Is Stereotype Threat?" Reducing Stereotype Threat, October 17, 2015. http://www.reducingstereotypethreat.org/definition.html.

"Who We Are." Girls Who Code, July 7, 2015. http://girlswhocode.com/.

Wilding, Faith. "Where Is the Feminism in Cyberfeminism?" *n.paradoxa*, no. 2 (1998): 6–13. http://www.ktpress.co.uk/pdf/vol2_npara_6_13_Wilding.pdf.

Wilson, Jason. "Hate Sinks." *New Inquiry*, February 6, 2014. http://thenewinquiry.com/essays/hate-sinks/.

"WMC's Research Shines Light on Gender Bias in Major U.S. Broadcast, Print, Online, & Wire Outlets." Women's Media Center, April 3, 2014. http://www.womensmediacenter.com/press/entry/wmc-research-on-gender-bias-in-major-us-media.

"Women in National Parliaments." Inter-Parliamentary Union, April 3, 2015. http://www.ipu.org/wmn-e/classif.htm.

Woolley, Emma. "Time to Make 'Revenge-Porn' Sharing a Criminal Act in Canada." *Globe and Mail*, July 24, 2013. http://www.theglobeandmail.com/technology/digital-culture/time-to-make-revenge-porn-sharing-a-criminal-act-in-canada/article13386714/.

Wu, Brianna. "Gamergate Death Threat Is a Slam Dunk for Prosecutors: Will They Act?" *The Mary Sue*, May 20, 2015. http://www.themarysue.com/will-prosecutors-act-on-gamergate-death-threat/.

———. Twitter post, 2:52 p.m., July 28, 2015. https://twitter.com/Spacekatgal/status/626102993318989825.

———. Twitter post, 2:54 p.m., July 28, 2015. https://twitter.com/Spacekatgal/status/626103329865789441.

Wyer, Mary, Mary Barbercheck, Donna Cookmeyer, Hatice Örün Öztürk, and Marta Wayne, eds. *Women, Science, and Technology: A Reader in Feminist Science Studies*. New York: Routledge, 2013.

Yiannopoulos, Milo. "Feminist Bullies Tearing the Video Game Industry Apart." *Breitbart*, September 1, 2014. http://www.breitbart.com/london/2014/09/01/lying-greedy-promiscuous-feminist-bullies-are-tearing-the-video-game-industry-apart/.

———. Twitter post, 7:22 p.m., February 20, 2013. https://twitter.com/Nero/status/304385532367106048.

———. Twitter post, 8:15 p.m., February 20, 2013. https://twitter.com/Nero/status/304398843435446272.

Zhang, Xiaoyun. "Sharing Block Lists to Help Make Twitter Safer." Twitter, June 10 2015. https://blog.twitter.com/2015/sharing-block-lists-to-help-make-twitter-safer.

Index

Women's House, 190

women's imprisonment, 9

women's networks, 189–90

women's speech, 13, 19, 96

Women's Square, 190

women's strategies, 160

Wondermark, 145

Working to Halt Online Abuse (WHOA),
92, 108, 243

Wu, Brianna, 78, 147, 174, 194

Xbox Live, 95

xoJane, 71, 139

Yiannopoulos, Milo, 126, 151

YouTube, 181

zines, 218

Zoe post, 141

CPSIA information can be obtained
at www.ICGtesting.com
Printed in the USA
FSOW01n0752031216
28115FS